John Tomkinson comes from Stoke-on-Trent in the English Midlands. He was educated at the University of Wales (Lampeter) and the University of Keele in Staffordshire. He holds an MA in History and an MA and a PhD in Philosophy from the University of Keele.

A British qualified and trained teacher, he has enjoyed forty years experience teaching History to students from primary to undergraduate level, has experience of both the British and US systems of education, and of teaching in international schools. He taught IB History for nearly twenty years and for most of that time was an examiner.

Today he lives in retirement in Athens, and writes on various subjects.

By the same author for the IB:

In the series Themes in *Twentieth Century World History for the International Baccalaureate*:

      Wars and Warfare

      The Cold War

Also:

Studying History for the International Baccalaureate

Study Skills for the International Baccalaureate

The Enterprise of Knowledge: A source book for Theory of Knowledge

Single-Party States

John L. Tomkinson

Anagnosis
Athens, Greece

Anagnosis
Harilaou Trikoupi 130
145 63 Kifissia
Athens, Greece
Website: www.anagnosis.gr

Fifth Edition
© Anagnosis 2011
ISBN 960-88087-3-1
978-960-88087-3-7

First published 2005
Reprinted 2005
Second edition 2006
Reprinted 2006
Reprinted 2007
Third edition 2008
Reprinted 2009
Fourth edition 2009
Reprinted 2010

Photoset and printed by:
K. Pletsas - Z. Karadri O.E.
Harilaou Trikoupi 107
Athens
www.typografio.gr

Teachers' Preface

The teacher of history for the course of the International Baccalaureate has a very difficult task. Some problems are shared with teachers of other subjects, while some are unique to history.

The IB course is a short one: two academic years means considerably less time than two calendar years, when the final examinations are held in May or November. In addition, many IB students are studying in a language which is not their mother tongue.

Unlike the "newer" Group Three subjects, where it is assumed that students enter the course knowing nothing about the subject at all, and where the requirements of the examination are based entirely upon what can reasonably be accomplished in such a short time, it is assumed that history students will already have a long background in the subject when they enter on the course. The standard of the examination is necessarily set high, because the grades awarded have to be comparable with those of long-established university entrance examinations which are the final stage in a long period of education and training in the discipline.

Yet in practice IB History students, particularly those in international schools, come to the subject from very different backgrounds. Their experience of history in their previous schools may not provide any useful foundation for their IB studies at all; and it may even be counterproductive. In his book *Lies My Teacher Told Me: Everything Your American History Textbook Got Wrong*, James W. Loewen quotes a colleague teaching history in college as saying that he sees his first job as disabusing his charges of what they learned in high school. "In no other field does this happen. Mathematics professors, for instance, know that non-Euclidian geometry is rarely taught in high school, but they don't assume that Euclidian geometry was *mistaught*... [H]istory is the only field in which the more courses students take, the stupider they become." In many countries, the study of history in schools has been reduced to the rote of learning selective "basic facts" and stories, or it is so imbued with nationalist ideology as to be worse than useless.

The history teacher is thus pulled from both ends. On the one hand his/her pupils may have no useful background in the subject at all, or one which is actually counterproductive, and they may not be working in their mother tongue. On the other hand, he/she has to prepare students in a very short period of time for examinations which are marked to a standard which matches those of students who have usefully studied history in their mother tongue over many years. This means that the history teacher has very speedily to instill in his/her students a new way of looking at the subject, teach new skills and provide basic facts, yet at the same time provide a level of analysis which will enable the students to obtain the best grades of which they are capable.

There is no shortage of excellent texts for school history, but few are designed to provide for the wide range of levels and backgrounds which the IB course needs to encompass. Either they are designed for lower level examinations, and provide basic facts and an elementary introduction to analysis, or they provide adequate analysis, but assume knowledge of basic facts. This small series of books is an attempt to fill that void, by providing both basic facts and a range of analysis, which will enable the students to make the transition to a level appropriate to their abilities as quickly as possible.

The books may usefully be employed as an accompaniment to a course taught in class, the numbered paragraphs providing a handy means of reference. Students may use the text as a model upon which to construct their own notes. The texts may function as revision notes for examinations. Each individual note usually contains a single idea which can be identified by a key word or phrase. If the student identifies these key words by highlighting or underlining them, then the very process of making the decision about which words to choose will ensure active consideration of the points covered, and the process of committing facts and theories to memory will have already taken place. Running the eye over the highlighted words wshould enable recall of the entire set of ideas. Some particularly important key words have been highlighted in bold; but in most of the notes students have been left to make their own choices.

Like most books designed for use in schools, these do not have detailed references. Students should be warned that this makes them unsuitable for use as research sources for internally assessed studies or extended essays; although used as initial reading they may provide the student with some idea of the issues to be confronted, in approaching some aspect of a particular topic.

Attention has been paid to the development of the students' vocabulary, with the needs of those not working in their mother tongue in mind. Science students spend much of their time becoming acquainted with the technical vocabulary of their subject. By contrast, students of history are frequently quite unaware of the need to assimilate a special vocabulary at all, because history books do not have the immediate opacity that science texts present to the uninitiated. A good grade in university entrance examinations such as the IB, requires that the student demonstrate evidence of wide reading. Without an adequate command of the terminology of history, such reading may be superficial, ill-assimilated, and of limited use. Even those students who understand such terms in context may be unable to use them confidently, if at all, in their own essays and examinations, without some explicit focus upon their meaning. Dictionaries have their uses as works of reference, but there are few students so highly motivated, or so Spartan in character, as to work their way through a dictionary of relevant terms. I have tried to focus upon the meaning of key terms which dominate the study of the themes covered in each volume. This should make the students more aware of the complex conceptual issues at stake in the subjects they are studying, and might also go some way towards dragging students away from narrative, and focusing their attention upon ideas and issues.

Finally, History should never be a "dead subject" concerned entirely with the past, with no relevance to the burning issues of the day. These books are offered to help students see the relevance of what they study to understanding today's world, to be more intelligent and critical in their reading of contemporary situations, and so come to grips with the living issues of the day in a confident and thoughtful manner.

John L. Tomkinson
Athens 2005

Note on the Fifth Edition

The text of this edition has been extensively revised. The number of "optional" single-party states has been reduced, so as to allow greater focus on the more popular topics. All the ancilliary material has been placed online [see page 8].

Contents

Course Relevance

1. States, Governments and Ideologies: General, Paper 2
2. Lenin's Russia; Paper 2; Paper 3 (Europe)
3. Stalin's USSR: Paper 2, Paper 3 (Europe)
4. Mussolini's Italy: Paper 2; Paper 3 (Europe)
5. Franco's Spain: Paper 2; Paper 3 (Europe)
7. Hitler's Germany: Paper 2; Paper 3 (Europe)
8. Khrushchev's USSR: Paper 2; Paper 3 (Europe)
9. Brezhnev's USSR: Paper 2; Paper 3 Europe
10. Mao's China: Paper 2; Paper 3 (Asia)
11. Authoritarianism, Fascism and Totalitarianism: Paper 2

IB teachers and students will be aware that the various options on the IB History course overlap extensively.

The following is covered in the companion volume *Wars and Warfare:*

Hitler's Foreign Policy

The following Single-Party States are covered in the companion volume *The Cold War:*

Castro's Cuba
Khrushchev's Foreign Policy
Brezhnev's Foreign Policy
Gorbachev's USSR, in "The End of the Cld War"

Online Resources

Additional resources for each of the topics covered in this book which are updated from time to time are freely available to all our readers on the publisher's website for IB books at www.anagnosis.eu. These include:

General advice on writing history essays
Notes on writing essays on wars and warfare
Useful quotations
Hints on understanding or dealing with the topics covered in the book
Bibliographies of secondary and printed primary sources
DVDs
Online primary sources, including videoclips
Links to websites with useful content, including videoclips

This website is frequently updated, and will repay periodic revisits.

Publisher's Note

This book has been produced independently by the author and publisher, and it is not endorsed by the International Baccalaureate Organisation.

Karl Marx

States, Governments and Ideologies

States and Governments

1. The state is the basic unit of political organisation in the modern world. A **sovereign state** is one which is independent of all others. It is represented by its head of state, flag, anthem, etc.

2. Political thinkers in the past compared the complex structure of the state, with the human body; and the way in which its parts worked together as its "constitution", by analogy with the human constitution. Thus the way in which a state is governed, the powers of, and relations between, the various institutions and officials is called its **constitution**(1). This constitution (1) is determined by **basic laws** which lay down the powers and duties of the various institutions and officials. These basic laws are themselves collectively referred to as the constitution (2). They are usually set out in a legal document, which is itself also called the constitution (3).

3. During the nineteenth century constitutions (2,3) were granted by kings, ensuring the **rule of law**; a state of affairs in which everyone, however mighty, had to obey the laws. The rule of law is opposed to **arbitrary government**, where the powerful do as they wish with impunity.

4. **Sovereignty** within a state lies in those institutions or persons which exercise ultimate power.

5. States are of three kinds: unitary states, federal states and confederations.
    (a) In **unitary states**, the central government alone has sovereignty. Local governments have power only insofar as the central government confers power upon them; e.g. France and Italy.
    (b) In **federal states**, sovereignty is shared between central government and the highest level of regional government. The regional, or state, governments have powers of their own which cannot be taken from them as they are written into the basic laws of the country. e.g. USA, Germany.
    (c) In **confederations**, sovereignty rests with local governments, and not with the central government. The central government only has such powers as the local governments have conferred upon it. Switzerland is a confederation of self-governing cantons.

6. The **head of state,** king or queen in a monarchy and president in a republic represents the nation, both to the other citizens of the state and to other states.

7. Traditionally monarchs based their right to rule, their **legitimacy**, upon the claim that God had chosen and authorized them to rule. This was called the **divine right of kings**. In modern times it was recognised that monarchs should themselves be subject to the constitution of their country.

8. The head of a state may, or may not, also be the head of its government. In the UK the head

of state is Her Majesty the Queen and the head of government is the Prime Minister. In the USA, by contrast, the President is both head of state *and* head of the government. The president of a country will always be the head of state, but he may, or may not, also be the head of the government. The head of government is usually called the prime minister: in French-speaking countries the premier, and in German the chancellor.

9. There are states where the most powerful person in the country holds only a minor or no official government position. Such a figure will hold his power by virtue of his past contribution to national life, or because of his relations with various powerful factions within the country, such as army leaders. In single-party states, the head of the Party may be more important than the head of state or the head of the government, e.g. the USSR..

10. The **executive** part of the government consists of those officials and institutions which administer, or manage, the country. In its higher reaches, the executive usually consists of the **cabinet**, comprising the chief ministers of the country under the Prime Minister or President.

11. The **legislative** part of the government has the main function of making laws. In the UK the legislature is called Parliament, in France the National Assembly, and in the USA Congress. Some legislatures have distinctive names: e.g. in Russia, the *Duma.* Legislatures are either **unicameral,** consisting of one chamber, or **bicameral,** consisting of two.

12. Some constitutions, e.g. that of the USA, deliberately keep the powers of government separate (the **separation of powers**). This is true of countries which have a **presidential system of government**, where the president is elected by the people. In virtue of his election, he/she runs the executive independently of the legislature. In other countries, such as the United Kingdom, these powers are inextricably mixed up. This is true of countries which have a **parliamentary system of government**, where the prime minister and the other ministers, are members of the legislature, and exercise power in virtue of their ability to command a majority in the legislature.

Changes of Government

1. Governments in democratic countries are changed by the holding of elections. Elections for the legislature are generally of two types: majority systems and proportional systems.

2. In elections held according to a **majority** (or "first past the post") **system**, the country is divided into areas called constituencies. In each area, each party is represented by a single candidate. That candidate wins who receives the most votes. This system tends to allow governments to be formed with clear majorities in the legislature. However:
(a) Since the majorities in different constituencies may be of varying sizes, using such a system it is possible for the party with the largest vote across the country to lose the election.
(b) It is also difficult for minority parties to gain any representation at all, since to gain a single seat they must win a constituency with a majority of votes cast there. Thus the use of the majority system leads to two party dominance, e.g. USA, UK.

3. In elections by a **proportional system**, many different methods may be employed to ensure that the proportion of candidates for each party which are elected reflects as closely as possible the proportion of votes cast for each party. However:
(a) Often there is no clear winner in an election by proportional representation, since no party commands a majority in the legislature. The party leaders form a **coalition** government after a period of bargaining in which they trade policies and posts in the government;
(b) Coalition governments are sometimes unstable, since internal disagreements may lead a coalitions to break up.

4. When a significant number of people within a country gather together armed forces and attempt to overthrow and replace the existing ruler or government by force, this is a **rebellion**.

5. Lacking popular support, those seeking to replace a government may do so in a manner which involves the citizens as little as possible. Plotters seize control of the state without warning, so that no one is able to prevent them. A sudden seizure of power is called a ***coup d'état:*** in Spanish-speaking countries a ***pronunciamiento,*** and in German a ***Putsch***. Those who govern may seek to do so unhampered by the constitution, and rule arbitrarily. Thus members of a government or armed forces may themselves launch a ***coup d'état***. They are in the best position to do so.

6. When people rise up with the intention not merely of replacing the existing government, but also of fundamentally changing the political and economic nature of society, we have a **revolution**. Such fundamental changes may come about without violence or bloodshed, in which case we may speak of a **peaceful revolution,** or a velvet revolution.

Political Ideologies

1. Much of political life is given its character and direction by political ideologies

2. Ideologies are **framework theories**. They provide a set of assumptions about society, and human nature, the nature of economics and the purpose of political activity.

3. Because they provide frameworks for thought, the most familiar and widespread beliefs and values within a particular society are determined by a dominant ideology.

4. Most people may not be aware of the existence and function of the dominant ideology in their own society. This is because the assumptions upon which they are founded have become so widely accepted, and are held defensively, no one usually questions them. Yet they *are* highly questionable. **Implicit ideologies** permeate society, and their values saturate the mass media.

5. Ideologies set limits to our thought. They determine which questions can be asked, and which answers are acceptable. Questioning ideologies is not normally permissible, since, they are usually held with strong emotional commitment, and are fiercely defended in a partisan manner.

6. The prevalent ideology within a society is usually designed to justify the existing social and economic arrangements, and justify the privileges of existing elites and their exploitation of other groups. In this way, **implicit ideologies** are systems of propaganda, designed to persuade under-privileged and disadvantaged groups to accept a value system which justifies their exploitation.

Implicit Ideologies
Conservatism

1. The ***ancien regime***, the traditional society of pre-revolutionary Europe, was dominated by hereditary monarchs and hereditary land owning aristocracies. The ideology of conservatism portrayed this situation as "natural"; i.e. as both necessary and desirable.

2. Conservatism asserts that there are different classes of people in society who are "naturally" (i.e. by birth) suited to perform different tasks, and therefore to fulfil different roles in society.

3. Society functions well only when the people of these different classes perform those roles within society which are appropriate to their several natures, in the interests of the harmony and well-being of the whole, and do not aspire to perform functions for which they are not suited.

4. Some of these tasks, and therefore the roles of those who perform them, are superior to others, and for this reason those who are by nature suited to perform them deserve special privileges.

5. With privileges also go certain obligations and responsibilities, called *noblesse oblige*, which it is the duty of the privileged to perform, such as giving charity to the poor.

6. Privileged people are entitled to exercise authority since, through inheritance, their nature, privileges and authority ultimately come from God. Thus to question the authority of privileged classes, is to question the judgements of God himself, and is a sin.

10. Government is essentially good, since it is the chief instrument of those classes born to control and care for society. Resisting the will of the government is fundamentally wicked.

Liberalism
1. Liberalism arose among, and was fostered by, a mercantile industrial class of capitalists who, during the industrial revolution, began to replace the hereditary land owning aristocracy as the dominant group in society. The source of their power and privilege lay in their wealth.
2. Liberalism thus attempts to show that it is "natural" that:
   (a) some people should possess great wealth, and that others should lack it;
   (b) that great wealth should bring privilege, including the power to govern and exploit others.
3. The possession of wealth is the major indication of a person's value and importance in society. Those who have acquired wealth have in general done so justly, and have a moral right to the privileges which this wealth buys for them. Thus envy of the rich by the poor is inappropriate.
4. Unrestricted **competition** and the **free market** produces the most just distribution of wealth. This is because free competition favours those who are already wealthy, and in the best position to compete successfully.
5. Individual liberty is a supreme value and must be safeguarded. (This means much for the rich, although little for the poor, since a rich man is free do lots of things with his wealth, while a poor man must work as much as he can simply in order to stay alive.
6. Government is generally a bad thing, which should be as limited as possible, because it interferes with individual liberty (i.e. the liberty of the wealthy to enjoy their money). It does so by:
   (a) levying of taxes;
   (b) enforcing regulations which interfere with the pursuit of profit, the ultimate standard of value in society (e.g. regulating safety in workplaces) and the unrestricted enjoyment of wealth.
7. Liberalism is the dominant ideology in the world today.

Reformist Ideologies
1. **Reformist ideologies** are advanced on behalf of the majority in society, who do not enjoy special privileges of birth or wealth.
2. They propose:
   (a) a **critique** of existing society;
   (b) a description of what an **ideal** society would be like;
   (c) a set of **prescriptions** for getting from the existing situation to an ideal, or better, one.

Socialism
1. Historically, socialism is a reaction to the injustices of the capitalist economic system.
2. All real wealth is created from nature by human work, or labour (harvesting, manufacturing, etc).
3. Those who produce wealth, the workers, benefit least from it, since most is taken from them.
4. Some people produce nothing, but do perform useful or valued services for others (e.g. nurses).
5. Those who most benefit from the enjoyment of wealth neither produce anything nor perform services for others. Their only labour is to appropriate the wealth created by others for themselves. Thus they are social parasites (e.g. currency, commodity and property speculators.)
6. These differences lie at the basis of the social class system, whereby the worker enjoys the lowest status, the least security, and the fewest opportunities in life; while social parasites who produce nothing and perform no useful services for others enjoy the highest status and security and the most opportunities for the enjoyment of wealth and leisure.
7. These inequalities are systematically transmitted from generation to generation through the

inheritance of land, wealth and connections, and the purchase of educational advantages.

8. In order to justify the capitalist system, liberalism values highly selfish individualism, ruthless competition, and material greed, the suppression of human cooperativeness and compassion, and the undermining of the sense of community; arguing that man is "naturally" selfish.

9. Production is organised for profit rather than for need, and so may be wasteful and destructive of the environment, while genuine needs may not be met, because it would be insufficiently profitable for a capitalist to invest in meeting them.

10. Peoples' lives are left at the mercy of the blind trade cycle (boom and bust), which periodically generates mass unemployment, with consequent waste of human resources, poverty and squalor.

11. Great wealth gives power, and so gives some people unacceptable power over others.

12. By contrast, a socialist society would be one in which:
    (a) the means of production and distribution of wealth would be in common ownership;
    (b) there would be near equality of wealth, hence of power;
    (c) no class system or exploitation of some groups by others;
    (d) competition would be replaced by cooperation for the common good, so that human nature would no longer be distorted by greed or poverty but improved by cooperation;
    (e) production would be for need and not profit, so conserving environmental resources;
    (f) the wasteful chaos of a competitive free-for-all would be replaced by rational planning.

13. Socialists disagree about how to get from the existing capitalist system to a socialist society:
    (a) **social democrats** believe in working to extend the franchise, then electing socialist parliamentary representatives, who would bring about a peaceful social revolution;
    (b) **syndicalists** wish to use the trade unions to bring down capitalism by strikes and industrial espionage, and then to provide the organisational basis of a new social order;
    (c) **revolutionary socialists** believe that elites will never voluntarily give up their privileges, and will use force to keep them (police, etc.), so that there is no alternative to violent revolution.

Marxism

1. Marxism is a form of revolutionary socialism developed by Karl Marx in the middle of the nineteenth century. It was an attempt to place socialism on a strong intellectual base by developing a systematic body of doctrine, using categories (framework and basic ideas) taken from the philosophy of G. W. F. Hegel.
    (a) Hegel held that the wide sweep of the past reveals that the universe has passed through a series of distinct stages, from pure matter, through sentient life to intelligent life.
    (b) The various stages of evolution are inevitable, since at each stage, conflict between existing forces (called "thesis" and "antithesis") gives rise to a synthesis, which gives the distinctive character to the next stage of development. The idea that the future is determined in advance is called **determinism**. The belief that conflict is the engine of this development is called **dialectic**.

2. Karl Marx's political ideas were set out in *The Communist Manifesto* (1848) and *Das Kapital* (1867) and other writings.

3. Marx applied Hegel's concept of inevitable evolution to the successive stages of human history. He held that history is a dialectical process, in which each stage is succeeded by a contrasting one with which it interacts, creating a synthesis of the two that constitutes a next stage, and so on.

4. Marx believed that it is the manner by which individuals in a society create wealth out of what is found in nature, and distribute it, which defines a society. This is the real engine of history. Thus Marx's philosophy is known as **dialectical materialism**.

5. Since these relations are determined for humanity at each historical stage, Marx's philosophy is also a form of **determinism**.

6. The present historical stage is that of **capitalism**. Under capitalism, one class (the **proletariat**) works, while another class (the **bourgeoisie**) appropriates for themselves most of the fruit, or products, of this labour – the wealth which the workers have created.

7. The wealth created by the proletariat, together with the means to produce this wealth, does not belong to them, and is not controlled by them, but is owned by the capitalists who employ them. This deprives the workers their independence and detracts from their humanity, reducing them to the status of "hands." To refer to the ownership, by one class, of the work of another, Marx used the term "**alienation.**"

8. Like all previous stages of history, capitalism contains within itself internal conflicts, and cannot survive. It will inevitably bring the class struggle to a critical point. Since industries tend to service each other, by a natural process industrialization tends to concentrate the oppressed working masses in large **conurbations.** (Assembly line factories require "feeder" factories to manufacture parts they assemble). In the industrial conurbations both the injustice of their misery and their strength (which lies in their numbers) will inevitably become apparent to them. When that happens, the proletariat will spontaneously unite to change the system by force. This act of forceful change is **the Revolution**.

9. When the Revolution occurs, the proletariat will take over the means of production and distribution of wealth, (the **dictatorship of the proletariat**), **and** use them for the benefit of those who labour, and establish a classless society.

10. The state, which is an instrument of oppression, a means by which the bourgeoisie oppress the workers, will no longer be necessary, and will wither away.

11. Marx believed his form of socialism to be uniquely "**scientific**" because it was based upon an objective analysis of social relationships.

12. Marx's analysis was refined and elaborated after his death, with significant departures being made from the original orthodoxy. These revisions of Marx's doctrines are often known as forms of "**revisionism**."

Anarchism

1. Anarchism arose out of the same social *milieu* as socialism and shared many of the ideas of the socialists. For that reason, many nineteenth-century radicals are not easy to classify as socialists or anarchists. They may themselves have been unable, or unwilling, to say which they were.

2. While socialists see the essence of society's ills in inequalities of wealth (which inevitably lead to inequalities of power); anarchists see the essence of society's ills in inequalities of power (which inevitably lead to inequalities of wealth). Anarchists believe the suffering of the majority to stem from the increasing powers assumed by nation states, as these are exercised with impunity by governments, police and law courts.

3. These who control nation states can launch wars and use the mechanisms of the state to conscript people to fight in them against their will, imprison and execute them. They can fix the tax system to suit themselves and their cronies, and they can do these things while beyond the effective reach of ordinary citizens, and at no personal cost to themselves.

4. Only in a society without rulers and ruled, can men be free and happy, acting not according to laws imposed from above, but according to the dictates of their own consciences.

5. The centralized state should be replaced by a confederal system of autonomous local communities and industrial associations, bound by mutual contracts arising out of mutual interests, with arbitration replacing courts of justice.

6. Like socialists, anarchists divide over how the present situation can be remedied, some favouring an evolutionary approach, and others a revolutionary path.

(a) Those who favour a revolutionary approach argue that the powerful will never voluntarily allow their privileges to be taken away. The only way to destroy the oppressive state system and the entrenched privileges of powerful would be by force. **Terrorism** causes the authorities to overreact, and reveal themselves as the oppressors they are, provoking revolution.

(b) Those who favour an evolutionary approach argue that the increasing devolution of power by the transfer of more and more powers from central governments to lower and lower tiers of local government, would in time secure the withering of the state and the creation of self-governing communities, where individuals will be able to enjoy freedom from oppression.

Ideologies and Political Parties

Do not confuse ideologies with political parties, which often bear the same names. Political parties are means of gaining and retaining power. Leaders of political parties will change the ideology their party professes to suit the climate of the day. Thus most political parties today are liberal in basic ideology, including the US Republican and Democratic parties and the British Conservative and Labour (Socialist) Parties.

Incomplete Ideologies

Incomplete ideologies do not present believers with a complete picture of society or a complete set of values. Instead, they focus upon one aspect of society only, and so may be combined with the other ideologies in different ways to serve different interests at different times.

Racism
1. Racism is the belief that all people "naturally" belong to a particular genetically defined group.
2. Some races are superior to others because of their inherited qualities; and, on the basis of this superiority, deserve greater privileges; while inferior races properly have fewer rights.
3. During the nineteenth century almost everyone was a racist. Most of the land surface of the globe was under the rule of white Europeans, or people of white European descent. It seemed self-evident to most people that this was because of the cultural superiority of the white race, which had developed because of their inherited superior intellectual and physical qualities.
4. The man-made disaster of the First World War, undoubtedly attributable to the "superior" races, began to shake the faith of educated non-whites in the colonies; but it did not make an impression on the masses until their initial victories of the Japanese in the Second World War.

Nationalism
1. Nationalism has proved one of the most pervasive and powerful ideologies of recent centuries among the general population. Although it has abated in Europe, where it first appeared, and is seen as a major cause of past wars, it is rampant in the USA.
2. The ideology of nationalism must be distinguished from sentiments which are frequently confused with it. **Patriotism** is the love of one's country, its landscape, its people, its customs and institutions. Sometimes this can turn into **chauvinism**, an aggressive, competitive "My country right or wrong" attitude, similar to the loud but unthinking support of his team by a fanatical team sports fan. **Xenophobia**, or fear and hatred of foreigners, is the dark side of chauvinism.
3. According to the ideology of **nationalism** mankind is "naturally" divided up into distinct

nations. Everyone is born into, and belongs to, a nation, a distinctly identifiable group of people.

4. The only legitimate form of political organisation for the nation is the nation state. Each nation has the right to national territory, and a sovereign nation state. Multi-national states are anomalous.

5. The nation state commands the highest loyalty of the individual, and its government has the right to demand anything from its people, up to and including their lives.

6. So deep is the influence of this ideology that to many people these things will seem self-evident. In fact they are products of the French Revolution. Before this period, we might find patriotism, chauvinism and xenophobia, but it was generally believed that it was right for rulers to have control over the areas they had inherited or won by conquest, irrespective of the ethnic origins, languages, religions, customs, or even the wishes, of the people who lived there.

7. Within a nation state, various groups will disagree about how it is to be organised. Conservatives, liberals and socialists will argue about the proper form of its political, social and economic organisation. For this reason, nationalism is an incomplete ideology, so nationalists may be conservatives, liberals, or socialists, etc. as well.

8. The main problem with this ideology is that its central concept, "the nation," is incoherent. If we ask "What makes a nation?" there is no clear answer. In the nineteenth century, people would have replied "race" or "blood." But we now know from DNA testing that because of migrations of people in the past, only few nations (e.g. Icelanders) can be identified as sharing a common ancestry. Few nations have a universal, as opposed to a dominant, mother tongue, or religion. "Culture" is a vague term, in which a large part is played by language and religion. Other aspects of culture, such as the way people build their houses or cook their food, depend upon local conditions, and so tend to vary from region to region within states.

9. A common response to this is to force people into a mold so that they will *appear* to possess cultural unity, by the persecution of minorities and the suppression of minority languages.

10. The demand that each nation have its integral national territory also leads to:
    (a) nations attacking their neighbours to "liberate" their "unfree" fellow-nationals;
    (b) the forming of independence or separatist movements by minorities seeking either national self-determination or the annexation of their part of their state by an adjacent state of their own nationality, which resort to terrorism or rebellion.

Social Darwinism

1. Human beings and human societies are subject to the same laws of natural selection that Charles Darwin had discovered, namely the survival of the fittest.

2. This process of natural selection would naturally result in the survival of the best competitors and in continuing improvement of the breeding stock of the population.

3. War, and social and economic hardship are integral parts of this process, since they purge society of the unfit and prevent them from breeding, and so weakening the race or nation.

4. This natural process is thwarted by values such as charity and social concern, which secure the survival of the "unfit." The survival of the poor, subnormal, disabled, incurably sick, aged and weak should not be aided, since it lowers the quality of the breeding stock.

5. The state should intervene to protect the fitness of the race/nation e.g. by selective breeding, (**eugenics**). The unfit should be prevented from breeding, and the fit encouraged.

6. The dominance of one race or culture over another was thought to be a sign of "fitness" and superiority, so Social Darwinism was thought to justify imperialism, racism, conservatism and liberalism.

Vladimir Ilyich Ulyanov
(Lenin)

Lenin's Russia

"There is no other man [than Lenin] *who is absorbed by the revolution twenty-four hours a day, who has no other thoughts but the thought of revolution, and who even when he sleeps, dreams of nothing but revolution."* (A Menshevik opponent)

Russia Before the Revolutions

Background

1. At the beginning of the twentieth century, Russia was the least developed, economically and industrially, of the Great Powers.
2. The system of government was **autocracy.*** The all-powerful ruler, the tsar, recognized no constitutional limits on his power, and claimed to derive his authority directly from God.
3. Throughout its history, Russia had passed through:
   (a) long periods of turning in upon itself, away from the West, in order to develop its own distinctive Orthodox culture, an inheritance of the medieval Byzantine tradition.
   (b) short periods of openness to the West, when bursts of reform and modernisation would be imposed upon the country from above.
4. At the beginning of the nineteenth century, the peasants still cultivated the land in small strips using primitive techniques. The *mir* or village council would redistribute these strips periodically, so as to ensure that each family enjoyed a fair share of the good and bad land. The country people were serfs,* who were tied to the land, and had to perform forced labour.
5. Serfdom was abolished by Tsar Alexander II in 1861, but this emancipation* was arranged in a manner designed to inconvenience the landowners as little as possible. The peasants had to make redemption payments* for their land, while each *mir* was collectively responsible for all the peasants' debts. Thus the peasants were still tied to the land, but now by debt; and it was almost impossible for them to consolidate their holdings, and make them more efficient.
6. Since the emancipation of the serfs, local assemblies, known as ***zemstvos,**** had been set up, and had enjoyed some powers of local government, and had introduced some reforms.
7. During a period of intensive industrialisation in the 1890s, many peasants began to leave their villages during periods of the year when there was little agricultural work, to labour in the mines, and in the factories in the towns.

Reformers and Revolutionaries in Russia

1. Many people in Russia were dissatisfied with the autocracy as it was and sought change. They fell into three groups:

   (a) Those who believed in the autocracy, but who wished to **reform it** in order to make it more efficient and better able to survive in the modern world;

   (b) Those who wished to limit the power of the autocrat by the adoption of a **constitution**. Many among the middle classes wished Russia to follow the democratic west. These liberals dominated the *zemstvos*.

   (c) Those who wished to **abolish the monarchy** completely as part of a social revolution, and replace it with something else. These were the **revolutionaries**.

   Most of the *intelligentsia** were inclined to **socialism** or **anarchism**. Many of these thought that the future of Russia lay in the hands of the peasants. These **populists** looked to native Russian traditions to provide the way forward. Some of these believed that the *mir* was an institution around which a socialist system could be built.

2. Revolutionaries became very popular in Russia. Geoffrey Hosking calls them "a kind of alternative establishment." One group of populists, **The People's Will**, turned to terrorism as a means of bringing about revolution, and assassinated Tsar Alexander II in 1881.

3. **Marxism** was brought to Russia by **Georgy Plekhanov**, who believed that in order to achieve socialism this industrially backward country would have to pass through two distinct stages:

   (a) a **bourgeois revolution:** which would result in the establishment of a democratic republic, and the development of capitalism;

   (b) a **proletarian revolution:** but only after mature capitalism had generated a numerous proletariat which had attained a socialist consciousness.

4. The Russian empire, which stretched across the north of the Asian landmass was a **multi-national empire** no less than the overseas empires of Britain and France. Many of the non-Russians within the empire, such as the Poles, were **separatists,*** and desired their own independence.

5. Against all those who wanted change (reformers, revolutionaries and separatists) were those who wished to move in the opposite direction and strengthen the most traditional aspects of the autocracy. These **reactionaries*** were headed by Konstantin Pobedonostsev, who held that the Russian Orthodox Church lay at the heart of what it was to be Russian, and was the bulwark both of the established order and of the unity of the nation.

6. Pobedonostsev persecuted **religious minorities**, e.g. Catholics, Lutherans and Orthodox Old Believers.* Following the assassination of Tsar Alexander II, the Jews were singled out for special persecution. They were:

   (a) confined to an area known as the Pale, in Poland and Western Russia.

   (b) forbidden to sit on the *zemstvos*.

   (c) excluded from the legal profession

   (d) Many were forced into ghettoes*

   (e) Quotas limited their entrance to secondary schools

   This was an example of anti-Semitism.*

7. The **Okhrana**, the Tsarist political police, watched all radicals* and separatists carefully.

   (a) Censorship was all-pervasive.

   (b) Critics of the regime were exiled to Siberia. This was not particularly harsh, since the exiles were not locked up. They were maintained by state pensions, and were allowed to have their families join them.

   (c) Those who committed terrorist crimes, and a few plotters, were executed.

Lenin: the Revolutionary

1. Vladimir Ilyich Ulyanov, later known as Lenin, was born into a provincial middle-class family. His mother was the daughter of a physician, and his father, although the son of a serf, became a school inspector. His eldest brother Alexander, a student at the University of St. Petersburg, was hanged for participating in a plot to assassinate Tsar Alexander III. Lenin studied law at Kazan University, and despite getting into trouble with the authorities, he graduated in 1891.

2. He practised law in Samara in 1892-93 and St. Petersburg from 1893, working as a public defence counsel. In practising law, he saw how the legal system was biased against working people, and built up associations with the Marxists there.

3. In 1895 Lenin and others united the Marxists of St. Petersburg in the Union for the Struggle for the Liberation of the Working Class. But in December Lenin was jailed for 15 months with three years exile in Siberia. There he met older exiled revolutionaries, read philosophical and political works, and married Nadezhda Krupskaya, a fellow revolutionary.

4. In January 1900, he went to Munich to join Plekhanov and Martov to publish *Iskra* (*The Spark*), which they hoped would unify the various Marxist groups scattered throughout Europe into a single "Social Democratic Party."

5. Many of the Russian intelligentsia believed that Marxism was inapplicable to Russia because an industrial proletariat was almost nonexistent. Lenin followed Plekhanov in believing that Russia would first have to pass through the stage of bourgeois revolution, to establish a bourgeois state, which would then be industrialized. Only when a genuine industrial proletariat had been created would a socialist revolution be possible.

6. Lenin argued that if the peasants revolted and divided all the land among the *mirs*, the result would not be socialism but capitalism, because of the free market in agricultural produce. He believed that in order to achieve socialism, the market system would have to be abolished. In *The Development of Capitalism in Russia* (1899), he pointed out that the peasantry was dividing into a well-off rural bourgeoisie (*kulaks**), middle peasants, and an impoverished landless rural proletariat. The last two classes could become allies of the small Russian industrial proletariat.

7. In *What Is To Be Done?* (1902), Lenin argued that the proletariat could not grasp that it would be necessary to overthrow capitalism in order to win complete emancipation unless its **level of awareness** was raised. This could best be accomplished by a political party which would act as the "**vanguard* of the proletariat**."* Lenin believed that it was the right time to found such a party, but a congress held in Minsk in 1898 failed when most of the delegates were arrested.

8. It was decided that the Second Congress would meet in Brussels (1903), but police pressure forced it to transfer to London. The main issues discussed were:
   (a) eligibility for membership
   (b) the character of party discipline
   Lenin insisted upon **democratic centralism**, or absolute party discipline. According to Lenin the party had to be a highly centralised body organised around a small, ideologically homogeneous core of professional revolutionaries, who would be elected to a central committee by the party congress. "Give us an organisation of revolutionaries," Lenin declared, "and we will overturn Russia!"

9. Although Lenin found himself in the minority in the early sessions of the Second Congress of what was then named the **Russian Social-Democratic Workers' Party (RSDWP)**, a walkout by his opponents left him with a small majority. Thus, paradoxically, the members of Lenin's group were called **Bolsheviks** (majoritarians), while their opponents, led by Martov (including Plekhanov and Trotsky) were dubbed **Mensheviks** (minoritarians). The RSDWP had split into two opposing factions.

The Crisis of 1905

1. The efficiency of an autocracy depends upon the character and abilities of the autocrat. Tsar Nicholas II, who had reigned since 1894, was weak-willed and probably not very intelligent. The Tsarina, Alexandra, was German and unpopular. Soon after his accession Nicholas dismissed as "senseless dreams" the aspirations of the *intelligentsia** to share in the work of government.

2. Unrest developed during the Russo-Japanese War (1904-5) which was a series of disasters for Russia, revealing the autocracy as incompetent.
   (a) Influential liberals organised a **banquet campaign** to publicise demands for reform;
   (b) Students and workers held **demonstrations;**
   (c) **Terrorist attacks** took place on officials.

3. On Sunday January 9th, "**Bloody Sunday**", a monarchist priest, Father Gapon, led a large crowd to present a petition to the Tsar at the Winter Palace in St. Petersburg. They were demanding:
   (a) improvements in working conditions;
   (b) the abolition of redemption payments on the peasants' lands; (which had impoverished many)
   (c) freedom of the press;
   (d) democracy, in the form of a parliament or *Duma.*
   The Tsar was not in residence, but the guards fired on the crowd, killing over two hundred.

4. Protest and disorder increased:
   (a) A general strike broke out.
   (b) Revolutionary committees called **soviets** were set up in factories and other workplaces in St. Petersburg and elsewhere. These functioned as:
      (i) places where the workers could engage in political debate
      (ii) emergency municipal governments

5. The unpopular Tsar was perceived by many as:
   (a) an incompetent war leader;
   (b) ultimately responsible for the massacre of "Bloody Sunday."

6. The Tar was forced to make concessions in the **October Manifesto**, when:
   (a) he accepted the idea of a constitution in principle;
   (b) agreed to the election of a *Duma.*

7. The soviets were suppressed at the end of the year by the police, and leading members of the St Petersburg soviet were arrested. This led to bloody clashes.

8. Tsarism survived this crisis because:
   (a) The troubles were spontaneous, lacking co-ordination and leadership.
   (b) The Tsar had the backing of the army, and with the end of the war with Japan, troops could be moved into the cities;
   (c) Liberals had been alarmed by the establishment of the soviets and the strikes, and moved to support the government;
   (d) Tsar Nicholas was, on this occasion, prepared to compromise: dividing the opposition and defusing tension.

9. During the troubles of 1905, Lenin was in Switzerland. The Mensheviks argued that the proletariat must ally with the bourgeoisie to create a bourgeois revolution. This would bring the bourgeoisie to power, whereupon the RSDWP would act as the party of opposition, preparing the way for a future socialist revolution. Lenin rejected this. He declared that:
   (a) The proletariat was the driving force of revolution and its only reliable ally the peasantry.
   (b) The revolution in Russia need not necessarily stop at the first stage (of the bourgeois revolution). A Russian bourgeois revolution might trigger the already developed western European industrial proletariat into launching a Socialist revolution in their own countries.

Reform and Reaction 1905-10

1. Russia had at last acquired a parliament: the ***Duma.*** The electoral system for the First *Duma* was rigged so that landowners and the middle classes would be over represented. The main groups represented were:

   (a) The **Kadets** of the **Constitutional Democratic Party** (**KDs**). Influenced by the West, they favoured the introduction of liberal democracy. They wished for either:

       (i) a constitutional monarchy on the British model, or

       (ii) a parliamentary republic on the French model.

   (b) **The Socialist Revolutionaries (SRs),** the successors of the populists. They had only vaguely thought out aims, but they were inclined to violence. They were popular among the peasants.

   (c) **The Social Democrat Labour Party (SDs)** a Marxist party divided between its two factions, the Bolsheviks and the Mensheviks, popular only among the small industrial proletariat.

2. When the **First *Duma*** met, it demanded:

   (a) a more just and representative electoral system;

   (b) the right to approve the appointment of the Tsar's ministers;

   (c) the confiscation of the large estates.

   After ten weeks the Tsar had the *Duma* dispersed by troops.

3. The Second *Duma* (1907) suffered a similar fate.

4. The franchise was then restricted to exclude peasants and urban workers.

5. The Third and Fourth *Dumas* were conservative, and so lasted longer; but they were largely irrelevant since they had been deprived of power.

6. This treatment of successive *Dumas* did not spark revolution because:

   (a) Most revolutionary leaders had been imprisoned or exiled after the troubles of 1905;

   (b) The economy improved during 1906.

7. The Tsar's minister, Peter Stolypin, negotiated a loan from the French.

8. Stolypin attempted improvements in agriculture, and output rose sharply between 1906 and 1914.

   (a) By 1914 about 10% of the peasants had consolidated their strips into one holding.

   (b) Many had transferred their land to hereditary tenure, so that they could hand it on to their children.

   (c) Many households formed cooperatives* to purchase seeds, equipment and fertilizers, or to market their produce.

   (d) Many peasants from the more densely populated regions of Russia had migrated to Siberia and northern Turkestan, where they were offered subsidies for travel, free land and specialist advice.

   Stolypin's real aim was to undermine revolution in the long term by laying the basis for a more prosperous peasant agriculture, which would create a class of rich peasants (***kulaks***), who would have a stake in the *status quo** and so be inclined to resist revolution; while the landless peasants would form a pool of labour to man the factories in the towns.

9. The government also sought to widen its support by welfare reforms:

   (a) Basic trade union rights were introduced in 1906.

   (b) Health insurance was introduced in 1912.

10. While the non-Russian peoples of the empire made considerable political and cultural gains during 1905-06, these were largely reversed after 1907.

    (a) Ukrainian nationalism gained ground and spread from the professional strata to embrace a growing number of peasants and workers.

    (b) In Poland:

        (i) After 1907, Russian was restored as the language of instruction in all schools;

      (ii) Local government assemblies were introduced, but with artificially stacked Russian majorities.

      (c) The Finnish Diet was reduced to the status of a provincial *zemstvo,* and Finland was placed under direct rule from St. Petersburg.

      (d) With the new electoral law of 1907 nearly all Muslims lost their representation in the *Duma.* Many of Muslim leaders emigrated to Turkey, drawn by the Young Turk Revolution of 1908.

      (e) In Central Asia, industrialization and the colonization of the grazing lands by immigrants from European Russia caused resentment which was to break out in open rebellion in 1916.

11. Despite some moderate reforms, the Tsar had become more unpopular during 1905-14:

      (a) The memory of "Bloody Sunday" had permanently alienated many.

      (b) The reforms offered were "too little, too late."

      (c) In time, Stolypin, the chief agent of reform, lost the confidence of the Tsar, and was assassinated in 1911. The Tsar was believed to be implicated in the shooting, which took place in his presence at the opera. It was believed Stolypin had become too liberal for the reactionaries.

      (d) Tsar Nicholas was preoccupied with the health of the Tsarevich* Alexei, who suffered from haemophilia, a condition in which the blood is deficient in clotting agent, so that any bleeding and bruising is dangerous and painful.

      (e) The Tsarina was heavily influenced by the Rasputin, a self-professed "holy man" who could relieve the suffering of the young Tsarevich (the young heir to the throne) using hypnotism. Despite his reputation for drunkenness and bad behaviour he became a powerful influence at court. In 1912 the *Duma* petitioned for his banishment, but without success.

      (f) Even the aristocrats began to despair of the autocracy.

12. In April 1912, 270 strikers in the Lena goldfields were shot. Industrial unrest increased, with:

      2,000 strikes in 1912

      2400 in 1913

      over 4000 in Jan-Aug. 1914

Richard Freeborn wrote that by July 1914 in St. Petersburg, these disturbances "assumed the proportions of incipient revolution with street demonstrations, shootings, and the building of barricades."

13. Between 1905 and 1914, the combination of repression and modest reform by the tsarist regime led to a decline of party membership in the RSDWP. Despair over the possibility of a successful revolution undermined party morale.

14. The split between Bolsheviks and Mensheviks became official and final at a Party Conference at Prague, in 1912, when Lenin proclaimed that the Bolsheviks were the *only true* RSDWP. After that date, each faction maintained its separate central committee, party apparatus,* and press.

Russia during the First World War

1. The outbreak of war brought a reduction in the number of strikes, greater national unity in Russia, and strengthened support for the monarchy. The *Duma* allowed its sessions to be suspended, and voluntary organisations were created to lend support to the war effort. All the Bolsheviks in Russia were arrested.

2. While Socialist parties throughout Europe rallied behind their governments, Lenin, who arrived in Switzerland in September 1914, joining a small group of anti-war Bolshevik and Mensheviks, virtually cut off from contact with Russia called for the creation of a new, Third, International composed of genuinely revolutionary Socialist parties; and called upon the workers to "transform the imperialist war into civil war." This policy found few supporters; even some Bolsheviks supported the war.

3. In *Imperialism, the Highest Stage of Capitalism* (1917), Lenin explained the causes of the war as due to the expansionist character of imperialism, a consequence of capitalism. At the end of the nineteenth century, a small number of banks dominated the advanced countries, and these had brought the rest of the world under their control. These banks could earn great profits on investments in colonies and client states. In 1914, rival coalitions of imperialists launched the war to take a greater share of these profits. Socialists supported their national governments because they were better paid workers, who received, in return, a tiny share of the colonial profits. For this, they had betrayed their exploited comrades in the colonies.

3. The Tsar forbade Russians to drink alcohol (mostly vodka) for the duration of the war. As a result, the government lost the revenues it earned from alcohol sales. It printed money to make up the loss, causing inflation.

4. The surprisingly swift Russian invasion of East Prussia in August 1914 was a failure, and nearly 150,000 Russians were taken prisoner. However the invasion did cause the Germans to withdraw troops from their western front, undermining the working of the Schlieffen Plan* and enabling the French to win the First Battle of the Marne.

5. The entry of Turkey into the war on the side of Germany was a major setback for Russia.
   (a) It created a new front in the Caucasus;
   (b) By closing the Straits,* it reduced the supplies that the Allies could deliver to Russia.

6. When the Central Powers launched a spring offensive in 1915, the Russian army was short of munitions. The Germans and Austrians were able to occupy the whole of Poland and begin advancing into the western provinces and the Baltic region.

7. These military reverses, together with an acute shortage of munitions, provoked the *Duma* to seek to compel the government to become more responsive to public opinion. In the State Council a "Progressive Bloc" was formed to bring about the formation of a "government enjoying public confidence," whose ministers would be drawn in part from the *Duma* itself. The bloc called for political reform, including:
   (a) the freeing of political prisoners;
   (b) the repeal of discrimination against religious minorities;
   (c) the emancipation of the Jews;
   (d) autonomy for Poland;
   (e) the elimination of the remaining legal disabilities suffered by peasants;
   (f) the repeal of anti-trade-union legislation;
   (g) the democratisation of local government.

8. In August 1915 the Tsar announced that he was taking personal command of the army. This had the effect of making him personally responsible for all future failures in the war effort.

9. Nicholas found it difficult to co-ordinate the war effort from his headquarters in Mogdilov, yet he insisted that all power remain in his own hands. He made frequent ministerial changes, known as "ministerial leap-frog." It was generally, and probably incorrectly, believed that this was under the influence of his wife and Rasputin. Anti-monarchical feeling grew.

10. The murder of Rasputin in December 1916 by an aristocratic clique, paradoxically exposed the monarchy to increased criticism by removing a convenient scapegoat.

11. Although the fronts were stabilised, and industry reorganised to concentrate on necessary military production, a food shortage was caused:
   (a) Ten million men, about one third of the male agricultural labour force, were in the army.
   (b) More grain than usual was needed because soldiers' rations were higher than average peasant consumption.
   (c) The food transportation system to the cities almost collapsed because of the diversion of

transport to other needs.

(d) The German and Turkish blockade choked off most imports. In consequence, prices rose and famine loomed.

12. Strikes began in the summer of 1915 and increased during 1916, culminating in a large strike at the Putilov Armament and Locomotive works in Petrograd (the name given to St. Petersburg during the war).

Timeline of the Approach of Revolution	
1898	Foundation of the Russian Social Democratic Labour Party
1901	Foundation of the Social Revolutionary Party (SRs)
1903	Second Congress of the Russian Social Democratic Workers' Party
	Lenin establishes Demcratic Centralism
	Split between the Bolsheviks and the Mensheviks
1904	Russo-Japanese War
1905	Near Revolution - Bloody Sunday
1906	Peter Stolypin becomes Prime Minister
1911	Assassination of Stolypin
1912	Final split between the Bolsheviks and the Mensheviks
1914	Outbreak of the First World War
1915	The Tsar takes personal control of the direction of the war

THE RUSSIAN REVOLUTIONS

Calendar Note
The two Russian revolutions of 1917 are still known as the February and October Revolutions in Russia, although they took place in March and November in the rest of the world. This is because at that time Russia still used the old Julian calendar which was thirteen days behind the Gregorian calendar, long since adopted elsewhere in the Western world.

The February/March Revolution

1. A food shortage developed in Petrograd due to:
   (a) the conscription of peasants into the army;
   (b) scorched earth tactics adopted by the Russian Army;
   (c) failure of the government adequately to manage the transport of supplies to he cities;
   (d) members of the Duma despaired at the incompetence of the Tsar's government. Some began to consider removing the Tsar.
2. The **February Revolution** began among the food queues of the capital, when people started calling for an end to autocracy. Workers from most of the major factories joined the demonstrations.
3. The Tsar dismissed the Duma again, but the Duma continued to sit. When workers marched on the Tauride Palace, where the Duma was sitting, the members decided to support them.

4. Cossacks summoned to disperse the crowds refused to obey orders, and troops in the city garrison mutinied. The usually loyal professional troops had been diluted, due to the needs of the war, with discontented conscripts who were often related to the people they were called upon to shoot.

5. Mobs seized public buildings, took over police stations and emptied the prisons.

6. The workers and soldiers spontaneously re-created the **Soviets of Workers' and Soldiers' Deputies**, as in the troubles of 1905. Soon their example was followed in many other towns and army units throughout the empire. Initially the soviets were dominated by Mensheviks and Socialist Revolutionaries (SRs).

7. By agreement between the Petrograd Soviet and the Duma, a **Provisional Government** was formed on March 1st. Headed by Prince Lvov, it consisted mainly of Kadets (liberals) and Octobrists* (conservatives), although the socialist Alexander Kerensky joined it as Minister of War.

8. Tsar Nicholas was advised to abdicate by several generals and a committee of the Duma, and no significant forces moved to defend the monarchy. **The Tsar abdicated** on behalf of himself and his son in favour of his brother, Grand Duke Michael, who refused the throne. Thus Russia became a republic.

Analysis

The February Revolution was:

(a) a spontaneous reaction to the chaotic food and transport situation;

(b) a revolt of the bourgeois liberals and constitutionalists against the autocracy;

(c) a revolt of industrial workers;

(d) a revolt of peasants;

(e) a general revolt against the war.

The Period of Dual Power

1. The provisional government had to try to govern in uneasy partnership with the soviets, a situation known as "**dual power.**"

2. The Provisional Government:

(a) gave independence to Poland and local autonomy to Finland and Estonia;

(b) released all political prisoners;

(c) abolished censorship of the press, the Okhrana, the tsarist police and security services, and the death penalty;

(d) announced reforms:

(i) freedom of speech and assembly;

(ii) a humane code of civil rights for soldiers;

(e) announced the future election of a **Constituent Assembly***

It was also decided to:

(f) continue the war;

(g) postpone the problem of land settlement (the peasants wanted the land of the great landowners) for the Constituent Assembly.

3. There followed a general breakdown of authority.

(a) Some soviets declared their cities "soviet republics" and/or formed paramilitary units.

(b) Factory committees took over many factories.

(c) Many of the *mirs* seized and divided land among the peasants.

(d) In military units soldiers' committees claimed the right to elect officers and approve their orders. Discipline began to disintegrate.

Because of its liberal approach to law and order, the Provisional Government had given up the means by which it could enforce its will upon the population.

4. The Soviet soon proved that it had greater authority than the Provisional Government. On March 1st (March 14) the Petrograd Soviet issued **Order No. 1**, which directed the military to obey only the orders of the Soviet and not those of the Provisional Government. The Provisional Government was unable to countermand this order. Even at this stage, all that prevented the Petrograd Soviet from declaring itself the government of Russia was fear of provoking a right-wing coup.

5. Marxists interpreted the February/March Revolution as a bourgeois revolution. The Mensheviks in the soviets, believing that a period of bourgeois rule was necessary before a true socialist revolution could be launched, were prepared to work with the Provisional government.

6. In April Lenin returned from exile in Switzerland. The Germans allowed him to travel to Petrograd via Germany and Sweden in a sealed train, hoping that he would cause further chaos in Russia.

7. In his "**April Theses**" Lenin argued that what was happening in Russia *could* become a genuine socialist revolution, and that the Bolsheviks must be ready to take power on behalf of the workers. He urged the Bolsheviks to:

(a) withdraw their support from the Provisional Government;

(b) call for immediate withdrawal from the war;

(c) call for the distribution of land among the peasantry;

(d) organise workers, soldiers, and peasants and to strengthen the Soviets so that they could eventually seize power from the Provisional Government;

(e) demand the nationalisation of the banks;

(f) and soviet control of the production and distribution of manufactured goods.

Lenin presented his *Theses* to a Bolshevik committee, which rejected them. The Bolshevik newspaper *Pravda* published them, pointing out that they were Lenin's own ideas and not official policy. Nevertheless, within a few weeks the party's seventh all-Russian conference (May 7-12 [April 24-29, old style]) adopted them as its program, along with the slogans: **"Peace, bread, land,"** and **"All Power to the Soviets."**

8. In June a new offensive was launched on the instigation of Minister of Defence Alexander Kerensky. There was a complete collapse of army morale and discipline. Hundreds of thousands of troops deserted. For some time a German counter-attack threatened Petrograd itself.

9. Although some Bolsheviks still had reservations about the *April Theses*, they became very popular among the workers and soldiers of Petrograd. Workers and soldiers using the Bolshevik slogans staged demonstrations and riots known as the "**July Days**". They demanded that the Soviet assume power. Many other revolutionaries had began to join the Bolsheviks, including Leon Trotsky, a former Menshevik. But Lenin was afraid of attempting to take power too soon:

(a) the Party had not planned for it;

(b) it might provoke a right-wing military coup that they would be unable to resist.

10. To undermine Bolshevik popularity and reduce the threat of a coup d'état, the government produced "evidence" that Lenin had close political and financial ties with the German government. A public reaction set in against the Bolsheviks; their leaders were arrested. Lenin fled in disguise to Finland; but others, including Trotsky, were jailed.

11. In August, **General Lavr Kornilov** attempted to overthrow the provisional government. He had been commissioned by Kerensky to strengthen discipline in the army, but he turned around with his troops to "restore law and order" at home. This was the much-feared right-wing coup attempt. It was foiled when:

(a) Kerensky immediately denounced Kornilov.

(b) In Petrograd former soldiers were fashioned into the paramilitary **Red Guards** under the leadership of Leon Trotsky. Fearing Kornilov's imminent arrival in Petrograd, Kerensky armed them.

(c) Railwaymen refused to transport Kornilov's troops into the capital.

(d) Soldiers south and west of Petrograd fraternised with his men, and urged them not to attack the city.

Sensing possible mutiny among his troops, Kornilov withdrew them.

12. The Kadets left the government, weakening it. Prince Lvov resigned and was replaced by **Kerensky**. More Socialist Revolutionaries (SRs) and Mensheviks were taken into the Provisional Government. Kerensky postponed:

    (a) the elections for the Constituent Assembly;

    (b) and consequently, land reform.

This increased his unpopularity.

13. Disorder, anarchy and violence increased across the country.

(a) Food shops were looted.

(b) Many peasants murdered their landlords and seized land.

(c) Many employers shut down factories on the excuse of raw material shortages in order to discipline workers who were pressing for better wages and conditions. The workers took the factories over, and set up factory committees to manage them.

(d) Murders of officers and desertions from the army became common.

Kerensky used troops against the population, making him even more unpopular.

14. Support for the Bolsheviks grew among the urban population. They soon came to control the Petrograd and Moscow soviets and many others.

15. The Provisional Government had been fatally weakened by:

    (a) continuing disorders and lawlessness at home;

    (b) its own abandonment of the means of coercion;

    (c) its postponement of the division of land amng the peasants;

    (d) continued defeats in the unpopular war;

    (e) the rival authority of the soviets.

16. In Finland, Lenin decided that it was time to seize power. The party should prepare an uprising to depose the Provisional Government and take power through the soviets. In *The State and Revolution,* he wrote that until 1917 revolutionary Socialists believed that a Socialist system could take the form of a parliamentary republic. But the Russian Revolution had produced the soviets, set up by workers, soldiers, and peasants, and excluding the middle classes. These soviets were more genuinely democratic than bourgeoise parliaments, which usually excluded working people.

17. Yet Lenin once again found himself in a minority within the party. Zinoviev and Kamenev argued against a revolution at this point, on the grounds that the Bolsheviks were not yet strong enough to hold power alone.

The October/November "Revolution"

1. Lenin secretly returned to Russia, entered Petrograd in disguise, and attended a meeting of the Bolshevik Central Committee on the evening of October 23. After a marathon 10-hour debate he won a majority in favour of preparing a coup d'état, so that the Second All-Russian Congress of Soviets, scheduled to convene the next evening, would be presented with a *fait accompli.**

2. Steps were taken to enlist the support of soldiers and sailors to aid the Red Guards for the take-

over. Trotsky led the preparations from the Smolny Institute as newly elected chairman of the Petrograd Soviet.

3. During the night 24th -25th October [6th-7th November] soldiers and Red Guards assembled. On the morning of the 25th, the Aurora gave the signal by firing on the Winter Palace, and they occupied key points in the city, meeting with no resistance. During the night of the 25th-26th they surrounded the Winter Palace. Early in the morning of the 26th all the members of the Provisional Government were arrested, except Kerensky, who had fled to the US embassy.

4. When the All-Russian Congress of Soviets met on the evening of 25th they recognised the end of the Provisional Government and the new **Council of Peoples' Commissars (Sovnarcom)**, headed by Lenin. The Mensheviks refused to accept the coup and walked out, leaving the Bolsheviks with a small majority with the support of the Left SRs. They turned the Congress into a legislature.

5. It took a week of fighting for the Moscow Soviet to take control there, and the rest of the month for most other cites to be secured.

6. This was not a genuine revolution but a **coup d'état** by a minority party, although it had the support of large sections of the population in the cities.

Reasons for the Success of the Coup

1. At the time, conspiracy theories abounded:
   (a) Western observers saw the coup as the successful outcome of a German plot to take Russia out of the war.
   (b) Most widespread was the theory of an international Jewish conspiracy. (Trotsky, Zinoviev and other prominent Bolsheviks were Jews.)

2. The Bolshevik success has often been put down to Lenin's fashioning the Bolshevik Party as a disciplined and well-organised instrument for seizing power. Lenin had always planned for the coup, and the Bolsheviks knew exactly what they wanted to do. However:
   (a) Despite Lenin's wishes, internally the Bolshevik party was quite democratic. Everything was discussed in the Central Committee, and Lenin's ideas had been frequently dismissed as extreme.
   (b) Between the February Revolution and the October coup, the Bolshevik Party had been swamped by new members, and was, paradoxically, in the process of turning into the mass party, favoured by the Mensheviks, which Lenin had sought to avoid.

3. The Provisional Government had been challenged by the existence of the soviets from the start, and its unqualified legitimacy* had never been accepted by the majority of the population.

4. The Provisional Government insisted upon unpopular policies:
   (a) postponing the land question;
   (b) staying in the war.
   which weakened its support among the increasingly radical population and increased that of the Bolsheviks who opposed those policies.

5. In turn this increased Bolshevik representation in the Petrograd and Moscow Soviets.

6. In August the moderates left the Provisional Government, leaving Kerensky isolated.

7. The failed coup attempt by General Kornilov boosted support for the Bolsheviks in Petrograd and led to the arming of the Red Guards by Kerensky..

8. Lenin had been prepared to compromise his principles, courting popularity by accepting popular policies, e.g. by supporting the peasants' land seizures, which he did not approve of.

9. Despite several false starts, Lenin finally judged well the moment of maximum hostility to the Kerensky government.

10. The Bolshevik Party alone was untainted by compromise with the Provisional Government,

which the people had rejected.

11. Leon Trotsky managed and carried out the coup successfully.

Timeline of the Revolutions (Old Style Dates)	
1917	
Feb 23	Rioting breaks out in Petrograd
26	Troops mutiny in Petrograd
27	The Tsar dissolves the Duma, but it refuses to leave
Mar 1	Establishment of the Petrograd Soviet
2	Provisional Government set up under Prince Lvov
	Tsar Nicholas abdicates
April	Lenin's April Theses published
June	First All-Russian Congress of Soviets meets
August	Attempted coup of General Kornilov
Sept	Trotsky becomes head of the Petrograd Soviet
Oct 7	Lenin returns to Petrograd and presses for Revolution
23	Kerensky closes down the Bolshevik Press
25	Bolshevik coup in Petrograd
	Second All-Russian Congress of Soviets approves Lenin and Sovnarkom as government of Russia
26	Storming of the Winter Palace

The Establishment of the Soviet State

1. Lenin intended to build a socialist society, but he did not yet have the means to coerce a partly ignorant and partly reluctant public.

2. After the coup the government was entrusted to a **Council of Peoples' Commissars (Sovnarcom),** headed by Lenin, while the All-Russian Congress of Soviets became a legislative body.

3. The main problems which Lenin's government faced were:
   (a) The Bolsheviks were a small minority in the country, with no support in the countryside.
   (b) Lenin had criticised Kerensky's postponement of the elections for the Constituent Assembly, so he could hardly postpone them himself.
   (c) The war was still going on.

4. The first step was to reform the Russian economy in accordance with socialist principles. Immediately Sovnarcom issued a series of edicts:
   (a) In **the Decree on Land,** 540 million acres of land was seized from rich landowners and the Church, without compensation, for distribution to poor peasants.
   (b) **The Decree on Workers' Control of the Factories** simply recognised what was already happening.
   (c) A **Supreme Council of the National Economy** was created to plan the economy.
   (d) Nationalization* of banks and foreign trade effectively introduced **state capitalism**.
   (e) Wages were fixed and an eight-hour day introduced.
   (f) All foreign debts were repudiated.
   (g) Comprehensive social insurance was announced.
   (h) The **Decree on Nationalities** recognised the right of non-Russian peoples to secede from Russia. There were already moves towards independence in the Baltic, Ukraine and Caucusus.

The purpose of these edicts was:
    (i) to gain popularity with the masses;
    (ii) to begin the building of a socialist society.
However, the right of workers on factory committees was limited to representation; direction and decision-making were to be the prerogative of the Party.

5. In order to fix the election for the Constituent Assembly, the KDs were first made illegal. The Bolsheviks won 168 out of 700 seats, while the Social Revolutionaries (SRs) held 380. When the Assembly convened it was surrounded by Red Guards. After some anti-Bolshevik speeches, the Assembly was abolished by a decree of Sovnarcom, and dispersed by the guards.

6. Further reforms were then introduced:
    (a) Private inheritance was abolished in April.
    (b) Major industries were nationalised in June.
    (c) Mortgages were abolished in August.

7. In July 1918 a **constitution** for the Russian Socialist Federal Soviet Republic was created.
    (a) Sovereign authority was vested in the All-Russian Congress of Soviets.
    (b) They elected a Central Executive Committee, which in turn elected a Council of Peoples' Commissars as the government.
    (c) The capital city was moved to Moscow.
    (d) The name of the Bolshevik Party was changed to that of Communist Party.
    (e) Other Soviet Republics were founded e.g. in the Ukraine and Azerbaijan, and alliances concluded with them. Bolsheviks were installed to govern them.

War and Peace

1. It was thought that the revolution in Russia would be followed by similar revolutions in other countries. There would soon be no old-fashioned states for the Foreign Ministry to do business with. Leon Trotsky, Commissar for Foreign Affairs, announced "I will issue a few revolutionary proclamations to the peoples of the world, and then shut up shop."

2. The Bolsheviks renounced the wartime alliance. In the **Decree on Peace**, the Bolshevik government called, unrealistically, for a peace without land transfers and indemnities. Lenin needed to end the war to:
    (a) fulfil the promise he had made to do so;
    (b) consolidate Bolshevik power.

3. An armistice was arranged with Germany for Dec. 22nd. Negotiations followed, managed by Trotsky, but proceeded slowly. The Bolsheviks were deliberately dragging their feet. On Jan. 7th, 1918, Trotsky asked for adjournment, still hoping for the long-awaited world revolution to break out. There was a mutiny in the Austrian fleet and a general strike in Berlin, but both were easily suppressed. The Bolshevik leadership now faced a choices between three alternatives:
    (a) to defy the Germans, and risk conquest and the overthrow of the regime;
    (b) to relent and sign over half of European Russia to German control;
    (c) to continue to stall, pursuing what Trotsky called "neither war nor peace," while awaiting the expected outbreak of revolution in Germany.

4. In the meantime the Germans and Austrians concluded the **Brotfrieden** ("bread peace") with representatives of the Ukraine. When Bolshevik forces entered the Ukraine the Germans broke off talks and ordered their army to resume its advance. The French ambassador offered the Bolsheviks aid if they would fight the Germans, but Lenin ordered immediate capitulation.

5. Germany presented harsh peace terms, and on March 3 the Bolsheviks signed the **Treaty of Brest-Litovsk.** The Bolsheviks were forced to recognise the independence of the Baltic States

(Estonia, Latvia and Lithuania), Poland and the Ukraine. They surrendered:

    (i) 34% of Russia's population,

    (ii) 32 % of its farmland,

    (iii) 54 % of its industrial plant,

    (iv) 89% of its coal mines,

    (v) virtually all of its cotton and oil.

With these economic gains, plus the release of troops, who could now be shifted to the Western Front, the Germans hoped that victory could be achieved there before American soldiers began to arrive in significant numbers.

6. The signing of the treaty caused great discontent on the left wing:

    (a) The Left Socialist Revolutionaries (SRs) resigned from Sovnarcom.

    (b) There was also considerable opposition within the party itself.

Lenin still considered that he was "giving up space to gain a little time"; time for the revolution to spread to Germany and the other countries of Europe. When it did, there would be no more hostile governments to deal with. Worker would join hands with worker across the national borders to create a new world order. The disadvantageous Treaty would simply become irrelevant.

The Russian Civil War

The Causes of the Russian Civil War

1. There were many groups in Russia opposed to the Bolshevik take-over of the country:

    (a) Counter-revolutionaries:

        (i) Those who supported the Tsarist system in some form;

        (ii) Those who wished for a Western style state: either a constitutional monarchy or republic;

        (iii) ambitious generals who saw the opportunity to gain personal power;

    (b) Non-Russian nationalists, who saw an opportunity to gain national liberation;

    (c) Revolutionaries who resented Bolshevik domination:

        (i) the Social Revolutionaries (SRs);

        (ii) the anarchists.

2. Following the Treaty of Brest-Litovsk, with its massive sacrifice of territory, the opponents of Lenin and the Bolshevists found common cause:

    (a) The Whites, including all counter-revolutionaries: supporters of the Tsar, the landlords or democracy.

    (b) The non-Bolshevik left: left SRs and anarchists: who had been alienated by Lenin's dissolution of the Constituent Assembly and by the Treaty of Brest-Litovsk.

3. By summer 1918 different factions of the "Whites"* had set up provisional governments:

    (a) Admiral Kolchak set up a "White" government in Siberia.

    (b) General Denikin held the Caucasus region.

    (c) General Wrangel held Crimea.

4. At the same time, the Left SRs attempted a coup and set up a government at Samara on the River Volga. Attempts were made to assassinate Lenin and leading Bolshevik officials.

5. The Czechoslovak Legion, comprising POWs from the Austro-Hungarian Army who had fought against the Germans under the Provisional Government. Following the peace of Brest-Litovsk, they had been permitted to leave the country by way of the Trans-Siberian Railway and Vladivostock, on the Pacific Coast. When attempts were made to disarm them, they seized control of the Trans-Siberian Railway and set up their own administrations.

THE TREATY OF
BREST-LITOVSK

(March 1918)

SWEDEN

FINLAND

Petrograd

ESTONIA

RUSSIA

LIVONIA

Moscow

LITHUANIA

GERMANY

Warsaw •   • Brest-Litovsk

POLAND

• Kiev

UKRAINE

AUSTRIA-HUNGARY

6. In addition, Allied governments were opposed to the Bolshevik takeover:

(a) Fearful of revolution among their own populations, they hoped, in Churchill's words, "to strangle the revolution in its cradle."

(b) The repudiation of foreign debts and the confiscation of foreign assets had hurt and infuriated the French.

(c) The Treaty of Brest-Litovsk was a disaster for the Allies, who considered intervention in Russia:

(i) If they could link up with nationalist Russians and reopen the Eastern Front, they might save their exhausted armies in France from facing the full force of the Spring onslaught the Germans were launching in an attempt to break through the lines before the arrival of fresh American forces.

(ii) They might also save Allied war *materiel* that had stacked up in Russian ports from seizure by the Germans or Bolsheviks, and distribute it to Russians still willing to fight the Germans.

7. Britain, Japan, the USA, France, Rumania, Poland, Serbia and Greece sent troops to Russia.

(a) The French landed in the Ukraine, at Odessa.

(b) The British landed in the Murmansk region in the north.

(c) The Americans landed at Arkhangelsk, in the north, and in the Far East.

(d) The Japanese established themselves systematically in the Far Eastern provinces.

Direct intervention by Allied military forces involved about 200,000 soldiers.

The Course of the Russian Civil War

1. By August 1918, the Czechs and White allies captured Kazan, 400 miles from Moscow. Leon Trotsky, the Commissar for War, rushed to the area by rail to assemble a local force to block the road to Moscow. Not only did he raise a force, he recaptured Kazan.

2. With the end of the World War in November 1918, and the end of the pretext of reactivating the Eastern Front, it became clear that the real reason for foreign intervention was the desire of the capitalists to suppress the revolution.

3. Early in 1919 General Kolchak approached Moscow, the new capital city, from the Urals with three armies.

4. By this time, Trotsky had built upon the foundation of the Red Guards and created a Bolshevik Red Army to defend the Revolution. He accepted the assistance of many officers from the old Tsarist Army. They were not given their uniforms or right to receive salutes back, but they were called commanders, and under the supervision of political commissars, could exercise full rights to command. The soldiers' revolutionary committees were abolished.

5. Kolchak was driven back in early summer.

6. The French in the Ukraine were:

(a) bewildered by the confused struggle between Bolsheviks, Russian Whites and Ukrainian nationalists;

(b) unsure of the loyalty of their own troops, who were absorbing revolutionary sentiments.

They withdrew their forces during March and April 1919, having hardly fired a shot.

7. The Americans and British in the Arkhangelsk and Murmansk areas did some fighting, using poison gas against the Bolsheviks, before withdrawing their forces in the early fall of 1919.

8. In October 1919, General Denikin took advantage of a cossack rising against the Bolsheviks in the Ukraine to conquer most of Ukraine. He advanced from the south and reached within 250 miles of Moscow before being defeated.

9. At the same time, General Yudenich made a thrust towards Petrograd from the Baltic region,

THE RUSSIAN CIVIL WAR
(March 1921)

Murmansk
British
Arkhangelsk
Americans
Foreign Control
FINLAND
White Control
Kolchak
Petrograd
BOLSHEVIK RUSSIA
Iudenich
Moscow
Trans-Siberian Railway
Samara
POLAND
White Cossacks
Poles (later)
UKRAINE
Kiev
White Control
Denikin
Odessa
ROMANIA
Wrangel
French
British
Turks
British
Baku
Foreign Control
TURKEY

before being driven back.

10. General Pyotr N. Wrangel launched an attack from the Crimea in 1920, but failed. By November 1920, the Whites had failed, and the danger to the Bolsheviks was over.

The Russo-Polish War

1. Taking advantage of the chaos in Russia to increase their own territory and influence in the region, the Polish Army invaded under **Marshall Pilsudski** in 1920, advancing as far as Kiev.
2. In response, the Red Army drove the Poles back almost to Warsaw. In doing so the Red Army was joined, for what were essentially patriotic reasons, by many officers of the old Tsarist Army who had not previously fought in the Red Army.
3. The Russians expected that Polish workers would rise against the bourgeoisie and participate in the World Revolution. But in Poland nationalism proved stronger than socialism.
4. The French sent assistance to Poland under **General Weygand,** and Polish resistance stiffened.
5. Polish and French troops then invaded White Russia and the Ukraine.
6. By the **Treaty of Riga (1921)** the Russians were forced to give up parts of White Russia and the Ukraine.
7. The Russo-Polish War demonstrated that relations between Soviet Russia and other states would be of the type normal between state powers, and not fundamentally affected by the Bolshevik character of the Soviet state.

War Communism

1. **War communism,** the mobilization of the state, party and people against the counter-revolutionary forces which threatened the government of the Bolsheviks. It was introduced in mid 1918 with the outbreak of the Civil War. Lenin enacted emergency decrees to take control of all the resources of the state:
   (a) all **large factories were nationalized**, virtually being placed under military control;
   (b) banks and credit were abolished
   (c) all private trade was banned
   (d) Lacking funds or goods to exchange against grain needed to feed the Red Army and the towns, and faced with the possibility of major famine, Lenin instituted a "**food dictatorship,**" a system of requisitioning grain surpluses without compensation.
   (e) special **production targets** were allocated to all enterprises
   (f) On "**Communist Saturdays**" workers had to work for one day extra without pay.
2. War communism was an attempt to establish total state control over the means of production and distribution. It was introduced:
   (a) ostensibly as an emergency measure because of the outbreak of the civil war. Lenin said: "War communism was thrust upon us by war and ruin... It was a temporary measure."
   (b) for ideological reasons, as a move towards building a socialist society.
3. Many peasants resisted the forced requisitions, which led to a drop in production and the development of a black market.*
4. Local Party officials carried the nationalization decree beyond the original intention of the government, including small artisan businesses, reducing their efficiency.
5. The Moscow government cracked down heavily on non-Bolshevik socialists. The Menshevik and Socialist Revolutionary deputies were expelled from the central and local soviets and prevented from engaging in any organised political activity.
6. The **PanRussian Extraordinary Commission for Struggle against Counter-Revolution (Cheka)**, a committee for fighting counter-revolution, was created, headed by the Polish

Bolshevik, Felix Dzerzhinsky. It was originally formed to:

(a) control banditry,

(b) keep watch on anti-Bolshevik conspiracies, whether from the Whites, the counter-revolutionaries, or the non-Bolshevik Reds.

It came to employ a staff of 30,000 to run a political police force and its own army. During early 1918 it rounded up and imprisoned many prominent SRs and anarchists.

7. Eventually, in September 1918, the government proclaimed a campaign of "Red terror," which authorized the shooting of hostages, and gave increased powers to the Cheka of summary arrest, trial, and the execution of suspects.

8. During this period many of what would later be thought of as the **distinguishing characteristics of the Soviet system** were set:

(a) Industrial production was paramount, since socialism could only be built after pro-duction was able to meet everyone's needs. (This was known as **productionism**).

(b) **a siege mentality**: the belief that all other powers and classes were dangerous enemies against which the Bolshevik state had to struggle to survive. At times this amounted to collective paranoia.

The Reasons for Bolshevik Success

1. The quality of Lenin's leadership:

(a) Although the economy had collapsed, Lenin managed to mobilise sufficient resources to sustain the Red Army and workers in industry.

(b) By admitting the right of the non-Russian peoples to secession, he won the forbearance of the non-Russian nationalities, because the Whites did not recognise that right. This prevented the disintegration of the empire, and allowed it to remain a multinational state.

(c) By making the industrial workers the new privileged class, favoured in the distribution of rations, housing, and political power, he retained their loyalty.

(d) Giving into the peasants' demand for the land from the gentry, church, and crown, without compensation, he won over the peasants.

2. Trotsky was a brilliant war leader. He increased the Red Army from half a million to five and a half million men. During the various campaigns he moved from one front to another in an armoured railway train, directing efforts and boosting effort and morale.

3. The Whites:

(a) Lacked unity and could not co-ordinate their efforts. Stephen J. Lee points to the "amazing variety of anti-Bolshevik regimes" which were set up at the beginning of the war;

(b) They frequently worked against each other, in an attempt to place themselves in an advantageous position relative t the others after victory over the Reds;

(c) Were associated with the foreigners, and so appeared unpatriotic to fellow Russians;

(d) Were associated with capitalists, who were suspected of wishing to exploit Russia's resources for their own profit;

(e) Were associated with the landlords. On the territories that they won, they restored landed property to the previous owners and punished peasants who had dared seize the land. Although the peasants' detested the Soviet's grain requisitioning, when forced to choose between Reds and Whites, they chose the Reds;

(f) Treated potential opponents with great severity, imposing a "White Terror" on the areas they occupied;

(g) Were committed to preserving the unity of the empire, and so were unable win the nationalist movements among the non-Russian peoples to their side;

(h) were violently anti-Semitic, killing perhaps 100,000 Jews in the Ukraine, alienating the Jewish population.

4. Foreign intervention was ineffective because:

(a) J L H Keep points out that , the war on the Western Front took priority, so no full scale invasion took place.

(b) The various Allied expeditions were uncoordinated.

(c) The soldiers were war weary.

(d) Many of the foreign soldiers sympathised with the revolution. French ships in Odessa had to be withdrawn after a mutiny. British trades unions urged the withdrawal of British troops.

5. Holding the central core of European Russia throughout the war, the Reds:

(a) Held the industrial heartland, which contained most of the military stores.

(b) Held the centre of the railway system, and so could communicate and move men and equipment more easily than the Whites, whose bases were on the periphery and so were cut off from one another.

6. The morale of the Bolsheviks was always high because they confidently expected that the Revolution would quickly spread to the rest of the developed world.

7. Little credit can be given to **war communism**, which:

(a) increased the unpopularity of the Bolsheviks, especially among the workers and peasants who were their natural allies;

(b) reduced the efficiency of their own economy.

The Results of the Civil War

1. The breakdown in normal services and production entailed by:

(a) The First World War;

(b) The First Revolution, and the disorders which followed;

(c) The Civil War;

(d) The Russo-Polish War;

led to a widespread famine which caused five million deaths.

2. Between 1914 and 1926 some fourteen million people died prematurely. There were millions of refugees and orphans.

3. Among the early victims of the Civil War were the members of the former imperial family. Nicholas II, his wife, and his children had been moved in the spring of 1918 to Yekaterinburg. The local soviet feared that Nicholas might be liberated and become a rallying point for counter-revolutionaries, so on the night of July 16-17th, 1918, all the members of the family were taken to the cellar of their prison house and shot.

4. In 1920, when the Civil War was for all practical purposes over, industrial production was about one-quarter of what it had been in 1913, and the number of employed workers had fallen by roughly one-half.

5. Since the civil war gave Russians only two alternatives, and one was not acceptable, the civil war might be said to have kept the Bolsheviks in power despite their unpopularity in 1918.

6. The political system which emerged victorious from the civil war, was one in which the soviets had been pushed to one side. All power belonged to the Communist Party, members of which occupied all the posts in the Soviet of People's Commissars, and the key posts at all the lower levels of government. The party itself was governed by its Central Committee, dominated by Lenin.

7. The style of Bolshevik government was dictated by the needs of emergency. Robert C. Tucker notes that this was based upon the **militarisation** of the Party:

(a) ready to resort to coercion;

(b) rule by administrative *fiat;*

(c) highly centralised and disciplined administration;

(d) summary justice.

8. The Communist victory was a defeat for the various nationalist movements of the non-Russian peoples. The Communists proclaimed the right of self-determination, but in practice they imposed Russian hegemony on them.

The New Economic Policy

The Origins of the New Economic Policy

1. The end of the civil war led to increased opposition among various groups which had previously supported the Bolsheviks.

2. War communism had been unpopular with the peasants, who saw no reason to produce food which was taken from them without compensation, and so they began to produce only enough for their own needs. This caused severe food-shortages, aggravated by a severe drought during 1920-1. Famine led to widespread peasant disorders.

3. Early in 1921 urban workers held strikes and demonstrations. A "Workers Opposition" was formed within the party under the Peoples' Commissar for Labour, Shylapnikov, calling for a return to the purity of original ideals.

4. Revolts broke out in several regions, e.g. the Eastern Ukraine and Western Siberia.

5. In March 1921 there was a mutiny by the sailors at the Kronstadt Naval Base. They had taken part in the October Revolution, but had become disenchanted with the Bolshevik government. They formed a Provisional Revolutionary Committee and demanded:

   (a) "soviets without Bolsheviks,"

   (b) the release of non-Bolshevik socialists from prison,

   (c) the end of the Communist Party's dictatorship,

   (d) the establishment of political freedoms and civil rights.

   (e) economic liberalization

   Leon Trotsky and Mikhail Tukhachevsky led a force that crushed the rebels in ten days, shooting or imprisoning the survivors.

6. There followed a mass arrest of Mensheviks and SRs across the country.

7. However, Lenin decided to retreat from war communism and from the move towards a fully socialist system temporarily in order to avoid another revolution. This economic relaxation was called the **New Economic Policy (NEP)**:

   (a) Peasants were allowed to sell any surplus produce for profit after paying tax.

   (b) Small-scale private enterprise was allowed once more. Over 90% of all enterprises were returned to their original owners. The state was to control only "the commanding heights of the economy."

   (c) Incentives and bonuses for workers were introduced.

8. The NEP was viewed by the Bolsheviks as a temporary measure:

   (a) to prevent another revolution;

   (b) to allow the economy to recover;

   (c) to give a breathing space for the Communists to solidify their political control before continuing to move further along the road towards socialism.

9. In consequence of the new policy:

   (a) Some *kulaks* built up large and profitable farms.

   (b) Private traders, or **Nepmen,** began to flourish in the cities.

The NEP Years

1. A controversy arose over the role of the trade unions. It was decided that a monopoly of power must be retained by the party. This was called the "**dictatorship of the party**".
2. During 1923 prices fluctuated wildly in the **scissors crisis**. The government imposed price controls, which stabilised the situation.
3. Lenin accompanied economic liberalisation with intensified political repression.
   (a) In 1922 the Cheka was abolished and replaced by the GPU (the State Political Administration. Its powers were greater than those of the Cheka, since, in addition to dealing with political opponents and running the network of concentration camps (the **Gulag**), it was charged with spying on all economic institutions to prevent "sabotage" by Nepmen.
   (b) In 1922 the leaders of the Socialist Revolutionary Party (SRs) were subjected to a sham trial, and condemned to death on charges of counter-revolution. Only international protests caused their executions to be deferred.
   (c) The "Workers' Opposition," led by Bolshevik veterans who objected to the bureaucratization of the state and the elimination of workers from decision making, was suppressed when a secret clause in the party regulations forbade the formation of "factions," i.e. organised resistance within Communist Party ranks to the policies of the leadership. The leaders of the "Workers' Opposition" were purged.
4. In 1923 Russia adopted a new constitution, largely drawn up by Stalin.
   (a) The country was constituted the Union of Soviet Socialist Republics (USSR).
   (b) The Peoples' Commissars remained the government.
   (c) The Congress of Soviets, indirectly elected, remained the legislature.
   (d) The GPU was replaced technically) with the **Unified State Political Administration (OGPU)**.
5. By 1925 Nikolay Bukharin became the chief supporter of the NEP, while Leon Trotsky was opposed to it and Joseph Stalin was noncommittal.

Cultural Policy

1. As the Party-directed activities of the state expanded, most areas of culture were brought under state control, and effectively bureaucratized.
2. In 1920 the **Agitation and Propaganda Department** of the Central Committee (*Agitprop*) was set up to perform missionary work to the population. It came to:
   (a) supervise the entire educational system;
   (b) censor the arts.
3. Lenin personally was very hostile to religion:
   (a) Patriarch Tikhon of Moscow had condemned the Bolsheviks;
   (b) The Church was associated with the Tsarist regime, providing its ideological support;
   (c) The Churches and monasteries had been great landowners;
   (d) They had adopted attitudes which were: xenophobic, anti-Semitic* and obscurantist.*
   Religion was seen as outmoded and to be replaced by science. There was considerable persecution of the priests and monks and the closing of monasteries and many city churches at this time.

Foreign Policy

1. Relations with foreign powers were uniformly bad following the revolution and civil war.
2. In 1919 Lenin established the **Communist International (Comintern)**:
   (a) to spread radical ideas and revolutionary activities outside Russia;

(b) to counter or weaken anti-Soviet policies abroad.

3. During the Civil War many Western powers and Japan intervened against the Bolsheviks, violating Russian territorial integrity and, in the case of the British, using poison gas, to overthrow the regime:

    (a) ostensibly to strengthen the astern Front (although the war was over when most of them arrived;

    (b) to suppress the Revolution, since its success, and the setting up of a Socialist system of social justice for the majority would threaten the hold of ruling elites over their own populations.

4. In 1920 the Poles conquered parts of the western Ukraine. The Red Army drove them back and almost reached Warsaw, expecting Polish workers to rise and join them. However the Polish workers were nationalists, and with French assistance under General Weygand, Marshall Pilsudski recovered the lost territory, before the **Treaty of Riga** (1921) was concluded.

5. After the Civil War, Lenin decided to establish normal inter-state relations with foreign powers:

    (a) Trade pacts were concluded with fourteen countries, beginning with Britain.

    (b) The **Treaty of Rapallo** was concluded with Germany in 1922. This included secret provisions to assist Germany evade the terms of the Treaty of Versailles.

Lenin's Last Years

1. By 1922 Lenin began to fear that degeneration of the Soviet system was the greatest danger to socialism in Russia.

    (a) The state had expanded its functions from Tsarist times considerably. This required a large **bureaucracy**. The party and Soviet state were in danger of becoming hopelessly entangled in red tape and incompetence.

    (b) The Tsarist government bureaucracy had been inherited by the Bolsheviks. The leading Bolsheviks feared its ability to block or corrupt the Revolution, but realised that they needed its technical experts, known as *spetsy*.

    (c) The Party was usurping many of the functions of the government which it shadowed and directed. Its own bureaucracy grew. Many of its members were uneducated workers, soldiers and peasants who had joined after the revolution and risen through the ranks of the Party during the Civil War. It was more attractive to them than the state bureaucracy. Thus the party suffered from **careerism**.*

    (d) Leading Bolsheviks were displaying **Great Russian chauvinism*** towards the non-Russian nationalities in the reorganisation of the state in which Stalin was playing a key role.

2. In May 1922 Lenin had his first stroke. After his recovery he was alarmed at the growth of Stalin's power during the period of his illness. As general secretary of the Party, Stalin was rapidly concentrating immense power into his own hands. He was converting his administrative authority into political power. In December he suffered another stroke, leaving him partially paralysed.

3. Lenin foresaw a coming power struggle between Trotsky and Stalin for the leadership of the USSR following his death. He distrusted Stalin, and explained this in a letter known as the **Testament of Lenin**, formally *Letter to the Congress, on Dec. 23-26, 1922, and Jan. 4, 1923*, addressed to a future Communist Party Congress. It contained proposals for changes in the political system and assessments of party leaders, including:

    (a) the enlargement of the Central Committee;

    (b) the warning that the most serious threat to unity within the Central Committee was the strained relationship between Stalin and Trotsky.

    (c) Lenin asserted that Stalin was not cautious enough to be entrusted with the large amount of power he had accumulated and that, although Trotsky was the most capable individual on the

Central Committee, he was too self-assured and overly inclined toward purely administrative functions.

The document has been interpreted as an attempt by Lenin:

    (i) to guide the party's choice of his successor;

    (ii) to undermine the efforts of colleagues who, he thought, were trying to usurp his power;

    (iii) to ensure a collective leadership of the USSR after his death.

4. A postscript, dictated after Lenin had become convinced that Stalin was not only mishandling the suppression of dissent in Georgia, but was being abusive to his wife, Krupskaya, proposed that the Congress remove him from the post of secretary-general.

"Stalin is too rude, and this shortcoming, though bearable in internal relations amongst us communists, becomes quite unbearable in a General Secretary. I therefore suggest to you, Comrades, that you remove Stalin from his post and replace him with someone who is superior to Stalin in this respect; namely is more tolerant, more loyal, more polite, and more attentive to the needs of the comrades, etc. This may seem a trifling detail. But as regards avoiding a split in the party and as regards the relations between Stalin and Trotsky, this is not a mere detail, but a detail which might one day acquire decisive importance."

Several copies of the *Testament* were made and sealed, with instruction that they were to be opened by Lenin personally or, in case of his death by Krupskaya.

5. After March 1923 Lenin was deprived of speech after a further stroke. Zinoviev, Kamenev and Stalin drew together to prevent Trotsky from becoming Lenin's successor. Subjected to a campaign of defamation, he left for the Caucasus.

6. In that year the Union of Soviet Socialist Republics (USSR) was created with a new constitution, including former parts of the Russian Empire. The Communists proclaimed the right of self-determination, but in practice they imposed Russian hegemony on them.

7. Lenin died in January 1924. His body was embalmed and displayed in a mausoleum in Red Square. Petrograd was renamed 'Leningrad' in his honour.

Assessment of Lenin's Rule

1. Lenin had:

(a) fashioned the Bolshevik Party as a small, dedicated party of revolutionaries, to conform with his own assessment of what was needed. In the event, this met with only limited success.

(b) adapted Marxism to suit the Russian situation. e.g. When he saw that the Russian peasants wanted to take the land for themselves, he changed his views and sided with them;

(c) placed the Bolsheviks as spokesmen of the mass of the Russian people during the confused period of dual authority, subordinating his ideology to the requirement to gain public support;

(d) after much wavering he had chosen just the right moment to launch a *coup d'état;*

(e) instituted the initial moves towards building socialism in Russia;

(f) brought the country through a civil war and foreign invasions;

(g) prevented the total break up of the multi-national empire;

(h) left a model of efficient organisation for:

    (i). revolutionary activity and the taking over government; and

    (ii) the mobilisation of society;

in the Bolshevik Party he had created, which others (including fascists) were to follow.

2. However:

(a) He had split the Russian Marxists by his insistence upon his own ideas for the Party;

(b) He presided over enormous suffering, with 20 million lives lost;

. (c) Because of his identification of socialism with modernisation, among Russians the

Timeline of Lenin's Rule (New Style Dates)	
1918	
Jan 29	Lenin dissolved the Constituent Assembly
Mar 3	Treaty of Brest-Litovsk concluded
Mar 10	Lenin and Sovnarkom moved to Moscow
May	Civil War began - War Communism instituted
June	Foreign intervention began
Aug 30	Assassination attempt injured Lenin
Sept	Bolsheviks defeated the Czechs and captured Kazan
1919	
March	Kolchak launched White offensive
Aug	Deniken launched White offensive
Sept	Yudenich launched White offensive
Nov	Last foreign troops withdrawn from Russia
1920	
Jan	Poland invaded the Ukraine
Dec	Last White army defeated in the Crimea
1921	
Feb 23	Kronstadt Mutiny began
Mar	Treaty of Riga concluded
Mar 17	New Economc Policy initiated
1922	
May 26	Lenin's first stroke
Dec 30	Union of Soviet Socialist Republics (USSR) inaugurated
1923	
Jan	Lenin completed his *Testament*
Mar 9	Lenin suffered a third stroke and rendered unable to speak
Oct	Scissors Crisis
1924	
Jan 21	Lenin died

development of industry became the chief immediate goal of the leadership of the state and party:

 (i) to fulfil the needs of the people;

 (ii) to build up a strong proletariat.

This belief in the need to increase production at all costs is known as **productionism**.*

(d) He set the character of the Bolshevik regime as a totalitarian* police state, by:

 (i) his own authoritarian style and personality;

 (ii) his insistence upon **democratic centralism;**

 (iii) his outlawing of **factionalism*** within the Party;

 (iv) refounding the secret police and founding the *gulag;**

 (v) his reliance upon Joseph Stalin for the performance of high-level administrative tasks.

(e) He died leaving many problems unsolved:

 (i) whether the USSR would have a mixed economy or state control:

 (ii) whether the peasants would own and farm their own land, or whether the state would own the land and employ the peasants:

 (iii) the growth of the Party and state bureaucracies with the development of careerism:*

 (iv) the leadership succession.

Glossary

anti-Semitism prejudice against Jews

apparatus the staff and organisation of the party

autocracy the system of rule by a monarch who has no limitations on the exercise of his power

black market illegal market established to avoid rationing

capitalism the economic system which allows for the operation of unrestricted markets, and so gives advantages to the wealthiest in proportion to the wealth they possess

careerism joining the Bolshevik Party in order to further one's career

Central Committee the governing body of the Russian Social Democratic Workers' Party (RSDWP)

chauvinism aggressive nationalism

Cheka The Pan-Russian Extraordinary Commission for Struggle against Counter-Revolution – the Soviet political police, successor of the Tsarist *Okhrana*, set up in 1918.

Comintern The Communist International , an organisation set up to coordinate foreign Communist parties under Moscow's direction

Constituent Assembly an assembly elected to draw up a constitution, after which a first regular government could be elected

cooperatives cost, equipment and profit-sharing enterprises designed for mutual self-help

counter-revolutionaries those working to overthrow a revolution

democratic centralism Lenin's idea that the Central Committee will decide policy and all other party members will follow their dictates obediently

Duma the name of the Russian parliament

emancipation the act of freeing one in servitude

factionalism disagreement within the Party and with the chief party organs. Lenin made it a reason for expulsion in accordance with democratic centralism.

fait accompli a situation already brought about.

ghettoes areas of cities set aside for alien populations, in this context Jews

GPU the State Political Administration, the second name of the Bolshevik secret police

gulag the network of Soviet labour camps

haemophilia a deficiency of the blood which prevents it from clotting. Bleeding from cuts and bruising (bleeding under the skin) may be very painful and lead to death.

intelligentsia the formally well-educated section of the population

Kadets (KDs) members of the Russian liberal party

kulaks wealthy peasants, whose land was sufficiently profitable to allow them to employ others to do their work

legitimacy possessing the legal right to exercise authority

Marxism the political philosophy of Karl Marx, a form of revolutionary socialism based upon categories taken from G. W. F. Hegel's dialectical philosophy [See Chapter 1].

mausoleum a large monumental tomb

nationalization converting a privately owned enterprise into state property

NEP The New Economic Policy, stepping back from socialism (esp. war communism)

Nepmen private traders, who were enabled to work and prosper from the New Economic Policy

nomenklatura **lists** list of names of politically sensitive posts, and those trusted to fill them

obscurantist opponents of enlightenment, and clear and rational thinking.

Octobrists conservatives content with the degree of liberalisation of the Tsarist regime provided by the October Manifesto (1905)

OGPU the Unified State Political Administration, the third name of the Bolshevik secret police, set up in 1923

Old Believers a sect of Orthodox Christians who had refused to accept reforms

Peoples' Commissars ministers in the Soviet government

productionism the belief that improving production is the key to creating the conditions for the building of socialism, focus upon increasing production

proletariat a technical Marxist term for the industrial working class

Provisional Government: a temporary government, to take charge of affairs until a Constituent Assembly can be elected

radicals those demanding substantial changes

reactionaries those demanding a return to earlier forms of government and society

redemption payments payments due from the peasants for the right to work their land

Schlieffen Plan the German war plan devised to avoid fighting a war on two fronts, by which the German Army would have six weeks in which to defeat France before the cumbersome Russian Army would be able to launch an attack upon Germany

separatists those who wish their region to become an independent state

serfs a peasant who is legally compelled to work on the land for his master

Sovnarcom: the Council of Peoples' Commissars, the original government of Soviet Russia

Social Democrats (SDs) the Russian Marxist party

Social Revolutionaries (SRs) members of a non-Marxist socialist party

soviets revolutionary councils of workers and soldiers, later institutionalized

status quo the state of affairs as it is at present

Straits the waterway between Europe and Asia, joining the Mediterranean and Black Seas at Constantinople (Istanbul) and the Dardenelles

totalitarianism a regime which seeks to control all aspects of the lives of the people

vanguard an advance guard, those who lead the way

Whites the counter-revolutionaries

zemstvos local councils in which the peasants organised village farming matters

Joseph Vissarionovich
Dzhugashvili (Stalin)

Stalin's USSR

I trust no one; not even myself." (Stalin)

Stalin's Rise to Power (1924-29)

Personal Background

1. Joseph Vissarionovich Dzhugashvili was born the son of a poor shoe repairer and a washer-woman in Gori, in Georgia, in the Caucasus.
2. He learned Russian while attending a church school at Gori, before attending the Tiflis Theological Seminary, where he trained to become a priest. There he read Karl Marx, and was expelled in 1899 for revolutionary activity. He then became a clerk in the Tiflis Observatory.
3. In 1900 he joined the political underground, organising demonstrations and strikes. When the Russian Social Democratic Workers' Party split into two factions, Menshevik and Bolshevik, in 1903, Dzhugashvili joined the Bolsheviks and became a follower of Lenin.
4. The Caucasus region, where Georgia is situated, has a long history of lawlessness and banditry, and Dzhugashvili became part of this, as a gangster organising protection rackets, extortion, arson, bank robberies and murders. It was this combination of ability, education, and ruthlessness which appealed to Lenin as important for his small dedicated band of professional revolutionaries. This background was suppressed when Stalin entered government, but has been uncovered by research in Georgia by Simon Sebag Montefiore in Y*oung Stalin* (Phoenix, London 2007)
5. Between 1901 and 1913, he was seven times arrested, imprisoned and exiled. The mildness of the sentences he was given, and the frequency with which he escaped, suggested to some that he was an *agent provocateur** in the pay of the Okhrana, the Czarist secret police. However no evidence of this has ever surfaced in the records
6. In February 1912 Lenin appointed him to the first Central Committee of the Bolshevik Party.
7. In 1913 he published an article under the name "Stalin", deriving from Russian *stal* ('steel') and briefly edited the new Bolshevik newspaper, *Pravda*, before undergoing his longest period of exile in Siberia from July 1913 to March 1917.
8. Returning to Petrograd on March 25, 1917, and taking up his position as an editor of *Pravda* once more, he argued that the Bolsheviks should co-operate with the provisional government;

but under Lenin's influence switched to the policy of armed coup.

9. When the coup d'état occurred in November 1917, Stalin played a much less prominent role than that of his chief rival, Leon Trotsky.

10. During the Civil War Stalin was Commissar for Nationalities and Commissar for State Control.

11. In 1922 he became General Secretary of the Central Committee. He was also member of the Politburo* and of many other committees.

12. From 1921 onward Stalin began to act independently, until, in 1923, Lenin wrote his political *Testament*, calling for Stalin's removal from the secretary generalship, which was sealed and a copy given to his wife Krupskaya.

The Power Struggle (1924-29)

1. On the death of Lenin, Leon Trotsky was the most prominent Bolshevik, and expected to be Lenin's successor. However:

   (a) He was a late entrant to the Party, having been a former Menshevik;

   (b) He was a Jew;

   (c) A brilliant, but arrogant, orator and war leader, he had never built up a loyal group of supporters, and was envied by the other leaders, who feared Bonapartism;*

2. On Lenin's death, Trotsky was in Sukhumi, in the south and Stalin failed to inform him in time for him to return for the funeral. Stalin himself delivered the oration. He was to promote an extravagant **cult of the deceased leader,** in which he posed as arch-priest.

3. Stalin should have been weakened by the *Testament of Lenin,* when it was read out at a meeting of the Central Committee. Four months after Lenin's death, and just before the 13th Party Congress, Krupskaya sent the *Testament* to the Central Committee, indicating Lenin's wish that it be given to the Congress. But the Central Committee was already dominated by Stalin, and they decided that the document should not be presented to the Congress. The Central Committee prohibited the publication even of quotations from it. As a result, its existence was soon forgotten within the USSR. However, a copy was given to the *New York Times,* indirectly by Krupskaya and published. At the 20th Party Congress (1956), Nikita Khrushchev quoted from the *Testament* in his secret speech to the Central Committee.

4. Stalin was in a strong position as against his rivals:

   (a) As party Secretary-General he controlled the growing party apparatus.*

   (b) He used his powers of appointment and promotion, controlling the **nomenklatura lists,** * to place his supporters in key positions, while relegating his opponents to isolation and impotence in distant parts of the country, where they could be kept under observation. (There were two lists at every level of government e.g. SSR,* oblast,* etc., one of politically sensitive posts to be filled by the CPSU secretary at that level, and one of candidates suitable to fill them).

   (c) Then he used Lenin's concept of **democratic centralism*** to turn disputes within the party to his own advantage. Those disagreeing with the policy of the Central Committee were accused of factionalism.* (See below)

5. The party divided between "right" and "left":

   (a) The "right", led by Bukharin, argued that agriculture was the key to growth, so the introduction of socialism should be slow "at the speed of a peasant nag".

   (b) The left, led by Trotsky, argued that to do this would be to strengthen the *kulaks* * and build up opposition to socialism. They argued that the pace of industrialization should be speeded up.

6. Zinoviev and Kamenev with their own followers joined with Stalin, using Bukharin's ideas to prevent Trotsky from taking over he leadership of the Party. The confrontation was ostensibly over Trotsky's view that they should:

(a) abolish private farming;

(b) industrialize rapidly;

(c) encourage revolutions abroad. (When that was achieved, the workers of western Europe would help the USSR with her industrialization.)

as opposed to following the more prudent policy of:

(d) maintaining the NEP;

(e) encouraging good relations with other countries to attract foreign investment and increase trade, and so "building socialism in one country."

The dispute was really over who would control the party. Trotsky resigned as Commissar. Although he kept his position on the Politburo, he was isolated and ineffective.

7. At the 14th Party Congress, there was a dispute between the "Right": Bukharin, Rykov and Tomsky, who wanted the NEP maintained, and the Left Opposition: Kamenev and Zinoviev, who wanted to move the revolution forward. When Kamenev attacked Stalin's policy of "building socialism in one country," they were condemned, and Kamenev was expelled from the Politburo.

8. In 1926 Kamenev and Zinoviev joined Trotsky as the "United Opposition", but were condemned for factionalism and expelled from the Party. Trotsky was exiled to Alma-Ata in Kazakhstan, while a chastened Kamenev and Zinoviev were allowed to apply to rejoin the Party.

9. In 1927 Stalin turned against the NEP.

(a) "Temporary" taxes were imposed upon profits, especially upon *kulaks*.

(b) 100% surcharges were levied on private goods sent by rail.

(c) Anyone guilty of "evil-intentioned" price rises was liable to the confiscation of his property. When Bukharin Trotsky and Rykov, the Right Deviationists" protested, they were expelled from the Politburo and the Party (1929).

10. On Dec. 21st 1929, Stalin celebrated his fiftieth birthday. This was a signal for the launching of his **personality cult.***

By this time the *vozhd*, or "boss", had outmanoeuvred all his rivals and held supreme power.

Timeline of Stalin's Rise to Power	
1912	Stalin appointed to the first Central Committee of the Bolshevik Party. Stalin appointed Commissar for Nationalities
1917	Stalin became Party General Secretary
1922	Lenin became an invalid
	Lenin wrote his *Political Testament*
	Lenin died - Lenin's *Political Testament* suppressed
1924	Left Opposition defeated - Resignation of Trotsky
1925	United Opposition expelled from the Party
1927	Right Opposition discredited
1929	Trotsky exiled

The Reasons for Stalin's Success

1. Initially Stalin had been very close to Lenin:

(a) he was a practical man, not concerned with fine points of doctrine;

(b) he was unswervingly loyal to Lenin.

2. Historians have argued that Stalin was underestimated by his rivals because he was an inconspicuous character who did not stand out or display special abilities. Trotsky described

him as a provincial mediocrity, and Sukhanov as "a grey blur" in 1917, Yet it is unlikely that the man who modernised and terrorized Russia and defeated Hitler was a mediocrity. Trotsky, who referred to him as "the party's most eminent mediocrity," also paradoxically prophesied to Smirnov in 1924 that Stalin would become "the dictator of the USSR." Now that Montefiore has revealed Stalin's early life (see above) it is clear that this judgement is false, and that historians have swallowed uncritically Trotsky's portrait of Stalin Yet as Montefiore points out, this probably owed more to Trotsky's own "vanity, snobbery, and lack of political skills" than to fact.

3. Many of the Bolshevik revolutionaries were also Caucasian gangsters, like Stalin, appreciated his proven abilities, and would have supported him against intellectuals and Jews.

4. He was a good tactician who understood the weaknesses and vulnerabilities of others, and was prepared to exploit them ruthlessly.

5. He was able to use his position as General Secretary of the Party, and their positions within the Party organisation, to consolidate power into his own hands:

(a) Using his power of making *nomenklatura* appointments:

(i) elevating trusted supporters to positions in and near Moscow;

(ii) blocking the promotion of those who could not be trusted;

(iii) appointing rivals to distant posts, where they could be isolated and watched.

(b) He was able to employ Lenin's insistence upon democratic centralism and his strict condemnation of factionalism within the Party to spy upon and have removed or demoted, those rivals of his who expressed any significant disagreement with official party policy.

Stalin's rise to power could be described as a "**bureaucratic coup**."

6. Stalin was unprincipled in being fully committed to no position, and so was able to change his position over policy when it was convenient to isolate his opponents. Thus he was able successively to use Lenin's strictures against factionalism to isolate and downgrade his chief opponents one by one.

7. His chief opponents banked upon the revolution spreading throughout the West. If this had happened in the least industrialised Power, then on Marxist principles the others could not be far behind. But it did not happen.

8. Stalin's main rival, Trotsky, failed to secure the succession because:

(a) Originally a Menshevik, he remained an outsider in the Bolshevik party;

(b) As a Jew he was considered an outsider in Russia;

(c) He was arrogant. He made enemies, and failed to consolidate his position within the party by building up a personal following;

(d) Because of his obvious talents, forceful personality and ambition, he was widely suspected of Bonapartism* among the leadership below Lenin, and so as Lenin's death approached he became an object of general suspicion and fear;

(e) Trotsky was prepared to criticise the Party for the growth of bureaucratization* and careerism;* This alienated many in the Party. By contrast, Stalin was very careful never to criticise the Party.

(f) He failed to act in a timely fashion to prevent Stalin's rise to power.

Stalin's USSR (1929-41)

The Collectivisation of Agriculture

The Reasons for the Collectivisation* of Agriculture

1. Soviet agricultural output was low because:

(a) the small peasant individual holdings were uneconomical;

(b) there was no real incentive for the peasants to produce food above their own needs and that of some local bartering.

2. Many in the Party were eager to move forward in the process of turning the SSR into a socialist country. Peasant private ownership of their land was not part of that ideal.
3. This was a barrier to Stalin's aim to industrialize. He needed agricultural output:
    (a) to feed the industrial cities cheaply;
    (b) to earn foreign exchange to purchase machinery.
4. In addition, Stalin saw the *kulaks* as class enemies who would resist socialism. *Kulaks* were wealthy or prosperous peasants who owned a relatively large farm and who were able to employ labour and lease some of their land. Before the revolutions of 1917, they played a central role in the life of the village. The NEP had favoured them. Collectivisation of the farms would destroy their influence.
5. In autumn 1927 it was rumoured throughout Russia that the capitalist powers were preparing to intervene militarily once again in the USSR. This was due to:
    (a) the coming to power of the anti-Communist Marshal Pilsudski in Poland in 1926;
    (b) The massacres of Communists in China by Jiang Jieshi (Chiang Kai-shek).
The peasants began to hoard grain in anticipation of higher prices being paid by the government. Stalin sent in military detachments to seize the grain under threat of prosecution for "speculation." This produced immediate results. Collectivisation would ensure greater control over produce.

The Implementation of the Policy of the Collectivisation of Agriculture
1. In 1927 the government began to increase *kulaks'* taxes and restrict their right to lease land.
2. In 1929 Stalin began the drive for the rapid and systematic collectivisation of the farms. Lands, livestock, grain and equipment were commandeered at gunpoint and the individual holdings merged into giant collective farms, (*kolkhozi*)*.
3. The *kulaks* opposed giving up their own farms, so at the end of that year a campaign to "liquidate the *kulaks* as a class" (*dekulakization**) was launched by the government. The *kulaks* were:
    (a) conscripted into the new industrial towns for labour;
    (b) deported to Siberia and abandoned to survive in uncultivated places;
    (c) interned in labour camps;
    (d) or simply shot.
4. Many peasants burned their farms and destroyed their livestock rather than see them confiscated. In spring 1930, because the consequences were so catastrophic, Stalin ordered a temporary halt to the campaign, blaming "excesses" by "overenthusiastic officials".
5. In 1931 collectivisation was resumed. By 1932 over 60% of all holdings had been collectivized. Much of the grain seized was sowing grain for the next season. When this was seized, famine was inevitable during the following year.
6. Some state farms (*sovnarkhozi*)* were introduced. In these, the state acted as employer and paid a wage. Stalin preferred them to *kolkhozi*. They were usually large single-crop farms.
7. Most were turned into collective farms (*kolkhozniki**), which were a compromise.
    (a) The *kolkhoz* functioned as a business. After paying its utility bills and the Machine Tractor Stations (MTS) for the use of its equipment, all profits (if any) were divided between the workers.
    (b) Each worker also had a small plot of land for his own use (*artel*). Surplus produce from this could be sold in the market.
    (c) The *kolkhozi* was set quotas of production to sell to the state at fixed prices;
    (d) workers were tied to the land by lack of an internal passport.
8. Machine Tractor Stations (MTS) were set up (in the average ratio of one to ten farms) to hold farm equipment to share between the farms, and to keep an eye on the workers (a member of the management of the MTS was usually a member of the security police).

The Consequences of the Collectivization of Agriculture

1. Famine resulted from the disruption. A military cordon was thrown around the Ukraine to prevent the news from leaking out. Stalin was later to admit to Churchill that collectivisation led to about ten million peasants suffering premature death. Meanwhile nearly two million tons of grain were sold abroad to raise foreign capital to purchase machine tools etc. needed for industry. It has been argued that the famine in the Ukraine was deliberate genocide of a potentially troublesome population, however Robert Service argued that:
    (a) Stalin needed their production, so genocide would not make economic sense;
    (b) The quotas for requisitioning of produce were cut three times during 1932 as the extent of the famine became evident.
2. Soviet agriculture was crippled and would never fully recover. The *kolkhozi* never became efficient.
3. The cottage industries upon which Russian relied for clothes, furniture and tools were destroyed.
4. The country churches were closed, and the buildings taken over for the use of the MTSs or the *kolkhozi*.
5. Age-old local folk traditions were swept away in a sharp break with past life, making this a real revolution..
6. Many peasants fled to the cities, and became available for the new factories Stalin was to build.

Superfast Industrialization

The Reasons for Superfast Industrialization

Stalin initiated a programme of rapid industrialization which would realise the potential of the USSR as a superpower, for several reasons:

1. Because of the identification of socialism with modernisation among Russians, the development of industry became the chief immediate goal of the leadership. Expressed in the form of the need to increase production at all costs, this is known as **productionism**. It became a symbol of the success of the revolution. Stalin was much influenced by this.
2. Stalin believed that industrialization was necessary in order to protect the revolution against external enemies such as the West and Japan, since military strength depended upon industrial strength. He said of the capitalist West in 1931: "We have lagged fifty to a hundred years behind the leading countries. We must cover this distance in ten years. Either we do that, or they crush us."
3. The centrally planned and controlled industrialization would give Stalin greater control over the industrial proletariat.

The Implementation of the Policy of Superfast Industrialization

1. Stalin claimed to have uncovered a counter-revolutionary conspiracy among the engineers of Shakhty in the Donbass Region. The public **Shakhty Trial (1928)** was an attempt to intimidate the skilled industrial workers.
2. In 1928 he authorised the implementation of the **First Five-Year Plan**, a crash programme of industrial development concentrating on he basics required for heavy industry: coal, oil, electric power stations, iron and steel works, and railways.
3. Some twenty-five million peasants were moved into industry. The internal passport controlled this mass movement of population.
4. Expertise as acquired by encouraging foreign usually German) engineers and technicians to work for fixed terms When the time came to pay them, they sometimes conveniently "disappeared.

5. Huge new industrial complexes, dams and hydroelectric power stations, etc. were built in virgin territory, e.g. iron and steel works at Magnitogorsk, tractor works at Gorki, and a hydroelectric dam at Dnepropetrovsk. At first the workers lived in shanty towns, and built themselves proper homes when the factory was in full production. The belief that "large is good" was a general one in those days, and by no means confined to Communists.

6. Every enterprise was given specific targets to achieve by Gosplan.* This created the **Command Economy.***

7. Pay differentials were introduced, with bonuses paid for overproduction. Workers who dramatically over fulfilled their norms became heroes, known as **stakhanovites**,* after the legendary achievement of the coal miner Alexei Stakhanov.

8. **Absenteeism** was punished, records being entered on each individual's workbook. In time, absenteeism and quitting a job became criminal offences. e.g. Absenteeism (being twenty minutes late without good reason) carried six months in a labour camp in 1940. Leaving a job was punishable by imprisonment. This was military discipline in the factory.

9. Compulsory **internal passports** and the need to register change of address to the police made it very difficult to change jobs and move home.

10. No account was taken of worker safety in the drive to achieve targets.

11. Underproduction was blamed on sabotage by class enemies and agents of foreign powers, or on incompetent management. During the early 1930s, about 75% of plant managers were purged.

12. The **gulag**,* or system of prison camps was extended, located largely in the Arctic (such as Kolyma and Vorkuta) where there were natural resources, but the climate was too inhospitable to support ordinary civilian populations. They became sources of slave labour.

13. A **Second Five-Year Plan**, begun in 1933, continued the emphasis on heavy industry: tractors, railway carriages and lorries.

14. A **Third Five-Year Plan** in 1937 was to concentrate more upon light industry and consumer goods, but by that time war was so likely that war materiel was produced instead.

The Achievements of Superfast Industrialization

1. The plans were successful. By 1940 the USSR was the world's second industrial power, had overtaken Britain in the production of iron and steel, and was within reach of Germany.

2. The extent of Soviet industrial activity had been extended to include new areas in the Urals and Siberia.

3. Stalin had managed to industrialize without using Western capital, and the loss of sovereignty that would have entailed.

4. The USSR avoided the effects of the World Economic Crisis and the Great Depression.

5. Stalin's "superfast industrialization" laid the foundation for the military defeat of Hitler.
   But:
   (a) everything was achieved at tremendous human cost. It is arguable that a comparable degree of industrialization would have come about in any case, and by means less savage, under almost any alternative regime.
   (b) Paradoxically, in the state supposedly created by an industrial workers' revolution, the working conditions of the industrial workers were a low priority because of:
      (i) the weakness of the trade unions;
      (ii) the character of the Soviet "war economy" which was continued indefinitely due to "external and internal threats";
      (iii) the bureaucratization of the state.

6. There were costly mistakes, e.g. the Belomor Canal, cut between the White Sea and the Baltic

using the labour of over 100,000 political prisoners, of whom at last 11,000 died, was too shallow and narrow for the warships for which it was partly designed.

7. Success was in infrastructure and heavy industry (which was needed most immediately). This became a fixed character of the Soviet economy, which was never extended successfully to the production of consumer goods.

The Great Terror

1. Despite the position of dominance Stalin had achieved in the USSR, his harsh policies were sometimes criticized, e.g. by Marteman Riutin. In 1933, Stalin tried to have Riutin executed, but was prevented by Sergei Kirov, head of the Leningrad Party, (He was shot anyway in 1937).

2. The 17th Party Congress (January 1934) was known as the **Congress of Victors**, since no "deviations" remained to be combated. Former opponents of Stalin had been readmitted to the party or were never expelled, and held minor posts. Many felt that some relaxation was due. Stalin seemed to many to be unsuited to leadership in a more peaceful era. A group of leading party figures considered replacing him as general secretary by Kirov, while retaining him in some honorary post. Some 166 delegates (out of 1,225) crossed Stalin's name out in the balloting for the new Central Committee. This was suppressed by Stalin's henchmen.

3. Stalin claimed to favour the new moderation proposed at the Congress, and there was a noticeable thaw. But in fact Stalin had felt threatened by his subordinates.

4. The OGPU, the secret police were reorganised in 1934 as the **NKVD** under Genrikh Yagoda.

5. On December 1 1934, **Kirov** was **assassinated** in the Smolny building at Leningrad, ostensibly by a disgruntled communist, whose access to his victim had been arranged by senior NKVD agents. It is generally thought that Stalin had arranged this murder through Yagoda. However, Christopher Read points out that:

   (a) Stalin behaved afterwards as though shocked and threatened.

   (b) Kirov's memory was honoured. He would have been the only one of Stalin's victims not to have been erased from history, but to have been honoured.

   (c) Isaac Deutscher thought that Stalin was not responsible for the murder, but took advantage of it.

   However,

   (i) Stalin's position had been threatened by the vote. Kirov himself remarked afterwards that he was "finished."

   (ii) It is difficult to see who would have dared do such a thing without his approval.

6. The law was tightened up, e.g.

   (a) Appeals against death sentences were abolished, so that executions could be carried out immediately;

   (b) Torture was made officially legal;

   (c) Anyone over the age of twelve was liable to the full force of he law, including torture and the death penalty.

7. Zinovyev, Kamenev, and their followers were arrested and sentenced to imprisonment for "responsibility for" (although not "direct involvement in") the murder of Kirov. Stalin's agent Andrei Zhdanov took control of Leningrad, and from 1935 to 1939 almost all Kirov's followers were eliminated.

8. Over the next four years ever-increasing circles of alleged plotters against the regime were exposed, all of them linked with the Kirov case. The country was submitted to an intensive campaign against hidden "enemies of the people."

9. There followed a series of public show trials. The first was the Zinovyev-Kamenev trial (1936).

Zinovyev, Kamenev, and others confessed to terrorist plotting with Trotsky and were shot.

10. In September NKVD chief Genrikh Yagoda was replaced by Nikolay Yezhov, from whom the **Yezhovshchina**, the worst phase of the terror in 1937-38, took its name. Yagoda had objected to the executions of lading Bolsheviks.

11. A new group, headed by Grigory (Yury) Pyatakov, was arrested for a second show trial in January 1937. This time the charges included espionage, sabotage, and treason, in addition to terrorism.

12. On Feb. 18, 1937, Stalin's old ally and Politburo colleague Ordzhonikidze committed suicide. He was reported to have planned to criticise the new repressions. Bukharin and Rykov were arrested. Virtually all the old Bolshevik leadership was arrested or executed.

13. From March 1937 the terror developed a mass character. To cope with the large-scale arrests, special extra-legal tribunals were set up, the NKVD "*troikas**," which sentenced hundreds of thousands of people to death in their absence.

    (a) The Communist Party itself was most ruthlessly purged. Of the 139 members of the Central Committee elected at the 17th Congress in 1934, 115 were arrested, and of the 1,966 delegates to that Congress, 1,108 were arrested. The local leaderships in Leningrad, in Ukraine, and elsewhere were almost annihilated. At the lower level, of the 2.3 million people who had been party members in 1935, just under half were executed or died in labour camps.

    (b) The army suffered heavier losses. In May 1937, after a story that Marshall Tukhachevsky was plotting a coup with the Germans had been transmitted by Reinhard Heydrich, head of the *SS* Intelligence Service (*SD*) to Stalin via Edvard Beneš, president of Czechoslovakia, Tukhachevsky and eight senior generals were arrested, tortured, and shot. Over the next two years almost all their senior colleagues were arrested, tried in secret, and executed. The officer corps lost about half its members, proportionally more than any modern army has ever suffered in wartime.

    (c) The cultural world was decimated. "Plots" were discovered in the State Hermitage Museum, the Pulkovo Astronomical Observatory, and throughout the academic world.

    (d) The purge also involved large numbers of the general public, sometimes for bizarre reasons, such as being philatelists or Esperantists. Some 5 million people were arrested, of whom no more than 10% survived.

    Citizens were urged to denounce each other. People were sent to the gulag for making a joke against Stalin During the **Yezhovshchina***, the USSR was submitted to one of the most brutal regimes of state terrorism in recorded history.

14. In March 1938 the third great Moscow Show Trial was held. Bukharin, Rykov, and Yagoda, confessed to several murders, including those of Kirov and the writer Maksim Gorky, as well as to treason, espionage, etc. Bukharin was accused of planning to murder Lenin in 1918, though he denied it. After the executions the only survivors of Lenin's last Politburo were Stalin and Trotsky, the latter in exile in Mexico. (Trotsky was killed by an NKVD agent in 1940.)

15. There had been 65 labour camps in 1922. During the NEP there was a reduction in the number of prisoners to some tens of thousands. But Stalin decided systematically to utilise the labour of prisoners for his programme of industrialization. By 1932 there were at least one million *zeks**, or political prisoners, and by 1935 more than two million. The camps were described by an inmate as "like Auschwitz without the ovens", the inmates being used as slave labour, e.g. on the Belomor Canal.

16. By the autumn of 1938 the terror was dislocating the life of the country, including the economy, so that production actually declined in 1938-39. Yezhov was arrested in 1939 and shot in 1940.

17. Lavrenty Beria took on the NKVD leadership, purged the NKVD itself, but supervised a general reduction in the purge of other groups.

The Consequences of the Great Terror

1. Estimates of ordinary Russians sent to the camps vary between 7 and 16 million, with some 2 to 17 million deaths. Since the opening of the Soviet archives, estimates have been revised upwards.

2. Both the industry, the governing party and the armed forces were denuded of able, experienced people. The purge of industrial ladder undermined the effectiveness of the Second Five-Year Plan. The purge of the army:
   (a) led to the initial defeat of the Red Army by the Finns in the Winter War;
   (b) encouraged Hitler to invade the USSR.

3.. By the 18th Party Congress (March 1939) all independence of mind on the part of any of the leadership had vanished. Thereafter the history of the USSR until 1953 was confined to Stalin's decisions and the attempts of his subordinates to gain his confidence. The purges had:
   (a) removed rivals to Stalin;
   (b) cowed the population;
   (c) removed many talented people;
   (d) created an atmosphere of subservient mediocrity which would hinder progress for decades.

The Reasons for the Great Terror

1. The Terror was supposed to be **ideologically driven**. Class conflict was intensified to destroy class enemies and saboteurs.

2. Isaac Deutscher and Christopher Read argue that the Terror had a rational explanation, that Stalin feared internal enemies. He was in the process of **removing rivals** to himself: both individuals and groups. They point out that the authorities systematically swept through certain groups. In particular, Stalin needed to eliminate all the old Bolsheviks and the army command. There is evidence that Stalin and Molotov thought the victims to have been guilty. However, most of the people arrested were probably innocent. Read thinks that this was due to the crudity of Stalin's methods, and the belief that it was better that the innocent suffer than that the guilty go free.

3. The Terror was **economically driven**. In order to accomplish Stalin's industrial goals a source of slave labour was needed. The camps were located largely in the Arctic (such as Kolyma and Vorkuta) where there were natural resources, but the climate was too inhospitable to support ordinary civilian populations. The system became a regular feature of Soviet economic life. By autumn 1938 the terror was not needed any more, since the camps were full. They just needed "topping up" occasionally.

4. Traditionally Russians valued a strong Tsar who would keep the nobles in order and preserve the unity and strength of the country, preventing foreign invasion. There is evidence that Stalin saw himself as the "strong Tsar", whose ideal was Ivan the Terrible. Eisenstein was commissioned to make a film of Ivan, who brutally unified the country, subordinating all classes and interests to his rule, drove back external enemies and expanded its borders. Stalin considered the film insufficiently sympathetic to the despot. In this case the purpose of the Terror was precisely to **terrorise the population** by arresting the innocent as well as the guilty, so that no one could feel himself safe.

5. Stalin needed to keep Hitler at bay until he was ready to face war with Germany. It has been argued that before making a temporary accommodation with Hitler to achieve this (the Molotov-Ribbentrop Pact), he had to eliminate the old Bolshevik and military anti-fascist groups who would have opposed it.
   However, The Terror began while Stalin seems to have still hoped for an anti-Nazi alliance with the West, and included more groups than those who might have opposed the Pact.

6. Explanations based upon the assumption that the Terror had a rational basis tend to lack credibility because of the large numbers of obviously innocent victims who fall into no category which threatened Stalin or the Revolution. Christopher Read suggests that the process got out of control:

(a) the authorities had quotas of arrests to meet, and officials were afraid that if they failed to meet their quotas, they too would be arrested. Thus 28% of those arrested had to be executed;

(b) The demand to implicate others fed the process, since failure to get the names of "collaborators" from those arrested , and to follow these up with fresh arrests, would reflect upon the authorities concerned;

(c) The purges created jobs for ambitious men by removing those above them in the hierarchy, and many may have denounced superiors for this reason;

(d) **Over zealousness** by "little Stalin's" lower in the system, sometimes settling personal scores, may have disguised the intentions of the authorities and allowed the policy to get out of control to some extent.

7. Many explanations are based upon **Stalin's personal psychology**. e.g.

(a) Khrushchev, who was a colleague, thought that it was an outcome of Stalin's **paranoia,** and his crude and brutal personality.

(b) Moshe Lewin considered it a search for inner justification by **externalising his betrayal** of the Party, by taking the country in an essentially counter-revolutionary direction, which, as a Bolshevik, he had constantly to lie about, even to himself.

Economic, Social and Cultural Developments (1924-41)

The Economy

1. Small-time capitalism was abolished, all private enterprises renationalized and the Nepmen abolished. Gosplan* became the dominant force in the economy.

2. The **Command Economy*** was created. Every enterprise was given specific monthly targets to achieve by Gosplan.*

Government

1. There was a massive growth in the state bureaucracy,* and in the party bureaucracy charged with supervising it. In 1924 the number of ministries and higher government agencies was 10, by 1940 it was 41, plus many state committees, such as Gosplan. Each of these bodies had their own *apparat*. This resulted in all the evils towards which bureaucracy tends:

(a) tendency to further unjustified growth

(b) with rising costs

(c) inefficiency

(d) nepotism

(e) corruption

(f) institutionalized timidity, inflexibility and narrow-mindedness

(g) false reporting of statistics

This arose from:

(i) the mind-set inherited from the tradition of Tsarist bureaucracy;

(ii) the centralisation of all planning, decision-making and administration;

(iii) the nationalisation of the means of production and distribution, and Stalin's etatism;*

(iv) the natural tendencies of all bureaucracies everywhere.

Special privileges began to be attached to bureaucrats; access to special shops, hospitals, etc. The

USSR ceased gradually to be a workers' state and became a bureaucrats' state.

2. The "cult of personality" of Stalin was developed. History was falsified on a massive scale to give him a major role in the Bolshevik underground, the Revolution, and the Civil War. The country was blanketed in adulation of the *Vozhd*, or "Boss".

Constitutional Reform (1936)

1. In 1936 Stalin introduced a new and overtly liberal democratic constitution for the USSR.
2. Ironically, all basic personal freedoms and rights were safeguarded and guaranteed by the state. This included a right to an old-age pension and sickness benefit.
3. Voting for the Supreme Soviet, the legislative body of the USSR, was by secret ballot. Trade Unions and other bodies could propose candidates for election, and the party would choose the best one to offer to the voters or their approval. The supreme soviet was divided into two houses: the Soviet of the Union, representing people according to population, and the Soviet of the Nationalities, representing the different states of the USSR.
4. The Supreme Soviet, which met twice a year, elected a smaller body, the Presidium, to consider the details of legislation, together with the Council of Ministers (a cabinet).
5. The leading role in the state was played by the Communist Party (CPSU), of which the sovereign body was the National Congress, which met every five years, and which elected a Central Committee to act for it. The Central Committee met twice a year, and elected a Politburo to act for it in between meetings. Stalin was its General Secretary.
6. The official ideology of the USSR was codified by Stalin under the name of Marxism-Leninism, and later became the official doctrine of eastern European communist parties. He simplified these ideas in his *A Short History of the Communist Party of the Soviet Union* (1938).
7. Ironically, this liberal constitution was introduced when Stalin was liquidating all opposition. The Terror was not affected. The constitution was:
   (a) to draw attention away from what was really happening
   (b) to curry favour with the democratic West in view of the rise to power of Adolf Hitler.
8. Stalin's real method of rule was based upon his own autocracy. He ruled over the country not through the government or the party, but through personal agents and through the security police (NKVD). The party, as an institution, actually declined under Stalin:
   (a) It was the chief victim of the Terror;
   (b) Between 1934 and 1952 there was only one party congress, in 1939.
9. The general secretaries of the Communist parties abroad imitated this essentially Leninist model, and strict hierarchical subordination became the norm throughout the Communist world.

Social Security

1. By the mid-1930s education, medical care and holidays with pay were becoming available for all.
2. Cohabitation, easy divorce and abortion were severely discouraged, reversing Lenin's socially liberal policies.
3. Motherhood was valued highly: mothers of ten children were decorated as heroines of the USSR.

Education

1. In 1929 it was specified that 70% entrants to higher technical education had to be children of workers in order to foster upward social mobility. This quota was abolished in 1935.
2. Discipline was reintroduced into education. Educational experimentation was ended. Rote learning, examinations and school uniforms were reintroduced.

3. This produced results. Illiteracy was cut from 50% in 1924 to 19% in 1939.
4. In history, strong rulers like Ivan the Terrible and Peter the Great were praised. The history of the revolution was rewritten so as to place Stalin at the side of Lenin throughout the crisis. This view was set out in *A Short History of the CPSU* (1938), every child's "bible" taught in the schools.
5. Organisations to further educate and control young people were created:
    >   The Little Octobrists
    >   The Lenin Pioneer Organisation
    >   The Young Communist League (Komsomol)

The Arts

1. Socialist realism was the only accepted style in art. Although apparently realistic (not symbolical or abstract), socialist realism portrays the workers and their labour in a way which glorifies them.
2. Writers were to glorify the victory of socialism. Novels of the five-year plan like Ostrovsky's *How the Steel was Tempered*, and Gladkov's *Cement* became the norm.
3. In music "melodies which could be whistled by a worker" were required. Prokofiev and other modern composers were attacked for "dissonance." Stalin's personal taste became the norm.

Religion

Official atheism was maintained.
1. In 1926 the League of Militant Atheists was formed to oppose religion.
2. In 1929 the Churches were forbidden to engage in any activities not strictly religious.
3. The greatest blow to the Orthodox Church came with the collectivisation of agriculture. The priests were expelled with the kulaks, country churches closed, and the buildings taken over for the MTSs or *kolkhozi*,. By the end of the 1930s only 2% of Orthodox churches were still in use.
4. During the 1930s most of the mosques were closed. The veiling of women, polygamy, and the pilgrimage to Mecca were forbidden.

The Military

1. In the Red Army the old tsarist ranks were reintroduced.
2. Uniforms and insignia were made more elaborate.

Timeline of Stalin's Rule 1923-41	
1927	Grain procurement crisis begins
1928	First Five-Year Plan launched - NEP abandoned - Shakty Trial
1929	Collectivisation of the farms and liquidation of the kulaks begins
1932–33	Famine
1933	Second Five-Year Plan launched
1934	"Congress of Victors" - Murder of Kirov
1935	Purge of Leningraders begins the Great Terror
1936	New constitution of the USSR
	Yezhovschina begins - Kamenev/Zinoviev show trial
1937	Purge of the armed forces
1938	Third Five-Year Plan launched - Bukharin/Rykov show trial
1939	Yezhov replaced by Beria - Terror ameliorated
1940	Trotsky assassinated

Foreign Policy (1924-41)

1. Stalin concentrated on building up socialism and power in the USSR. This seemed to foreign governments a more welcome strategy to that of Trotsky, who was calling for world revolution. Thus Stalin continued Lenin's policy of seeking recognition of the Soviet regime by foreign governments. The Comintern* sometimes encouraged subversion abroad, but if good relations with a capitalist state conflicted with support for local communists, Stalin always chose good relations with the state.

2. Stalin suspected the Locarno Treaties (1925) by which Germany accepted its new frontiers in the Treaty of Versailles in the West – but not those in the East – to be a plot against the USSR. Nevertheless, Soviet Russia signed the Kellog-Briand Pact to renounce war as an instrument of policy.

3. In December 1927 Stalin announced that capitalism had entered a new period of instability. The Great Depression of 1929 was the fulfilment of his prediction. He said that this would be followed by upheavals in many countries.

4 After 1931 Stalin became aware of the danger to the USSR from a newly aggressive Japan.

5. When Hitler was moving to take power, Stalin restrained the German Communists from helping the SPD to keep Hitler out of power, believing that the rise of the Nazis would hasten the collapse of capitalist Germany.

6. However, Hitler's elimination of all internal opposition showed that the Nazis were going to be able to retain power. Threatened by the Nazi-Polish Non-aggression Pact, the USSR joined the League of Nations in 1934.

7. Stalin now feared the possibility of a war on two fronts, against Germany and Poland in the West, and Japan in the East.

8. Stalin attempted to secure the USSR by:
   (a) During 1935 getting the Communists all over Europe to cease undermining social democrats and co-operate with other anti-fascist forces in anti-fascist **popular fronts**.
   (b) during 1936, signing security pacts:
      (i) the Franco-Soviet Pact,
      (ii) the Czech-Soviet Pact;

9. During the Spanish Civil War, Stalin provided:
   (a) advisers and money for the communists'
   (b) arms for the Spanish Government, which had to be paid for with the country's gold reserves;
   (c) received refugee children from areas threatened by Nationalist bombing.

10. During the mid and late 1930s, he sought to co-operate with the West against expansionist Nazi Germany. During the Sudetenland crisis he offered to sent troops to Czechoslovakia, but the USSR was not even invited to the Munich Conference, which resulted in further appeasement. This convinced Stalin that he would need to deal with Hitler alone.

11. During 1938-9 Soviet and Japanese troops clashed on the Manchurian and Mongolian borders. Stalin wished for security in Europe in case there was a Soviet-Japanese war.

12. In May 1939 he replaced the Jew Litvinov as Soviet Foreign Minister by Molotov. By June he was negotiating with the Nazis as well as with the West. On 23rd Aug. 1939 **the Molotov-Ribbentrop Pact** was signed. Openly, this was a ten-year non-aggression pact, but a secret protocol was appended. It said that if eastern European frontiers were to be "disturbed," the USSR would take Eastern Poland, the Baltic states and Moldova. This was a tremendous achievement for Stalin:
   (a) It secured the recovery of most of the land lost to Russia by the Treaty of Brest-Litovsk with-out a blow. This would be a buffer area in the event of an attack from the West.

(b) It gave the USSR temporary security in Europe in case of a Soviet-Japanese war.

(c) It gave the USSR time to prepare for a war with Germany.

(d) Hitler's invasion of Poland could be expected to lead to a long war with Britain and France, which would leave Stalin free to prepare to launch a surprise attack on a weakened and exhausted Germany when he was ready.

13. Hitler seized Danzig and attacked Poland on Sept. 1st. Two weeks later the Red Army attacked Poland from the East.

14. The USSR demanded bases in Finland as a safeguard against future German occupation of that country, and the ceding of territory near to Leningrad. The Finns refused, and the USSR attacked Finland in Nov. 1939 in the **Winter War.** Initially the Red Army was thrown back, but massive reinforcements were brought up, and in March 1940 Finland surrendered. In consequence of this:

(a) the USSR was expelled from the League of Nations

(b) dangerous deficiencies in the Red Army were revealed. As a result:

(i) many purged army officers in labour camps were reinstalled in their commands;

(ii) Hitler was encouraged in his plans to invade the USSR.

15. Moldova and the Baltic States were subsequently occupied. These areas were immediately "sovietised".

16. In 1941 Stalin concluded the Russo-Japanese Non-Aggression Pact. The Japanese had decided to expand into south-east Asia to create their Greater South-East Asia Co-Prosperity Sphere. This left Stalin free to concentrate on the threat from Hitler.

17. However, the speed with which Hitler reduced France, and the shelving or abandonment of his plans (if they ever existed) to conquer Britain, found Stalin unprepared for war in summer 1941.

18. The military build-up on the Germano-Soviet border and the warnings from Churchill, his generals and his spy in Tokyo, Richard Sorge, did not move Stalin to take any defensive measures. It is likely that:

(a) Stalin doubted that Hitler ever intended actually to attack the USSR unless provoked:

(i) It would open a war on two fronts, which had proved fatal to Germany in World War I;

(ii) It would be suicidal for Hitler to launch an attack on the day that Napoleon launched his failed attack, too late in the year;

(iii) He was gambling on attacking Germany before the USSR was itself attacked, and so had made only offensive preparations, almost useless for fighting a defensive war.

(b) He did not wish to provoke an early attack by hostile preparations.

(c) He suspected Churchill of trying to break up the Germano-Soviet understanding for his own purposes.

Timeline of Stalin's Foreign Policy	
1934	USSR becomes a member of the League of Nations
1935	Stalin supports creation of Popular Fronts
1936	Stalin signs security pacts with France and Czechoslovakia
	Stalin aids the Government in the Spanish Civil War
1939	Stalin replaces Litviov with Molotov - Nazi-Soviet Pact
	Soviet invasion of Poland
	Soviet invasion of Finland - the Winter War
1940	Stalin siezes the Baltic States and Bessarabia
1941	Stalin signs non-aggression pact with Japan
	German invasion of the USSR

The Great Patriotic War (1941-45)

[For a more detailed account of the Great Patriotic War,
see the companion volume in this series "Wars and Warfare]

1. Stalin had placed the USSR at a disadvantage in 1941, since:
   (a) He had purged the experienced army leadership during 1937-8. Marshall Tukhachevsky was preparing new plans and leaders to take advantage of mechanised warfare and fighter planes (CF *Blitzkrieg*)* just before he died. The plans were scrapped and the leaders chosen to put it into operation were purged. The principal fighter aircraft designer, Tupalev, was in a labour camp.
   (b) He had placed great reliance on the Molotov-Ribbentrop Pact to keep off a German attack on the USSR for the immediate future.
   (c) The old fortifications on the pre-1939 frontier had been dismantled, and new ones further west were never built on the new frontiers, because he was preparing an offensive, not a defensive, strategy.
   (d) Troops on the border were forbidden to do anything which might provoke Hitler, including the laying of mines and firing at intruders.

2. In May 1941 Stalin recognised the growing possibility of a German attack on the Soviet Union by appointing himself chairman of the Council of People's Commissars (head of the government). It was his first government office since 1923.

3. Stalin was planning to attack Germany:
   (a) His military dispositions were all offensive;
   (b) The Red Army trained only for attack;
   (c) The old border defences had been deactivated when Eastern Poland had been taken, and new defences had never been constructed.

4. Yet since he was not ready to attack Germany, and had no defences, Stalin was desperate that no excuse should be given to Hitler to attack. Thus the preparations which should have been made were strictly forbidden.

5. *Operation Barbarossa*, the German *Blitzkrieg,* surged into Soviet territory on June 22, 1941:
   (a) Losses of materiel were enormous. Most of the Soviet air force was destroyed on the ground.
   (b) Millions of soldiers were taken prisoner.
   (c) Part of the Red Army deserted.

6. Explanations of Stalin's inactivity include:
   (a) He did not think that Hitler would be so stupid as to initiate a war on two fronts.
   (b) The known date for the supposed attack was the date on which Napoleon had invaded Russia in 1812. It had been too late in the year, and this had led to disaster. He may have thought that Hitler would not deliberately make the same mistake.
   (c) He had gambled on being able to use another winter to build up his forces.

7. Stalin was shocked into temporary inactivity by the onslaught. However, he soon rallied and appointed himself supreme commander in chief. On 3rd July he went on the radio to rally the nation using the terminology of nationalism rather than communism. At the parade in Red Square to mark the anniversary of the October Revolution he reinforced this, making the war a war of nations rather than a war of classes, the "**Great Patriotic War**" against the Germans to defend "Mother Russia."

8. A **State Defence Committee (*GKO*)** was set up as the supreme war-making body, consisting of Stalin as its chairman and 5-8 members of the Politburo. The Supreme Military Command was *Stavka*, of which Stalin was also chairman.

9. Stalin was ruthless at this time in dismissing the incompetent, and in choosing the ablest people he could find, even taken out of the *gulag*.

10. A three-pronged assault was launched:
    (a) in the north through the Baltic States to take Leningrad;
    (b) in the centre to Minsk, Smolensk and Moscow;
    (c) in the south from Rumania through Southern Poland to Kiev, and then south to the Don Region and the Caucasian oil fields.
11. Initial disasters were due to:
    (a) the element of surprise and Stalin's lack of defence planning;
    (b) Stalin's interference in operational control;
    (c) hatred of Stalin's regime, particularly in non-Russian areas.
12. Stalin followed the usual Russian policy during an invasion of "giving up space to buy time". Resources were destroyed in front of the advancing German armies.
13. The war was to be one of attrition, and the Soviet economy was placed on a more efficient war footing than that of Germany. Russian enterprises were moved east out of the path of the advancing Germans into the Urals region.
14. The **mass evacuation of factories** and the workers who operated them to the lands in the east, out of reach of the German advance, allowed the Soviets to continue their manufacture of war supplies. During the first year of the war 1,500 enterprises were evacuated, e.g. an aircraft factory, which began assembling planes within two weeks of the arrival of the last pieces of equipment on the new site on the River Volga. Three weeks later, thirty aeroplanes had been completed. This tremendous effort is one of the great achievements of mankind, comparable with the building of the pyramids or landing a man on the moon, and incomparably more useful.
15. When the Germans menaced Moscow in the winter of 1941, Stalin remained in the threatened capital, helping to organise a great counter-offensive.
16. As war leader, Stalin maintained close personal control over the Soviet battlefronts, military reserves, and war economy. At first over-inclined to intervene with inept telephoned instructions, as did Hitler, the Soviet leader gradually learned to delegate military decisions. This enabled him simultaneously to be credited with all successes by the media, while avoiding responsibility for any setbacks.
17. The NKVD summarily executed soldiers who retreated. Relatives of soldiers who became POWs were refused all assistance by the state.
18. Members of various non-Russian nationalities considered of questionable loyalty were rounded up and forcibly exiled from their native territories.
    (a) In 1941 the Volga Germans and other Soviet Germans were deported, and the Volga German Republic was abolished.
    (b) In 1943-45 the same measures were applied to the Crimean Tatars, the Kalmyks, the Chechens, and several other Caucasian peoples. More than 2,000,000 people were involved, and premature deaths are estimated at about 500,000.
19. In September 1942 the Germans reached Stalingrad, which was important to Stalin because of its name. There the Soviets fought valiantly to save the city. As the Germans fought their way in, their armies were surrounded by three armies under Marshall Zhukov, and the besiegers became the besieged. On 31st January 1943, Field Marshall von Paulus and his surviving men surrendered.
20. In the north, the siege of Leningrad was lifted, and in the south the Germans were driven back on a wide front. The tide of war had turned.
21. In early July 1943 the Germans tried to attack at Kursk, but in the largest tank battle in history they were held. That was the last major German offensive. The Russian offensive began later in the month.

22. In a series of offensives, the Red Army drove the Germans out of Soviet territory, invaded the lands to the West, and reached Berlin, bringing the war to an end.

The Easing of Restrictions

During the war Stalin had found it necessary, in general, to ease the controls exercised over all aspects of life by the security police and the party:

1. In the Armed Services: Officers and men mostly belonged to two classes indifferent to, or hostile to, communism: the hereditary military caste and the peasants.

   (a) The party kept an eye on commanders by means of political commissars, responsible for the morale of the troops, who reported directly to the Central Committee, and often usurped the privileges of command. During the war these were downgraded to "assistant political officers" (*zampolity*), without any right to interfere in operational command.

   (b) The "commanders" of the Red Army were renamed "officers", and their conditions of service and status improved:

       (i) A proper career structure was introduced.

       (ii) Saluting, full-dress uniforms and insignia restored.

       (iii) Officers were given access to superior housing and shops.

   (c) Before the war the armed forces had been thoroughly purged. During the invasion able people were promoted, even from labour camps.

2. The Party:

   (a) Membership was given for distinguished military service, quite independent of political allegiance. By 1944, half of the party membership was in the army. Naturally, the political commitment of the membership declined with such dilution.

   (b) There were no meetings of the Politburo, Central Committee or National Congress during the war. The USSR was governed by the State Defence Committee (GKO).

3. Industry:

   (a) The chief need was the production of war materiels. This took precedence over everything else, reintroducing some market discipline into the system.

   (b) Local initiative was allowed.

   (c) Ten million people and 1,500 enterprises were moved out of the path of the invasion, creating new industrial heartlands east of the Volga and in the Ural Mountains. This huge endeavour, carried out under the most adverse of circumstances, is one of the most impressive feats of humankind.

   (d) Women and adolescents were rushed into the factories.

4. Agriculture: The need was to produce food at any cost.

   (a) The productive private plots could be extended into the land of the collective farm, and the machinery and resources of the MTSs and the *kolkhozy* were made available for use on them.

   (b) Many kolkhozy were converted to the "link" (*zveno*) system, by which a group of peasants would take over part of the land of the collective, work it themselves, meet the proportion of the target due from that area of land, and then take the rest for their own profit.

5. Ideology: Stalin appealed to traditional patriotism and nationalism to defend "Mother Russia" against the German invaders, dropping the class terminology of Marxist-Leninism.

6. Local Initiatives were necessary during the crisis. In the path of the advancing Germans Local Defence Committees were set up consisting of:

       (a) members of the local army front command,

       (b) the local soviets,

       (c) the local party organization,

(d) the NKVD.

They organised resistance, e.g. the defence of Leningrad. This had the effect of allowing tactical decisions to be made locally by those who had knowledge of the immediate situation.

7. There was some relaxation of control of the media, with more frank reports from the front by war correspondents to validate authenticity. This was to make the media more credible to the people. But controls remained strict, e.g. all radios in private ownership had to be handed in.

Stalin as a War Leader

1. A war leader should prepare his country for war. When Operation Barbarossa was launched the USSR was:

(a) partially industrially prepared, since the five-year plans had transformed the USSR's economic base, and the Third Five-Year Plan had been diverted to war production

(b) militarily unprepared, since Stalin had been banking upon time to prepare and launch an attack, not upon defence.

(c) the armed forces had been denuded of experienced leaders by the purges

(d) the army was forbidden from preparing for or responding to the initial German attack, and suffered immense losses of men and equipment as a consequence.

2. Initially, Stalin interfered with operational decisions, with catastrophic results. Thus in spite of the advice of his generals, he believed that the main thrust of the German advance would be in the Ukraine. No one dared to contradict Stalin, and the main force was concentrated in the Ukraine. Even when new military intelligence made it clear that Stalin was wrong, no one dared to inform him.

3. When his lack of knowledge and realism led to defeat, Stalin did not adjust his picture of reality; instead he blamed and punished scapegoats, usually the unfortunate officers at the front.

4. Stalin failed to get good advice from his General Staff, because they hastened to propose what he would wish to hear, and always agreed with him. Only Marshall Zhukov dare dispute with him.

5. Stalin never hesitated to sacrifice men without a second thought. He was wasteful of men and materiel.

6. Yet Stalin emerged as the most successful of the supreme leaders thrown up by the belligerent nations.

(a) The Five Year Plans provided a good base for transition to a wartime economy.

(b) That transition was remarkably efficient.

(c) The movement of huge enterprises east, out of the path of the invaders, provided the means for the subsequent defeat of Hitler.

(d) Stalin soon learned to leave military tactics to the local commanders.

The Effects of the Great Patriotic War

1. As a result of the war, devastation in the Soviet Union was immense. Losses are estimated at:

(a) 20-25 million premature deaths, including 7.5 million military fatalities. This is more than the enemy, and, in absolute terms, more than any other nation has ever suffered in history;

(b) There was massive destruction of the country's infrastructure, with 25 million people left homeless.

2. Under Stalin, the nation had driven out and defeated the invader, and extended its area of control over much of Central Europe. This victory relegitimised Stalin and Stalinism in the eyes of the Soviet people. It eradicated the memory of Stalin's failures and seemed to vindicate the need for his apparent cruelties. Therefore it helped to preserve Stalin's leadership and the Stalinist system.

Stalin's USSR (1945-53)

The Restoration of Controls

1. At the end of the war Stalin moved to reimpose controls over Soviet society to pre-war levels. The reasons for this were probably:
    (a) to ensure his own unchallenged supremacy;
    (b) to mobilise the country for centrally-directed reconstruction;
    (c) to prevent ideological "contamination" from outside the country.

2. The Armed Services:
    (a) Marshall Zhukov, the victorious war leader, was transferred to the distant military district of Odessa. Officers taken from the Gulag during the invasion and restored to their commands were put back there.
    (b) The right to elect (appoint) party secretaries in military units was transferred from the armed services command back to the party hierarchy.
    (c) Political commissars* were not restored, but officers were encouraged to improve their political training by attending special party schools from 1947. This was a compromise, acknowledging the higher standing of the military, and ensuring that officers would be party-minded without direct party supervision.

3. The Party:
    (a) Recruitment policy was tightened up after Oct. 1944. Applicants needed recommendation by a long-standing party member and a period of probation. This was the counter the ideological dilution of the Party which had taken place during the war, when party membership had been given as a reward for outstanding effort on the battlefield.
    (b) Party high schools were set up in SSR capitals providing courses for party secretaries at *gorod** and *raion** levels, a prestigious high school in Moscow to train appointees to higher level party posts, and an academy of Social Sciences to train the teachers. Thus a finely graded career structure for the cadres was created.
    (c) The Politburo and Central Committee began to meet again, but there was no meeting of the National Congress until 1952. This was an indication of the real low standing of the Party in Stalin's eyes. It was merely a justification and cover for his personal dictatorship.

4. Industry: Wartime labour regulations were not lifted, preserving military discipline in the factories.

5. Agriculture:
    (a) All the land of *kolkhozy* which had been taken into private cultivation during the war had to be returned to common ownership, and the wartime drift towards privatisation was reversed.
    (b) MTS and *kolkhoz* chairmen were forbidden to allow the peasants any more to use public facilities for private work (tools, fodder, etc.).

6. Ideology:
    (a) Day to day close supervision of the media, literature and the arts was reimposed. In all works dealing with the war the leading role of Stalin and the Party had to be stressed.
    (b) There was a purge of "bourgeois specialists" who "crawled on their bellies before bourgeois authorities." i.e. experts who acknowledged the expertise of others in their field, regardless of their political affiliations.
    (c) Academic trends alien to dialectical materialism were condemned.
        (i) In 1947 Zhdanov condemned the "Principle of Uncertainty" of particle physics.
        (ii) The "bourgeois science" of Mendelian genetics was outlawed in favour of the "progressive biology" of Trofin Lysenko, a discarded pre-Darwinian theory asserting that

characteristics derived from the environment might be transmitted by inheritance. This effectively destroyed large areas of botany, agronomy and zoology in the USSR.

(d) In all fields Russian prowess was glorified, even in defiance of the facts: e.g. it was falsely claimed, that Russians had invented the radio and the aeroplane.

This combination of Marxist ideology and chauvinism was probably designed to cut off the country's intellectuals from Western influence.

7. While maintaining the federal facade, Stalin became increasingly hostile to all the national aspirations of the non-Russian peoples. This was probably intensified by the fact that in the Western Ukraine and Lithuania anti-Soviet partisans continued to operate as guerilla fighters against the Soviet government as late as 1950.

8. Religion: Controls were reimposed. Seminaries, monasteries and churches were closed, and anti-religious propaganda resumed. Yet more freedom remained for Orthodox Christians than before the war.

9. Opposition:

(a) There was a purge and massacre of those who had supported Hitler, e.g. General Andrei Vlasov and KONR (the Committee for the Liberation of the Peoples of Russia).

(b) The nationalist "forest brotherhoods" of the Baltic States, comprising at one point 0.5% of the population, and guerrillas in the Ukraine, were suppressed.

(c) POWs returning from the west:

   (i) if Russian were put into labour camps,

   (ii) if non-Russian were usually shot.

(Conditions in German POW camps were often better than in the USSR. Stalin did not want discontent to spread).

10. Outside the USSR, in Soviet occupied Eastern Europe, Stalin conducted purges of the intelligentsia and show trials, and intensive Sovietization to ensure their obedience.

Reconstruction

1. Finance:

(a) The currency was reformed. Old roubles were exchanged for new at the rates of 1:1 in savings and 10:1 in cash, to penalise moonlighters and black marketeers.

(b) In 1947 rationing was abolished. Prices in retail outlets were fixed by the market, passing on to citizens the cost of food shortages.

2. Industry:

(a) In 1946 the Fourth Five-Year Plan was introduced. Only heavy industry achieved its targets: coal, oil, electricity, iron, steel, cement and tractors. Soviet industry remained imbalanced, achieving little in light industry or consumer goods.

(b) Factories were rebuilt on the sites of those relocated during the war, while the transferred workers were kept on the new sites, contrary to promises given to them when they relocated.

3. Agriculture:

(a) Many *kolkhozy* were amalgamated to form larger units so as to simplify control through the MTSs. Some were converted into *sovkhozy* or state farms, where the peasants were employed by the state and paid regular wages. These were usually large single crop farms.

(b) There was only very slow recovery. Compulsory seizures of food to feed the cities led to famines in the countryside, especially in the Ukraine, with cases of cannibalism. By 1952 there were fewer cattle on the USSR than in 1916. The grain harvest had not reached the levels of 1940. Half the country's vegetables, two-thirds meat, milk and potatoes and nine-tenths of the eggs were produced on the small private plots.

Later Policies

1. Early in 1946 the place of Malenkov as second in the party was taken by Zhdanov, while a group of "Leningraders" associated with Zhdanov were appointed to important posts.
2. A wave of attacks on leading writers such as the poet Anna Akhmatova and the satirist Mikhail Zoshchenko took place. They were accused of being "individualists." This became known as the **Zhdanovshchina**, as Zhdanov was in charge of ideology.
3. Zhdanov fell from favour and was demoted in the summer of 1948, Malenkov taking his position as Stalin's chief aide.
4. Zhdanov almost immediately died. All the leading soviet and party officials in Leningrad were arrested and executed. The reasons for Stalin's purge of Leningraders may have included:
   (a) Stalin had always been suspicious of Leningrad, traditionally a westward-looking city.
   (b) Zhdanov had created Cominform to co-ordinate the work of European communist parties under Moscow's control. The Yugoslav Party had just been expelled from it, so it had failed.
   (c) A Yugoslav delegation had visited Leningrad in 1947 and praised the work of its heroic defenders. Stalin may have been jealous. This is supported by the immediate closure of the Museum of the Defence of Leningrad, and by the removal of all Leningrad newspapers of the period in public libraries to restricted access.
5. Following the founding of the state of Israel, which Stalin initially supported, Soviet policy became increasingly anti-Semitic.
   (a) From 1950 throughout eastern Europe the emphasis of accusations against the leaders on trial changed from Titoism* to Zionism*.
   (b) The Jewish Anti-Fascist Committee, set up during the war to assist in the struggle against fascism, was dissolved. Its leader, the actor and theatrical producer Solomon Mikhoels, was murdered by the MGB (Ministry of State Security).
   (c) "Rootless cosmopolitans" with Jewish names, mostly critics and playwrights, were attacked in a new propaganda drive, and many were arrested.
   (d) In August 1952 leading Yiddish* writers were executed.
   (e) A plan was mooted for creating a new SSR for Soviet Jews on the shores of the Arctic Ocean.
6. In 1951 a purge began in Georgia, directed against Beria's closest followers. These were jailed in what was called the "**Mingrelian Affair**." This seemed to be directed at Beria, and his security empire, the NKVD, was cut into two:
   (a) the MGB (Ministry of State Security) responsible for the security police,
   (b) the MVD (Ministry of Internal Affairs) - police, public order and the Gulag.
   Beria was given only the MVD. The MGB was headed by men not associated with him.
7. In 1952 the 19th National Congress of the CPSU was held. The Politburo was replaced by a new larger Party Presidium of 36 members, swamping the older Politburo members by newcomers. Khrushchev interpreted this as indicating a wish to remove the old guard, who had become too secure, and replace them with newcomers when they were ready. Thus a new purge of the leadership was imminent. Stalin attacked Molotov and Mikoyan as deviationists and accused them of espionage for the USA and the UK respectively.
8. In Jan. 1953 the **Doctors' Plot** was "exposed." This was an alleged conspiracy of prominent Soviet medical doctors of "planning to wipe out the leading cadres of the USSR by medical means." Nine doctors, who had attended on major Soviet leaders, including Andrey Zhdanov, were arrested. The doctors, many of whom were Jewish, were accused of being in the employ of US and British intelligence services and international Jewry. It was reported that all of the doctors had confessed, and Beria's MVD was reproached with "lack of vigilance."

In his secret speech at the 20th Party Congress (1956), Nikita Khrushchev asserted that Stalin had personally ordered that the cases be "developed" and confessions "elicited." He considered that the "doctors' plot" was to signal the beginning of a new purge, which was to include members of the Politburo.

9. Thus at the beginning of 1953 there was a general feeling of crisis:

(a) Economic difficulties were acute:

    (i) there were no more windfalls like war reparations;

    (ii) living standards had not risen;

    (iii) goods were shoddy, and produced without regard for need or quality.

(b) Several groups felt threatened with an impending purge: the politburo, especially Beria, the and the other members of the Politburo, the Jews, and leading doctors.

(c) This may even have been felt by Stalin. Khrushchev heard him remark: "I'm finished. I trust no one; not even myself."

10. On March 6th, 1953 Stalin's death was reported. According to Khrushchev he had suffered a stroke on March 1-2nd.

[For Stalin's foreign policy after the Second World War and his part in the Cold War, see the companion volume The Cold War"]

Timeline of Stalin's Regime 1945-53	
1941	German invasion of the USSR
1943	Battle of Stalingrad
	Battle of Kursk
1945	Soviet invasion of Germany - fall of Berlin
1946	Zhdanovshchina launched - Fourth Five-Year Plan launched
1947	
1948	End of Zhdanovshchina - purge of Leningraders
1951	Mingrelian affair
1953	
Jan	"Doctors' Plot" uncovered
Mar	Death of Stalin

Assessment of Stalin's Leadership

1. Stalin turned the most backward of the Great Powers into a superpower. From an initially backward position following the world war, civil war, and famine, and appallingly ravaged during World War II, the Soviet Union was able, under Stalin's leadership, to:

(a) avoid the consequences of the Great Depression;

(b) play the major role in defeating Hitler;

(c) establish the USSR as the world's second most powerful industrial and military power, from 1949 a nuclear superpower, able to resist American dominance.

However:

2. It is arguable that a comparable degree of industrialization would have come about in any case, and by means less savage, under almost any alternative regime.

3. Although a high industrial output was achieved, very little of it ever became available to the ordinary Soviet citizen in the form of consumer goods or improved amenities of life.

4. The collectivisation of agriculture seems to have ruined Soviet agriculture for ever.
5. The highly centralized bureaucratized administrative system was a blunt instrument which initially obtained excellent results, but soon proved a disadvantage. In particular, the command economy would prove a system unresponsive to the needs of the population and impossible to reform from within without collapse. The effects of its collapse are being felt even today.
6. Millions perished in the anti-peasant terror of 1930-33 and the general terror of 1936-39 and later, or barely survived in the vast labour camp system. An individual peasantry no longer existed. The instruments of terror remained after his death, feared and barely controlled by the Communist Party, and only partially dismantled by Khrushchev.
7. Stalin's methods crushed initiative among Soviet administrators, physically destroying many. The party, state, administrative, and intellectual cadres had been largely destroyed, and replaced by intellectually and morally inferior personnel. Moreover, even these had been heavily purged, so that the ruling caste was motivated by dogma, fear, ambition, malice, and greed; a process described as "negative selection."
8. Stalin spread communism throughout Eastern Europe, but not by encouraging and fostering revolutions abroad, but imposing it by military conquest.
9. Stalin had been unable to prevent new forms of communism appearing, e.g. in Yugoslavia and China.

The Basis of Stalin's Rule

1. The exercise of force and power was supported by terror methods.
2. But it also depended upon a basis of consent:
   (a) Stalin projected himself as the successor of the Revolution and Lenin. This was stressed in Stalin's personality cult.
   (b) A "strong Tsar" was traditionally admired, as he would pretext the people from over-mighty aristocrats and foreign invaders.
   (c) People believed that they were surrounded by enemies and saboteurs, so that strong measures were needed to defend the country against them.
   (d) Resentments against the privileged, the intelligentsia and minorities were exploited.
   (e) Basic living standards improved.
      (i) The USSR escaped the consequences of the Great Depression.
      (ii) Basic social security, housing, jobs, health and education were introduced for all.
   (f) Upward social mobility was possible. This was assisted by the purges.
   (g) After the war there was pride in Soviet achievements:
      (i) industrialization,
      (ii) their victory over Hitler and the Nazis.

Stalin and Lenin

1. Historians dispute whether:
   (a) Stalin perverted Lenin's creation and turned it into a dictatorship, e.g. Roy Deutscher, Isaac Medvedev;
   (b) Stalin merely continued the logic of Lenin's policies, e.g. Robert Conquest, Alexander Solzhenitsyn.
2. In favour of the latter view:
   (a) Lenin's notion of democratic centralism laid the ideological foundation for Stalin's totalitarianism.*
   (b) Lenin's belief that disputes undermined the Party and that factionalism* should be illegal laid

the legal foundation for Stalin's totalitarianism.

(c) Lenin's foundation of the Cheka and the gulag laid the institutional foundation for Stalin's totalitarianism.

(d) Lenin's authoritarian style, his belief that only knew best what was to be done, and that only he could be trusted to supervise it, led to his effectively slipping into the role of the tsar. Given his popularity, in a country used to autocracy, this ensured that people would be accustomed to treating the leader of the Party as the tsar in modern dress. Thus, despite his obvious wishes to the contrary (expressed in his *Testament*), he created the role into which Stalin would later insinuate himself.

(e) The cult of Lenin's personality, a largely spontaneous growth, laid the foundation for Stalin's manufactured personality cult.

Glossary

agent provocateur a government agent posing as a revolutionary or demonstrator

apparat the Soviet Party and state bureaucracy

apparatchiks members of the Soviet Party and state bureaucracy

blitzkrieg an in-depth strike with tanks, mobile infantry and planes, designed to panic the defenders

bonapartism when a "strong man" takes advantage of the confusion to hi-jack a revolution

bureaucracy administration carried out by officials

bureaucratization turning an activity into something administered by officials according to set procedures

cadres full-time party activists

careerism joining the Bolshevik Party in order to further one's career

collectivization joining the individual farms of the peasants to create large collective farms

Comintern The Communist International

command economy centrally controlled economy

CPSU The Communist Party of the Soviet Union

dekulakization destroying the class of *kulaks*

democratic centralism Lenin's policy that the party would lead the working class

etatism belief in increasing the power of the state

factionalism disputing the views of the leadership of the Party

GKO the State Defence Committee

gorod an administrative area, an urban district or city

Gosplan the all-powerful Soviet central economic planning agency

Gulag the system of labour camps

KNOR The Committee for the Liberation of the Peoples of Russia

kolkhoznik worker on a collective farm

kolkhozy collective farms

kulaks wealthy peasants

MGB The Ministry of State Security, responsible for the security police, part of the former NKVD.

MTS Machine Tractor Station

MVD **The** Ministry of Internal Affairs, responsible for ordinary police, public order and the Gulag; part of the former NKVD.

NEP the New Economic Policy

NKVD People's Commissariat for Internal Affairs - the political police, the successor of OGPU

nomenklatura the lists of politically sensitive posts and of people suited to fill them

oblast province

personality cult the deliberate development of the practice of veneration of a person

politburo the most important subcommittee of the central committee of the party

political commissars Party officials appointed to oversee the orthodoxy of the institution to which they were appointed

raion an administrative area, a rural district

sovkhozy state farms

SSRs Soviet Socialist Republics

stakhanovites workers praised for setting an example of heroic productivity

Titoism following a line independent of Stalin (of leaders of Communist states)

totalitarianism a regime which seeks to control all aspects of the lives of the people

troikas three man tribunals set up to try suspects during the Terror

vozhd "The Boss" - the title by which Stalin was known during his period in power.

Yezhovshina the period which marked the height of the Great Terror when Nikolay Yezhov was head of the NKVD (1936-8).

Yiddish a language spoken by Central and Eastern European Jews

zampolity political commissars appointed to ensure the political correctness of the army

zeks political prisoners in the Gulag

Zhdanovshchina the period of cultural terror when Zhdanov was most influential

Zionist a Jew wishing to live in, or whose loyalty belongs to, the state of Israel

Benito Mussolini

Mussolini's Italy

"... [A] rabbit, a phenomenal rabbit; he roars. Observers who do not know him mistake him for a lion."

(Giacinto Serrati)

Background

1. Italian democracy had never known stability.
   (a) Between 1871 and 1900 there were no less than 22 governments. Many ill-defined political groups competed in the elections, and in order to form a government which could command a majority in the parliament political offices and favours were traded.
   (b) The powerful Roman Catholic Church was alienated from the Italian state by its loss of the Papal States in the mid-nineteenth century. Until 1904 Catholics were forbidden to vote.
   (c) Universal manhood suffrage* was only introduced in 1912, so that the mass of Italians had little engagement in politics.
   (d) There was a general perception that democracy in Italy was corrupt* and inefficient, because:
       (i) the politicians represented the interests of the upper and middle classes;
       (b) bribery, clientism* and vote-rigging was common.
   (e) Italian politicians were perceived to have failed to make the newly-united Italy into a Great Power with a significant overseas empire.
2. The First World War was not widely popular in Italy, and the Italians were not very successful in fighting it. They lost one million men and gained twelve miles of territory.
3. Many Italians were disillusioned at the end of the war
   (a) Many were discontented with the peace treaties, since Italy did not receive Fiume and part of Dalmatia, and some German colonies in Africa, areas which it was claimed had been promised in the Treaty of London (1915)
   (b) The economic situation in Italy was bad:
       (i) The war had been paid for by borrowing from the USA, and this debt had to be repaid.
       (ii) There were shortages, including of food, due to the number of agricultural workers in the army and dislocation of transport and commerce.
       (iii) Inflation caused hardship, as prices rose by more than 500%.
       (iv) It was difficult to sell exports.

(v) There were hardly any tourists, upon which many people depended for a living.

(vi) Many returning soldiers faced unemployment as war production was ended.

(c) There was a feeling that democracy was not working:

(i) Universal male suffrage and proportional representation* had been introduced for the 1919 elections. The three main parties: the Liberals, Catholics (PPI) and Socialists (PSI), were unable to work together, with the result that unstable coalition governments* were elected, which failed to last for any length of time.

(ii) Politicians in general were despised as incompetent and corrupt.

(d) Industrial relations were bad, with:

(i) a large growth in the membership of the trade unions;

(ii) increased strikes;

(iii) occupations of factories by workers;

(iv) the organisation of factory committees, which resembled the soviets of revolutionary Russia;

(e) Violence was never far from the surface in public life. During 1919 and 1920, known as the Biennio Rosso, or Red Years:

(i) looting of shops was widespread;

(ii) farm workers in some areas seized land and set up cooperatives.

(iii) Soldiers returning from the war began to seize the lands of absentee landowners.

(iv) Brigands infested the south, reinforced by army deserters, while the power of the Mafia and the Camorra was dominant in certain areas.

4. Despite the increased popularity of the left, the socialists were unable to form a strong government as they had split between the social democrats (PSI) and the revolutionary socialists, who formed the Italian Communist Party (PCI).

5. Many privileged groups feared revolution. The upper and middle classes, nationalists and Catholics demanded strong leadership to:

(a) establish law and order;

(b) discipline strikers;

(d) rescue the national honour;

(e) protect privileged elites, the monarchy and the Church from revolution.

Personal Background

1. Benito Mussolini was the son of a blacksmith, and in later years professed pride in his humble origins as a "man of the people." But his father was also a part-time journalist, and his mother a schoolteacher.

2. A disobedient, aggressive bully, he was twice expelled from schools for violence.

3. He was also intelligent, and passed his examinations without difficulty. He obtained a teaching diploma and for a time worked as a schoolmaster.

4. At the age of 19 he left Italy for Switzerland and lived from day to day, moving from job to job.

5. While earning a reputation as a political journalist and public speaker, he undertook propaganda for a trade union, proposing a strike and advocating violence as a means of enforcing demands. More than once he was arrested and imprisoned.

6. After writing in a wide variety of Socialist papers, he founded a newspaper of his own, *La Lotta di Classe* ("The Class Struggle").

7. In 1912 he was appointed editor of the official Socialist newspaper, *Avanti!* whose circulation

he soon doubled. As its anti-militarist, anti-nationalist, and anti-imperialist editor, he opposed Italy's intervention in the First World War.

8. Then he changed his mind and began writing articles and making speeches in favour of war. He resigned from *Avanti!* and was expelled from the Socialist Party.

9. Financed by a publisher who also favoured war against Austria, he became editor of *Il Popolo d'Italia.*

10. From 1915-17 he served in the army, and was wounded while serving with the *Bersaglieri* (a corps of sharpshooters). He returned home a nationalist anti-Socialist, and a man with a sense of destiny.

The Foundations of Fascism

1. As early as February 1918, Mussolini was advocating the emergence of a dictator to solve Italy's problems: "a man who is ruthless and energetic enough to make a clean sweep." Three months later, he suggested that he himself might be that man.

2. The following year the nucleus of an organisation prepared to support his ambitious idea was formed in Milan. Mussolini called this force the *Fasci di Combattimento*. It was made up of discontented former soldiers who:

    (a) wore black shirts in imitation of:

    (i) Garibaldi's red-shirts, (It was a cheap way to create a uniform);

    (ii) and the anarchist labourers of the Romagna;

    (b) adopted the salute of the ancient Roman army;

    (c) took as their symbol the *fascinae* of ancient Rome, the bundle of rods and an axe which symbolised the state's authority to exercise power;

    (d) as referred to as *Duce*, (or 'leader').

3. Membership of the **blackshirts** appealed to:

    (a) discontented ex-soldiers who wished for:

    (i) a sense of purpose, by "saving Italy" as they had believed they were doing during wartime;

    (ii) some dignity, symbolised by a uniform;

    (iii) some excitement (brawling with local leftists);

    (iv) the comradeship of the forces;

    (v) respite from the responsibilities and pressures of the family;

    (b) nationalists, who wanted to make Italy a great power;

    (c) the middle classes (esp. students) who feared loss of privileges in a communist revolution.

    They included a wide variety of political outlooks.

4. He was inspired by:

    (a) Garibaldi's "Thousand" redshirts;

    (b) The poet d'Annunzio's seizure of the Italian-speaking port city of Fiume from Yugoslavia. D'Annunzio briefly established a corporate state under his own dictatorship with elaborate uniforms, ritual salutes, and the intimidation of opponents.

5. Initially, the fascists declared themselves to be revolutionary, and opposed:

    (a) Socialists and the trades unions;

    (b) capitalists and big business;

    (c) the monarchy;

    (d) the Church.

6. Thus Mussolini proposed:

    (a) the election of a National Assembly to draw up a new constitution;

(b) replacing the existing system of weak parliamentary government with strong government;

(c) the abolition of the Senate (the upper house with members nominated by the king);

(d) universal suffrage (with men *and* women having a vote);

(e) the confiscation of war profits;

(f) the confiscation of church property;

(g) a guaranteed minimum wage;

(h) worker participation in managing the factories;

(i) agrarian reforms, by breaking up the great estates of the big landowners;

(j) a purge the left;

(k) support for the demands of war veterans;

(l) the achievement of Italy's war aims.

Apart from the nationalism, this was a radical left-wing agenda.

7. At mass rallies, Mussolini caught the imagination of the crowds with his charismatic* personality and powerful oratory.

8. The Blackshirts practised systematc thuggery, breaking up rival public meetings.

9. In the elections of 1919 the Fascists failed to win a single seat.

10. Mussolini promptly:

(a) abandoned republicanism;

(b) abandoned opposition to the Church;

(c) formed his movement into a legal political party, the **National Fascist Party (PNF)**

(d) and began to seek to appeal to privileged groups in society as a popular alternative to Communism and revolution.

This was an abrupt turn towards the right wing.

11. New Fascist groups were founded, and by autumn 1920 were busy:

(a) breaking strikes;

(b) dismantling labour unions and peasants' co-operatives;

(c) overthrowing local councils.

12. Mussolini soon proved himself a master of propaganda. Portraits of Mussolini suggested a coming saviour. The simplistic slogan "Believe, obey, fight" appealed to the unsophisticated.

13. The Fascists received considerable support among the peasants of Central and Northern Italy. Within a few months Fascist squad leaders controlled most of the rural areas of Central Italy.

14. In May 1921, when Prime Minister Giolitti called new elections, thirty-five Fascists were elected to Parliament as part of a government *bloc* of 275 deputies.

15. In October 1921 Mussolini relaunched his party as the *Partiti Nazionale Fascista* (PNF) a right-wing party based upon nationalism and anti-Communism. His new programme included:

(a) a guarantee of the right to private property;

(b) the privatisation of state controlled industries;

(c) the creation of corporations to represent all classes in resolving disputes in industry and on the land;

(d) the incorporation of all Italian-speaking areas outside Italy into the country;

(e) Italy assuming a dominant role in the Mediterranean.

This consolidated Mussolini's move to the right.

16. In the next few months, seeing Mussolini as a man who could capture the masses and protect them from Communism, the political establishment began to conciliate and finance him. Benefactors included Giovanni Agnelli of Fiat and Alberto Pirelli of the tyre company. The police, the army, and much of the middle class sympathised with Fascist disruption of Socialist trade unions.

The "Coup d'État"

1. The Italian government was insecure. D'Annunzio, a nationalist poet, together with a group of volunteers, had seized Fiume by force in 1921. The Great Powers ordered the government to remove him, by force if necessary, and they had obeyed. This was extremely unpopular.

2. In Feb. 1922 it took several weeks to form a new government under Luigi Facta, which was immediately paralysed.

3. Throughout the countryside a low level war was waged against opponents of the fascists by the Ras,* local Fascist leaders, occasionally killing them. Their trade mark was forcing politicians and officials who opposed them to drink castor oil in public, but sometimes opponents were killed. Sometimes they siezed local government offices and took them over by force. This disorder:
   (a) often had the support of local army and police leaders;
   (b) was not organised by Mussolini, but by the Ras in their own areas. Mussolini fared it woud be counterproductive.

4. In Parma, a deeply socialist city which had proved immune to the attractions of Fascism, the *Arditi del popolo* (People's Shock Troops), an anti-fascist organisation set up in June 1921, had prepared for resistance. When Blackshirt leader Italo Balbo led 20,000 Fascists on a punitive expedition to the city at the beginning of August, the united population resisted for six days before Mussolini called them off. The blackshirts had lost 39 dead and 150 wounded, while the defenders lost five dead and several wounded.

5. Later in that month the unions tried to seize power in a general strike. The Fascists:
   (a) burned left-wing printing presses;
   (b) helped keep essential services running and broke the strike;
   (c) and in so doing, demonstrated the ineffectiveness of the government and the effectiveness of the Mussolini and the Fascists.

6. Mussolini declared that unless the government prevented the strike, the Fascists would. "Either the government will be given to us," he threatened at a gathering of 40,000 Fascists in Naples, "or we will seize it by marching on Rome."

7. Later that day, Mussolini and other leading Fascists decided that in four days' time the Fascist militia would lead a "**March on Rome**" (recalling Garibaldi's famous "marches on Rome") in four converging columns. Mussolini appealed to the army not to interfere.

8. Prime Minister Facta asked the king to declare martial law, but Victor Emmanuel III refused:
   (a) ostensibly in order to avoid possible army disloyalty or even a civil war;
   (b) in reality it was because he had been shocked by the Bolshevik revolution in Russia and the execution of the royal family, and saw Mussolini as a protector.

9. The King then sent a telegram to Mussolini offering to make him prime minister, asking him to form a government, hoping to tame him by constitutional means. Mussolini accepted a place in a government with three fascists in the cabinet.

10. Mussolini became prime minister, therefore, in a more or less constitutional manner. He was appointed by the king, and he headed a coalition government that included Nationalists, Liberals, and two Catholic ministers from the Popular Party.

11. The Ras* insisted that the **March on Rome** go ahead as a symbolic victory parade. Italo Balbo, leader of the Blackshirts of Ferrara, declared: "We are going, either with you or without you." The March on Rome was subsequently portrayed in Fascist propaganda as a violent coup d'état to demonstrate that Mussolini was a "man of action."

12. Although Mussolini was prime minister, it was in a coalition government with only two other Fascists and only 7% of the deputies in the Chamber. He depended upon the support of the king.

The Road to Dictatorship

1. For eighteen months Mussolini ruled through the constitutional government machinery, although the creation of the **Fascist Grand Council** in December 1922 established a rival body to the Council of Ministers, and one from which non-Fascists were excluded.

2. He pursued a policy of "**normalisation**." The squads were incorporated into an official Voluntary Militia for National Security. Lower middle-class job seekers flooded into the Fascist Party, making it more respectable; the Nationalists also merged their organisation into it, bringing with them much respectable backing in the south.

3. In 1923 the passage of the **Acerbo Law** ensured that the group of parties with the largest vote would receive an absolute majority of the seats in parliament. This enabled the Fascists to:
   (a) attract most of the Liberal deputies into a "national alliance";
   (b) avoid the instability of past coalition governments.

4. In the April 1924 elections the Fascist-dominated bloc won 64% of the votes and 374 seats, doing well in the south. The opposition parties remained divided but won a majority of the votes in northern Italy:
   (a) The Socialists had by this time split into three rival parties, and none of them had much influence.
   (b) The Catholic Popular Party was disowned by Pope Pius XI and the Vatican, which saw Mussolini as a more effective shield against Communism.
   (c) The election was conducted in an atmosphere of intimidation and violence.

5. When the new Parliament met, **Giacomo Matteotti,** leader of the reformist Socialists, denounced the elections as a sham because of widespread intimidation of opposition candidates and voters. On June 10, 1924, Matteotti was murdered by thugs led by the assistant to Mussolini's press office. Mussolini was suspected of personal complicity. The press denounced the government, and the opposition parties walked out of Parliament.

6. For some time Mussolini's regime seemed in danger:
   (a) by autumn his Liberal supporters were drifting away;
   (b) the "normalisation" policy had infuriated Fascist extremists in the country, especially local bosses, the Ras, threatened with dismissal by the new militia commander, an army general. Some of the Ras threatened to murder Mussolini if he gave up his attempt to gain power. They demanded a showdown with the opposition, and he had to agree. On Jan. 3, 1925, he made a speech in the Chamber of Deputies accepting responsibility for Fascism and promising a tough crackdown on dissenters.

7. Mussolini sought to reassure privileged groups in society:
   (a) In the Education Act (1923):
      (i) crucifixes were returned to classrooms;
      (ii) religious education was made compulsory in primary schools;
      (iii) religious education was permitted in secondary schools;
      (iv) he expressed his intention to solve the problem between the Vatican and the Italian state;
      (v) and exempted the clergy from taxation.
   (b) During 1924-5 his finance minister, De Stefani, cut government spending and balanced the budget. (He also benefitted from an upturn in the world economy). This was reassuring to businessmen.
   (c) He cancelled decrees legalizing land seizures by the peasants, reassuring the large landowners.
   (d) In April 1926 strikes were banned and independent trades unions closed down.

8. As a result, he successfully negotiated increased powers from the king:
   (a) In 1925, Mussolini was made directly responsible to the king, and not to parliament.

(b) In January 1926, he was allowed to govern by decree, and was to issue many thousands.

(c) In November 1926, after several attempts on Mussolini's life, all political parties except the Fascist Party were abolished.

9. He increased his popularity and power over the country:

(a) The press was closely censored by the *Duce* personally, cinema newsreels became largely government propaganda, and the regime controlled radio broadcasting.

(b) Semi-compulsory Fascist youth movements were founded, such as the Sons and Daughters of the She-Wolf, to capture the loyalty of the young.

(c) New textbooks were imposed on the schools to glorify nationalism.

(d) The government also provided mass leisure activities, such as sports, concerts, and seaside holidays through an organisation of local clubs, known as Doplavoro, which was genuinely popular. It provided free holidays for workers and for poor children.

(e) During 1926 various new laws:

(i) increased police powers of arrest;

(ii) allowed the internal exile of politicians on islands.

(iii) established the political police (*OVRA*).

(iv) A Special Tribunal for the Defence of the State, run by militia and army officers, was set up to try anti-Fascist "subversives." It imprisoned or sent to exile on remote islands thousands of political opponents, and imposed thirty-one death penalties.

(f) Repression was carried out by the police and army, not by Fascist organisations. The Fascist regime was mostly run by the traditional élites in the military and civilian bureaucracy, which were linked to the royal court and the landowners:

(i) The prefects, mostly career civil servants, retained their dominance over local government.

(ii) The new *podesta* was nearly always a landowner or retired army officer rather than a Fascist.

10. Mussolini feared the rivalry of the Fascists more than any other group, so he sought to empty the Fascist movement of power.

(a) In 1922 Mussolini established the Fascist Grand Council, which gave him power of patronage over the Ras;

(b) In 1923 he founded the Voluntary Militia for National Security (*MSVN*) which was a national militia which absorbed the local militias, in an attempt to get them under his control.

(c) In 1927 Fascist functionaries were ordered to obey the local *podestas*.

(d) During 1926-29, with a compliant secretary of the *PNF*, Augusto Turati, some 60,000 of the most radical and militant Blackshirts were purged.

The Blackshirt militia, soon had little to do except engage in propaganda and parades.

11. Mussolini increased his power in the Chamber of Deputies.

(a) When they the Deputies who had walked out of the Chamber after the murder of Matteotti tried to return, in 1925, Mussolini would not allow them to take their seats.

(b) In 1928 a new electoral law abolished universal suffrage, and reduced the voting population from ten million to three million. During the election of 1928 electors could only accept or reject the list of deputies presented by the Fascist Grand Council.

12. By 1929 Mussolini had:

(a) established firm control over the Fascist movement, subordinating it to state authorities manned by traditionally privileged groups;

(b) gained the confidence and approval of traditionally privileged groups, including the middle classes, the Vatican and the Crown.

Timeline of the Rise to Power of Mussolini	
1914	Mussolini expelled from the Socialist Party
1915	Italy enters the First World War
1918	The *Fasci di Combattimento* (Blackshirts) set up
1919-20	The "Red Years"
1921	The Fascist Party founded
1922	The Siege of Parma
	Mussolini invited to become Prime Minister
	The March on Rome
1923	The Acerbo Law passed
	Mussolini invades Corfu
1924	Murder of Matteotti
1926	Mussolini given the Power to Rule by Decree
	Blackshirts purged
1928	Universal suffrage abolished

Reasons why Mussolini was able to gain power

1. Mussolini had exceptional gifts as a publicist: a charismatic speaker and persuasive writer. He was a superb self-publicist, presenting himself and his movement as more capable and powerful than they really were.

2. Mussolini took advantage of the situation at the end of the war, brilliantly exploiting the needs and fears of many different groups, e.g. fear of Communist revolution.

3. He was an opportunist, able to accommodate himself to the needs of the time, and always willing to compromise and even t contradict himself, to gain political advantage.

    (a) He dropped much of his early radicalism, especially his anti-clericalism* and republicanism. This enabled Mussolini to win the support (active or passive) of the traditional centres of authority: Church, army, police, landowners, businessmen, etc.

    (b) Mussolini was ruthless enough to use people and then dispose of them when it was convenient for him, especially the blackshirts, who had won the streets for him during the "Red Years," but whose violence, crudity and extremism became an embarrassment in later years.

4. The Italian people welcomed authoritarian rule. They were tired of:
    - (a) corrupt politicians;
    - (b) frequent changes of government;
    - (c) frequent strikes and riots.

    They were ready to submit to dictatorship, provided that the economy was stabilised and national honour was restored. Mussolini seemed to be the one man capable of bringing order out of chaos.

5. Socialists and communists could not co-operate to keep the fascists out.

6. Opponents consistently underestimated Mussolini.

The Fascist Ideology

1. Insofar as there was a coherent ideology of Fascism, it was influenced by Nietzsche, Hegel and Bergson. Its was a patchwork of:

    (a) Social Darwinism;*

    (b) Chauvinistic nationalism;

    (c) Hostility to liberal democracy;

(d) The need to avoid class struggle in the interests of national unity;

(e) The belief that the state is more important than the individual, and should control the lives of individuals as much as possible;

(f) The "leader principle";

(g) The belief that war is good, territorial expansion a sign of good national health and "Peace is absurd."

(h) Belief in the corporate state: a "third way" an alternative to capitalism and communism, in which "corporations" made up of representatives of each of the various interests in society settle conflicts of interest without the social disruption of class conflict.

2. This ideology, however, was unimportant in itself. Mussolini once said that when he started the Fascist movement "there was no specific doctrinal plan in my mind." He once criticised Hitler as "doctrinaire."*

(a) The Fascist ideology was merely a vehicle for Mussolini's rise to power. He added whatever would assist him in obtaining power and keeping it.

(b) The ideology provided a veneer of respectability to his movement and his regime.

(c) It was often inconsistent, but since people tended to accept what they wanted and ignored the rest, inconsistency was a strength, in that it allowed people with widely different viewpoints to accept Fascism.

"Fascism" and "fascism"

Italian Fascism was an invention of Mussolini. But Mussolini was a much admired leader world wide during the 1920s, and had many imitators who founded their own similar movements. These are collectively called "fascist" movements, and their ideology as "fascism".

In order to distinguish Mussolini's own ideology and movement from these imitators, it is useful to refer to Italian movement and doctrine as "Fascist" and "Fascism", and to refer to the Italian and other movements and their ideologies collectively as "fascist" or "fascism".

The Corporate State

1. Mussolini imposed Fascism onto existing institutions, creating a complex, illogical system, so that he could preside over a number of competing centres of power.

2. Propaganda always played a large role in the government of the Fascist state.

(a) Mussolini's control of the newspapers was absolute. He censored them himself.

(b) He said that cinema was the most important medium, and was the first leader to use it systematically.

(c) Parades and speeches were major sources of inspiration and entertainment.

3. In 1926 the lira was revalued in order to demonstrate the strength of the currency. As a result:

(a) Exports fell sharply;

(b) Unemployment rose;

(c) Wages were frozen or even cut;

(d) Prices fell.

However, the steel, electricity, and chemical industries expanded, as their markets were domestic, and they were helped by cheaper raw material imports. Industries producing textiles and food, which were reliant on foreign markets, declined.

4. Industry: Government subsidies were given to industry to increase production. This was especially successful in iron and steel, artificial silk and hydro-electric power.

5. Agriculture: The government aimed at self-sufficiency by encouraging grain production (known as "**the battle for wheat**"). A high tariff was reimposed on imported wheat, and grain prices were kept artificially high. Production rose sharply as northern farmers used more chemical fertilisers. In much of the south the climate was unsuitable for growing wheat, but vineyards and olive groves were ploughed up.

6. A massive public works programme was launched to:
   > (i) reduce unemployment;
   > (ii) and improve the infrastructure and of the country.

   This involved

   (a) building roads (*autostrada*), bridges, new towns, railway stations, sports stadia, schools, apartment blocks, etc.

   (b) electrifying railway lines;

   (c) The draining of the extensive Pontine Marshes between Rome and Naples destroyed the breeding grounds of malarial mosquitoes and so improved the health of the population;

   (d) Irrigating dry land;

   (e) Reafforesting mountains;

   (f) excavating and laying out archaeological sites, e.g. the Roman Forum, for the development of tourism.

7. After October 1925 the Fascist syndicates, or trade unions, were the sole recognised negotiators for workers' interests. Although strikes and lockouts became illegal, and wages fell between 1927 and 1934, the syndicates secured:
   > (a) a shorter working week;
   > (b) higher welfare benefits (such as family allowances in 1934);
   > (c) public works schemes;
   > (d) ran leisure and social activities;
   > (e) protected jobs.

8. Under Fascism medical care improved, with a decline in infant mortality.

9. In 1934 the Fascists finally set up 22 **corporations,*** mixed bodies of workers, managers and employers, to decide labour disputes and supervise wage settlements under the supervision of a fascist. Despite much rhetoric and propaganda about the **corporate state**,* they had little impact in practice and virtually none on industrial management or economic policy. They were a vehicle for the state and big business to settle matters to their own satisfaction, excluding the workers.

10. The only strong non-Fascist organisation in the country remained the Roman Catholic Church. Pope Pius XI had implicitly supported Mussolini in the early years as protection against Communist revolution, and was rewarded with a concordat* which settled the "Roman Question" at last. Since the Papal States and then Rome itself had been incorporated into Italy, the Popes had refused to recognise the Italian state. In February 1929, by the **Lateran Concordat**, concluded with Pope Pius XI:

    (a) Vatican City became an independent state.

    (b) Italy began paying a large financial indemnity to the pope for taking over his former lands.

    (c) The church was granted many privileges in Italy, including:
    > (i) recognition of church weddings as valid in civil law;
    > (ii) religious education in secondary, as well as in primary, schools;
    > (iii) freedom for lay Catholic organisations, such as Catholic Action.

Disenchantment

1. When the Great Depression came after 1929, deflation accentuated, although the government:
    (a) increased spending on **public works** and on welfare in order to provide employment;
    (b) propped up leading banks and large industrial companies by creating the Instituto per la Riconstruzione Industriale (IMI). As a result, the second largest state-owned industrial sector in the world was created, especially in banking, steel, shipping, armaments, and hydro-electricity. The companies were not nationalised; they operated in the market as private companies and had some private shareholders.
    Most industrial development took place in northern Italy. The South lagged behind.
2. During the invasion of Ethiopia in 1935-36, the Italian economy was subjected to sanctions by the League of Nations. This led to:
    (a) devaluation of the lira
    (b) a more extensive drive for self-sufficiency ("**autarchy**"); imports were replaced where possible by native products, and most exports were diverted to Germany and Switzerland or to Africa. Abyssinia became a drain on resources.
3. Over time, official cartels and monopolies were encouraged; and resources were shifted to heavy industry and armaments. All this led to:
    (a) budget deficits and big tax increases which were resented because they were mainly needed to pay for wars in Africa and Spain;
    (b) small businesses were squeezed out by the monopolies.
4. The Fascist bureaucracy flourished, reducing efficiency.
5. The obvious corruption of the governing clique,* without whose permits (available at a price) nothing could be done, was resented.
6. Living standards for ordinary Italians fell during the 1930s.
7. In 1934 family allowances were provided, later supplemented by accident and sickness insurance; but these wee not sufficient to compensate for lower wages.
8. Anti-Fascist feeling became more widespread after the mid-1930s.
    (a) Italy's increasingly close alliance with Adolf Hitler's Germany was also resented and feared, even by many Fascists.
    (b) The sudden decision of Mussolini to impose anti-Semitic laws in 1938 was resented as servile subjugation to Hitler.
    (c) The economy no longer functioned efficiently.
    (d) The inadequacies of Fascist government became more evident.
9. The various conservative groups, including the army, the civil service, the law, and the church, which in the mid-1920s had looked to Fascism to protect their interests, realised by the late 1930s that Fascism was unreliable and began to withdraw their support.
10. Organized anti-Fascist movements were illegal, and for a long time remained weak and divided.
    (a) The Communists had an underground organisation and some Soviet support and finance.
    (b) "Justice and Liberty," an alliance of Republicans, Democrats, and reformist Socialists founded by Carlo Rosselli and others in 1929, managed to build up a clandestine organisation.

Foreign Policy

The First Period of Aggression

1. When Mussolini first came to power he promised a strong foreign policy which would:
    (a) reverse the humiliations of the past, e.g. Adowa (1896) and the Paris peace settlement;
    (b) establish a strong Italy as the dominant power in the Mediterranean (*Mare nostrum*). He

encouraged Italians to think of themselves as the successors of the ancient Romans.

2. In 1923 three Italian officers working for the League trying to settle a boundary dispute between Greece and Albania were shot on the border from the Greek side. Mussolini first demanded compensation, and then bombarded and occupied Corfu. Greece appealed to the League of Nations, but Mussolini refused to acknowledge its competence and threatened to withdraw from the League.. The Powers then ordered Greece to pay what Mussolini demanded.

This is a very early instance of appeasement, and must have taught Mussolini that in any confrontation with them he could force the Allied Powers to back down merely by being determined.

The Period of Peace

1. After the Corfu Affair Mussolini followed a surprisingly peaceful and constructive foreign policy for a decade.
2. In 1924 he concluded the **Pact of Rome** with Yugoslavia, whereby Italy received the disputed town of Fiume.
3. In 1925 Italy signed the Locarno Treaties guaranteeing the western frontiers with Germany.
4. In 1928 Italy signed the Kellog-Briand Pact renouncing war as an instrument of policy!
5. Two treaties with Albania in 1926 and 1927 established the dominance of Italian influence in that country.
6. In 1927 Mussolini signed a treaty of friendship with Hungary, and in 1930 with Austria.
7. In 1929 a royal marriage strengthened relations with Bulgaria.
8. He supported Britain over its claim to the province of Mosul in Iraq from Turkey, and in return was given a small part of Somaliland and a non-aggression pact in 1933.
9. With the rise to power of Adolf Hitler, Mussolini supported the anti-Nazi chancellor Dolfuss in Austria, paying for the *Heimwehr*, Dolfuss' private army.
10. He signed **Rome Protocols** with Austria and Hungary in 1934, establishing:
    (a) increased trade links;
    (b) a common foreign policy.
11. After a meeting with Hitler in June 1934, Mussolini called him "that mad little clown".
12. When Austrian Nazis murdered Dolfuss in July 1934 Mussolini rushed four divisions of troops to the Brenner Pass to warn Hitler against using the assassination as a pretext for invading Austria. This had the desired effect, since Germany was still under-militarised.
13. When Hitler announced the reintroduction of conscription in Germany in defiance of the terms of the Treaty of Versailles Mussolini joined the British and French in the **Stresa Front** of April 1935, condemning Germany and guaranteeing the frontiers of Austria.

The Second Period of Aggression

1. Fascist Italy's first colonial war was a long, bloody campaign in Cyrenaica that lasted until the early 1930s, when Italy began developing Libya as a place of settlement for Italian peasants.
2. Mussolini was already moving towards a war in Abyssinia at the time of the Stresa Conference. Since the Allies did not mention it, he thought they would not mind if he went ahead.
   Mussolini wished to take Abyssinia (Ethiopia):
    (a) To obtain for Italy the last remaining uncolonised part of Africa;
    (b) For prestige;
    (c) To reverse the ignominious defeat of Adowa in 1896, when the Italians had been chased out of that country;

(d) Because Italy's existing colonies in the horn of Africa, Eritrea and It. Somaliland, were not rewarding;

(e) To divert public attention away from the effects of the depression in Italy.

3. He used as a pretext a quarrel over an incident which had occurred at the oasis of Walwal on the borders of Ethiopia with Italian Somaliland in Dec. 1934. In October 1935, 250,000 Italians invaded Ethiopia, using modern weapons, against the ill-equipped Ethiopians.

4. The King, General Badoglio and the Army were not initially in favour of the campaign. Only the Church was enthusiastic, as it provided an opportunity forcibly to convert the native Copts* of Ethiopia to Roman Catholicism.

5. The Emperor, Haile Selassie, appealed to the League of Nations. The attitude of western leaders was ambiguous. Public opinion was outraged, but the leaders:

(a) wanted Mussolini's help against Hitler in a reconstituted Stresa Front;

(b) Britain and France were militarily, economically and psychologically unprepared for war.

6. After Badoglio used poison gas against the Ethiopian tribesmen, the League imposed economic sanctions against Italy, which were ineffective as they excluded oil, coal and iron and steel – precisely those resources necessary to fight a war. The British did not close the Suez Canal to Italian men and arms, which they could easily have done.

7. The British Foreign Secretary Sir Samuel Hoare and the French Prime Minister Laval proposed a secret solution in Dec. 1935:

(a) Italy would receive two-thirds of Ethiopia

(b) In compensation, Britain would offer Haile Selassie a strip of territory to connect his remaining lands to the sea.

The **the Hoare-Laval Plan** involved giving Mussolini more territory than the Italians had actually conquered at that time. When the details became known to the public, outrage was so violent that the proposals had to be withdrawn.

8. In May 1936 Marshall Badoglio entered Addis Ababa. Haile Selassie went into exile. King Victor Emmanuel III became Emperor of Ethiopia. Ethiopia, Eritrea and Italian Somaliland were joined together to form Italian East Africa.

9. The League then abandoned its sanctions.

10 Had he been faced with oil sanctions, Mussolini said, he would have had to withdraw from Abyssinia within a week. The incident discredited the League of Nations and the idea of Collective Security. Mussolini resented the sanctions and being branded an aggressor, and began to turn towards Hitler, who had not participated in the sanctions.

11. In Ethiopia feudal chiefs continued violent resistance, while the Italians massacred hundreds of nobles, clergy, and commoners. Italian success was limited, in that they never subdued the mountainous hinterland.

The Axis

1. During the Spanish Civil War, Mussolini sent help to Franco:

(a) To assist in the creation of a grateful, right-wing militarist state in Spain;

(b) Which would threaten France's southern borders;

(c) To gain bases in the western Mediterranean, e.g. Palma de Majorca.

During this period Italy served on the Non-Intervention Committee and gained experience of:

(i) western appeasement;

(ii) co-operation with the Nazis against the democracies. e.g. Mussolini was given a stretch of the Spanish coast for the Italian Navy to patrol, to prevent unmarked (Italian) submarines attacking ships supplying the government forces.

2. An understanding with Hitler was reached which was known as the Rome-Berlin Axis.
3. In 1937 Italy joined Germany and Japan in the Anti-Comintern Pact to stand together against Bolshevism.
4. In March 1938 Mussolini accepted the *Anschluss** without protest.
5. Mussolini played a key role in securing the Munich Agreement which prevented war over Czechoslovakia, by presenting German proposals for a solution as his own neutral ideas.
6. Mussolini enacted anti-Semitic Laws in November 1938:
    (a) Marriages between Jews and non-Jews were forbidden;
    (b) Jews were barred from the civil service and teaching;
    (c) They were barred from membership of the PNF (one third of Italian Jews were members!);
    (d) Jewish children were expelled from state schools;
    (e) Non-Italian Jews were expelled from the country.
    These laws was unpopular with Italians, with the Papacy, and even with Fascists:
        (i) They were unjust;
        (ii) Mussolini was seen as servile to Hitler.
7. In April 1939, on Good Friday, Italian troops invaded Albania in an attempt to demonstrate his independence from Hitler.
8. In the Pact of Steel of May 1939 Mussolini entered into a full alliance with Hitler, promising him support in war.

Mussolini's Fall from Power

1. As war approached, various groups began to cool their support for Mussolini.
    (a) The Army was alarmed by his grandiose war plans and association with Hitler;
    (b) The Church was alarmed by his association with Hitler;
    (c) The upper classes were alarmed by his association with Hitler and the possibility of involvement in a general war.
    This was ameliorated to some extent by Hitler's victories in Western Europe.
2. On the outbreak of war in 1939 Hitler asked Mussolini to join him, in accordance with the terms of the Pact of Steel. Mussolini pleaded unpreparedness, but vowed to join if a long list of war materiels were to be supplied to Italy by Germany. As expected, this was refused.
3. In fact Italy was unready for war:
    (a) Italy lacked sufficient supplies of iron ore, coal and oil;
    (b) Less than one million troops were available;
    (c) The Italian Navy had no aircraft carriers.
    (d) The air force had no long-range bombers and only slow fighters.
4. With the fall of France imminent, on 10th June 1940, Mussolini declared war on Britain and France. Italian forces invaded Southern. France, but were ejected. After the surrender Mussolini asked for some French territory, and was given a few villages.
5. In September 1940, Italian troops invaded Egypt from Libya, but were driven back by the British, who then invaded Libya. These in turn were driven back by Rommel's German forces.
6. Italian troops in Albania invaded Greece in October 1940, but were thrown out. Greek forces then invaded Albania. Only when German troops invaded Greece did the tide of battle turn.
7. By June 1941 the British and Ethiopians had driven the Italians out of Ethiopia, and Haile Selassie had been restored to his throne.
8. When Germany's main effort was engaged in the invasion of the Soviet Union in 1942, General Montgomery and the British Eighth Army drove Rommel from El Alamein into Libya, while

other British and US forces landed in Tunisia to squeeze them from the other side. By May 1943 Axis forces in North Africa surrendered.

9. Sicily was invaded in 1943 by an Anglo-American Force. On July 24, at a meeting of the Fascist Grand Council a resolution was passed by an overwhelming majority dismissing Mussolini from office. Disregarding the vote Mussolini appeared at his office, and was arrested. Marshall Badoglio took over the conduct of the war.

Reasons for Mussolini's Fall from Power

1. Mussolini made drastic errors in seeking:
   (a) to involve Italy in the Second World War, when he had been warned by his Commission on War Production that Italy could not sustain war for the forseeable future. This made Italy totally dependent upon Germany.
   (b) to invade Greece and Egypt without thought of the consequences.
2. Mussolini never:
   (a) displaced the supreme authority in the state (the king);
   (b) had the army make the oath of allegiance to himself; (it was made to the king);
   (c) created a force entirely loyal to himself, (like the *SS* in Germany);
   (d) created a truly totalitarian society, because of the prior loyalty of many Italians to the Roman Catholic Church;
   (e) built up a sufficiently efficient intelligence service. He was taken by surprise by his own dismissal and arrest.
3. A true master of the art of propaganda, Mussolini made the fatal mistake of coming to believe in his own propaganda, particularly where this concerned his own "exceptional abilities."

The Prisoner of the Nazis

1. In September 1943 the Allies landed on the Italian mainland at Reggio and Salerno, and Italy unconditionally surrendered to the Allies.
2. The Germans decided to hold Italy from a line between Rome and Naples at Monte Cassino. Badoglio persuaded the King to declare war on Germany. A partisan struggle against the Germans and Fascists began in the German occupied areas of the country.
3. Mussolini was rescued from the Badoglio Government in Sept. 1943 by German parachutists and installed as puppet dictator of the **Republic of Salo** behind German lines.

Timeline of Mussolini's Decline	
1935	Mussolini invades Abysinnia
	The Rome-Berlin Axis
1936	Mussolini intervenes in the Spanish Civil War
1938	Anti-semitic Laws passed
1939	The Pact of Steel
	Mussolini invades Albania
1940	Italy enters the Second World War
1943	Mussolini forced to resign and arrested
	Italy surrenders to the Allies
	Mussolini rescued by the Germans - Republic of Salo founded
1945	Mussolini executed by Communist partisans

4. He was thereafter little more than a prisoner of Hitler. He was not free to travel and his telephone was tapped.
5. He returned to his earlier attitudes: anti-monarchist, anti-capitalist and in favour of the nationalization of key industries. But it hardly mattered.
6. His new regime commanded little public support. His government was a puppet of the Germans.
7. Italy was slowly liberated by the Allies from the south. On 4th June 1944 they entered Rome.
8. The Allies were held up at the Kesselring Line during winter 1944-5, but completed the liberation of Italy in late spring 1945.
9. Mussolini was captured and executed by Communist partisans on 28th April, 1945, while trying to flee the country with the departing German Army. His body was displayed hanging from a street lamp at a petrol station in Milan.

Assessment of Mussolini's Regime

1. When he came to power Mussolini was hailed as a genius and a superman all over Europe and in the United States, praised by, among others, Winston Churchill and the Pope. His achievements were considered by many as scarcely less than miraculous:
    (a) He had reinvigorated a divided and demoralized country;
    (b) He had carried out some important social reforms;
    (c) He had improved the infrastructure of the country;
    (d) He had solved the problem of relations between the Italian state and the papacy;
    (e) He had destroyed the power of the Mafia.
2. Mussolini might have remained a success until his death, except for his:
    (a) arrogance and an exaggerated belief in his own abilities;
    (b) ignorance of Italy's fundamental economic and military limitations;
    (c) dreams of empire and greatness through foreign conquest;
    (d) tying his own fate, and that of his country, to that of Adolf Hitler, whom he once called a "clown" and a "madman".

These faults led Mussolini himself, and his country, to disaster.

Glossary

charismatic able to command by force of personality

clientism a system of buying votes for favours

coalition government a government formed by an alliance of two or more parties

Copts Christians of the Egyptian Church

corrupt influenced by bribery and other special considerations, such as nepotism and croneyism

doctrinaire applying principles without regard for circumstances

Ras the local Fascist leadership

OVRA Fascist political police

PNF National Fascist Party

proportional representation an electoral system which ensures that the relative proportion of members of Parliament elected reflects the relative proportion of the total votes cast

universal manhood suffrage each man being able to vote in elections

Francisco Franco

Franco's Spain

"His head was a cemetery of dead ideas." D. A. Puzzo

Franco's Rise to Power

Personal Background

1. Although he came from a family with a naval tradition in Ferrol, Spain's northern naval base, Francisco Franco served with distinction in the army in the Moroccan War, being wounded in battle. He became head of the First Battalion of the Legion, famous for its brutality. In time he came to command the Legion. At the age of thirty-three he became the youngest general in Europe. When the military Academy was formed at Zaragoza, he headed it.
2. He found the establishment of a republic in 1931 repugnant, but prudently hid his feelings. When, in 1934, Carlist* and Alfonsist* representatives visited Mussolini as part of a plot to restore the monarchy, Franco stayed aloof. This made him an object of suspicion to many of the right-wing generals.
3. When there was a revolt of striking miners in the Asturias in the same year, and martial law was declared, using Moroccan mercenaries he ruthlessly crushed the disorders. After this, he was hated by the left wing.
4. As a reward, Franco was made Commander-in-Chief of Morocco and Chief of the General Staff.

The Conspiracy

1. With the triumph of the **Popular Front*** in the elections of 1936 Franco was made Commandant-General of the Canary Islands, a post he regarded as demotion and banishment.
2. When General Mola began a new conspiracy to overthrow the democracy, Franco joined in. All the members of the conspiracy were ***africanistas****, so that the coup could be described as a coup by colonial officers against their civilian superiors.
   (a) There would be regional risings, followed by a concerted attack upon Madrid.
   (b) The Head of State would be General Sanjurjo, although he would only be *primus inter pares.** General Mola would direct operations, and other generals would take over various regions of the country. Franco would become High Commissioner for Morocco.

3. For a long time the other conspirators were doubtful whether Franco would actually join them. On 12th July he sent a coded message to Mola saying that the time was not right.
4. On the same day, Calvo Sotelo was murdered. Fearing a coup, a delegation of Socialists and Communists demanded of Caseres that he distribute arms to the workers, but he refused.
5. Franco went to Las Palmas and the army in Morocco rose against the government.
6. Franco immediately issued a manifesto justifying the revolt, and sent representatives to Mussolini and Hitler to seek aid, as did General Mola.
7. During the initial days of the rising things did not go as planned. Sanjurjo, who had been in Lisbon, was killed in an air crash. Fanjul in Madrid and Doded in Barcelona were arrested. This considerably denuded the leadership of the conspiracy. Many civilian rightist leaders were also arrested, including Jose Antonio Primo de Rivera.
8. The Navy stayed loyal to the government, but on the advice of Admiral Canaris, Hitler and Mussolini responded positively to Franco's appeal for assistance, rather than Mola's, and Franco was able to transport his Moroccan troops to the mainland mainly by air.
9. Thus Franco effectively became the Junta* leader because of his international backing.
10. In July, Prince Don Juan de Borbón, third son of Alfonso XIII arrived in Burgos to join in the struggle. The anti-monarchist General Mola promptly sent him away. This undiplomatic conduct undermined Mola's position with the monarchists, and strengthened Franco's position.
11. In Seville on 15th August, Franco announced that the rebels had adopted the old monarchist flag – a popular move with monarchists. Mola had not even been consulted.
12. Franco quickly built up:
    (a) popularity among the mass iof people on the right wing;
    (b) a sycophantic* entourage;*
    (c) tight personal security;
    (d) a political apparatus to deal with Mussolini and Hitler.
13. On 21st September the junta met on an airfield outside Salamanca to choose a successor to Sanjurjo as their leader. Franco's brother Nicolas and others had formed a campaign committee to build up support for Franco. The most senior generals all had disqualifications, so Franco was chosen.
14. On 27th September Franco broke the siege of the Alcazar* of Toledo. This symbolic victory made Franco famous throughout the world.
15. On the next day the junta met again and decided on Franco's powers. He was to be:
    (a) Generalissimo;*
    (b) head of government of the Spanish state "as long as the war lasts." But when this decree was published, someone, probably Nicolas Franco, had taken out that important qualification.
16. On 30th September, the bishop of Salamanca published a pastoral letter declaring the struggle of the nationalists a "crusade".* The revolt had church support.
17. October 1st, Franco was installed as head of state in Burgos.

Franco as a War Leader

[A detailed treatment of the Spanish Civil War is to be found in the companion volume "Wars and Warfare".]

1. A personality cult* of Franco was launched. The title "*caudillo*"* was adopted, linking Franco to past warrior heroes and monarchs of Spain, such as El Cid and the Catholic Monarchs.
2. Nicolas Franco tried to form a political party as a Francoist power base, but dropped the idea when it threatened to split the Nationalists.
3. Franco:

(a) moved into the episcopal palace in Salamanca;

(b) held audiences in which people had to wear morning suits;

(c) travelled around accompanied by a bodyguard of Moorish cavalry;

(d) began to adopt royal prerogatives such as the right to enter churches under a canopy.

4. On 2nd November Jose Antonio Primo de Rivera was executed in prison. Franco, who had probably sabotaged plans to rescue him, refused to accept the fact of his death in order to bar his designated successor as head of the Falange, Manuel Hedilla, from taking over.

5. Manuel Fal Conde, President of the National War Junta of the Carlists began asserting the autonomy of the Carlists. With Mola's permission he set up a separate training camp for Carlist officers. Franco gave Conde 48 hours to leave Nationalist Spain or face a court martial.

6. When the pretender Don Juan asked Franco to be allowed to return to Spain to fight, Franco:

(a) refused on the grounds that "his life was too valuable to be risked";

(b) told the Falangists that it was because of his commitment to the Falangist revolution.

7. Taking advantage of a struggle for the leadership of the Falange between the followers of Juan Antonio Primo de Rivera, son of Jose, and Jose' designated successor, Manuel Hedilla, an illiterate fascist thug, Franco persuaded Hedilla to accept Franco as *Jefe nacional*, with himself as *de facto* head of the Falange.

8. As head of State and of the Falange, Franco then announced the fusion of the Carlists, the Falange and CEDA. Hedilla was first offered a minor role in the joint organisation and then arrested.

9. Franco proceeded with incredible caution in prosecuting the war. As a result, it was unnecessarily prolonged by at least one year. It is generally believed that this was to give him the time to consolidate his position as national leader, as against all possible rivals, before the war ended.

10. As the war dragged on it became increasingly necessary to create a formal state structure. All power was vested in Franco as head of a single party, called the Falange. The Falange as a fascist militia was thus castrated, and its ideological role increasingly displaced by the Church. **The National Council of the Falange**, modelled on Mussolini's Fascist Grand Council, was set up. Its members were chosen by Franco.

11. On June 3rd 1937, Mola was killed in a plane crash, removing Franco's chief rival.

12. In 1st April 1939 the Civil War ended, and Pope Pius XI thanked Franco for his "Catholic victory".

Timeline of Franco's Rise to Power	
1934	Franco crushes the revolt of the miners in the Asturias
1936	
July 17	Outbreak of the Spanish Civil War
July 26	Hitler decides to assist Franco
Sep 21	Franco chosen as head of the Junta
Sep 27	Franco relieves the Alcazar of Toledo
Oct 1	Franco installed as Head of State by the Nationalists at Burgos
1937	
Apr 19	Franco becomes *Jefe nacional* of the Falange
June 3	General Mola, Franco's chief rival, killed in an air crash
1939	
Apr 1	Civil War ends

The Franco Regime (1939-75)

The Victors

1. After the war Franco made no attempt at national reconciliation. Instead, he carried out reprisals against the opposition.
   (a) Many were executed, e.g. the novelist Federico Garcia Lorca disappeared at this time, and was probably executed by Francoists.
   (b) Hundreds of thousands of opponents of the regime were imprisoned in labour camps. Count Ciano estimated 200,000 prisoners in Madrid alone in 1939.
   (c) 500,000 went into exile, many fled to France and Latin America.
   (d) Basque and Catalan rights, including the languages, and all regional government, were suppressed.
   (e) Trade unions were prohibited and strikes suppressed.
2. Repression was institutionalised with the Law for the repression of Freemasonry* and Communism of February 1940. The vanquished were excluded from public life.
3. Franco continued to acquire power. By the *Ley de la Jefatura del Estedo* (1939), Franco acquired the right to make laws and decrees without consulting the cabinet.
4. The Cortes, reopened in 1943, was comprised of representatives of various important interests. Two-thirds were appointed by Franco or his ministers, and one third elected by Falangist groups from lists of approved candidates. Its powers were limited to approving legislation presented by the government.
5. Franco carefully distributed government ministries to the various centres of power and influence which had supported the Nationalist cause during the war: army leaders, Catholic leaders, Alfonsists, Carlists, Falangists, capitalists and landowners; effectively sharing power with them. This was done in an informal manner using patronage. Ideological splits were strongly discouraged.
6. These groups were represented in the single legal political party, the *Falange Española Tradicnalista y de las Juntas de Ofensiva Nacional Sindicalista* (FET de las JONS).
7. Franco called this representation of a coalition of interests "**organic democracy**."
8. The government kept strict control over the media.
9. The policies of autarchy:* state control of prices and industrial development within a protected national economy cut off from the international market stunted growth The national income fell back to the levels of 1900; industrial production and agricultural output stagnated. Real wages fell dramatically. The 1940s were years of near famine, of the black market, and of rural misery that caused migration to the shanty towns of the cities.
10. Economically illiterate, Franco announced that Spain would become rich due to:
    (a) massive (non-existent) deposits of gold;
    (b) the discovery of a cheap substitute for petrol (gasoline).

Neutrality

1. Franco dreamed of acquiring an empire in North West Africa by courtesy of the Third Reich.
2. After a meeting at Hendaye, Franco did not get what he demanded and refused to join the Second World War, although his sympathies clearly lay with Germany and Italy, but he depended upon the Allies for food and oil imports.
3. However, during the war Spain supplied Hitler with monitoring services, war material and air bases.
4. The "Blue Division" of 47,000 Falangist volunteers went to help the invasion of the USSR.

This:

(a) repaid Hitler for his help in the Civil War;

(b) helped the fight against Communism;

(c) removed troublesome Falangists from Spain.

5. From 1942 the USA began a practice of pre-emptive purchase of supplies from Spain needed by the Axis. Later they launched an oil embargo.

6. At the end of the war the Franco regime assisted Nazis fleeing to South America.

The "Siege"

1. The fall of Mussolini and Hitler left Franco exposed in a hostile world.

2. Franco faced immediate threats from;

(a) Some Republicans, not reconciled to defeat, conducted a guerilla war in the north and east of the country for some time.

(b) Many important monarchists drew up plans to replace Franco with a royal government and restore the monarchy. In the **Lausanne Manifesto** of March 1945, the chief pretender to the throne, Don Juan de Borbón:

    (i) denounced the totalitarianism of Franco's Spain;

    (ii) denounced Franco's Axis connections;

    (iii) called for the return of constitutional monarchy.

3. Franco made some purely cosmetic moves towards liberalisation, and stressed his standing firm against the Axis demands to take Spain into war.

4. At Potsdam, Spain was excluded from the United Nations Organisation.

5. As an ally of the Axis powers, in 1946 Spain was subjected to an international economic boycott. This caused great poverty and suffering in the country, and this time was known as **The Years of Hunger.** Only grain imports from Argentina prevented mass famine. This provoked a nationalist response and strengthened support for the regime inside Spain.

6. In 1947 after a referendum, Franco was declared Chief of State for life, with the power to appoint his successor. He began to assume more royal prerogatives, such as creating nobility.

7. Gradually the Falange's radical Fascist ideas were subordinated to the conservative and traditionalist values of Franco's regime. Membership in the Falange became indispensable to political advancement, but the movement ceased to be identified with its original radical ideology.

The Cold Warrior

1. By the Concordat* of 1951 the Vatican:

(a) recognised Franco's regime;

(b) the right to present bishops chosen from a list of three names submitted by the Papal Nuncio;

(c) turned a blind eye to Franco's harassment of his enemy, Cardinal Segura of Seville.

This was in return for:

(d) Catholic control over education;

(e) a determining role for the Church in social policy;

(f) the exclusive right to proselytise.*

2. With the development of Cold War paranoia in the USA, Franco became a valuable ally of the USA against communism. By the terms of the **Mutual Defence Pact** (1953) Spain received significant US aid and diplomatic recognition in return for accepting US bases in Spain.

3. With a monarchist majority in municipal elections in November 1954 Franco met Don Juan de Borbón and insisted that *his* heir, Juan Carlos, be educated under Franco's tutelage in Spain, or the succession forfeited. Don Juan agreed.

4. A programme of industrialisation during the 1950s and the development of tourism gradually raised the standard of living of the people.

5. Unrest appeared periodically in the form of strikes during 1951 in Catalonia and the Basque country, in 1957 in Madrid and the north, and in 1962 throughout many parts of the country.

6. The opposition to Franco was divided among monarchists, liberals, socialists, communists and separatists. The monarchists were divided between the Carlists and Alfonsists. The latter were divided between those who supported the liberal Don Juan (younger son of Alfonso XIII) and those supporting his son Juan Carlos. The separatists were divided by the very nature of their ideology. Franco was thus able to position himself as
   (a) at least offering stability;
   (b) preventing any of these rival groups from gaining power.

7. In 1957 Franco began to rely upon a new generation of technocrats,* particularly in managing the economy. Their religious and political credentials were guaranteed in that they belonged to, or sympathised with, the Catholic movement called *Opus Dei.** Its ambition was to protect Catholic Spain.

8. The International Monetary Fund (IMF) became involved in the running of the Spanish economy with the **Stabilization Plan** of 1959. Economic nationalism, protectionism, and the state intervention were abandoned in favour of an approach to a market economy and the opening of Spain to international trade and much-needed foreign investment. The Development Plan of 1963 was based on the encouragement of the private sector.

9. In 1961, the economy began to improve. Growth rates of 7.4 percent between 1962 and 1966, aided by a rapid increase in tourism, foreign investment, and the remittances of workers who had sought employment in other European countries followed.

10 During the early 1960s the Spanish economy grew faster than any other economy in the capitalist world except Japan. People spoke of the "Spanish miracle." This was due to:
   (a) recovery from a very low position;
   (b) capitalists were attracted by the low cost of labour and lack of workers' rights;
There was an exodus from the countryside and a dramatic fall of the population engaged in agriculture as Spain became a modern industrialised nation. By 1973 it was the world's ninth largest industrial power.

11. The policies of the technocrats were fiercely resisted by the Falange, who were gradually phased out of office and influence.

The Long Decline

1. After 1965 the main focus of opposition to the regime took the form of a battle for the legal recognition of workers' associations to replace the state-sponsored trades' unions.

2. The Basque separatist movement began a terrorist campaign, assassinating the Chief of Police in San Sebastian in 1968. By 1969 it was necessary to proclaim a state of emergency to cope with the unrest. In May 1973 the Prime Minister, Admiral Carrero Blanco, was assassinated in Madrid.

3. Workers disillusioned with the "official" syndicates run by the Falange set up their own trades unions to negotiate wage claims. There were many strikes.

4. Sections of the church were sympathetic to claims for greater social justice and responsive to the recommendations of the Second Vatican Council. Younger priests were sympathetic to the trade unions.

5. Separatism remained an intractable problem.

(a) Basque nationalism developed a terrorist wing, the **ETA** ("Basque Homeland and Liberty"). The Burgos trials of Basque terrorists in 1970 discredited the regime abroad and went some way to uniting opposition to Franco at home

(b) The Assembly of Catalonia in 1971 united the opposition with a demand for democratic institutions and the restoration of the Autonomy Statute of 1932.

6. In the 1960s, elements in the regime were increasingly troubled by its lack of legitimacy and the problem of the succession, given Franco's failing health. By the **Organic Law** (1969) Franco gave Spain a cosmetic constitution, and in the same year he formally recognised Juan Carlos de Borbón as his successor as king and head of state.

7. In June 1973 Franco abandoned the premiership to Admiral Luis Carrero Blanco. Carrero Blanco was assassinated by the ETA in December.

8. Under Carlos Arias Navarro there was a struggle between reformists, led by Manuel Fraga and the new foreign minister, Jose Maria de Areilza, who wished to open up the regime by limited democratisation from above, and the nostalgic Francoists. Arias Navarro gave in to the right, and his government was distinguished by its repression of the terrorist activity of the ETA in the Basque provinces and the execution of terrorists (September 1975) in spite of international protests.

9. The Roman Catholic Church gradually distanced itself from Franco. Catholic Action* and Opus Dei supported some social reform in order to ensure that the Church should retain its popularity. Franco interpreted this as the result of the infiltration of the Church by Communist and masonic* bishops and priests.

10. On January 12, 1975, prior to Franco's death, a law was passed permitting the establishment of other "political associations"; thereafter political parties began to proliferate.

11. Franco died in November 1975.

12. Following Franco's death, Juan Carlos became king and restored democracy to Spain.

Timeline of Franco's Regime	
1939 Apr 1	End of the Civil War
1940	Law for the repression of Freemasonry and Communism
Oct 23	Franco meets Hitler at Hendaye - keeps Spain out of the war
1945	Lausanne Manifesto
1946	Trade embargo against Spain instituted
1947	Franco declared Chief of State for life with right to appoint successor
1953	US-Spanish Pact of Madrid concluded
	Vatican Concordat concluded
	IMF Stabilization Plan launched
1959	Basque separatist movement (ETA) begins terrorist campaign
1969	Juan Carlos officially designated Franco's heir
1970	The Burgos Trials of Basque Separatists
1973 June	Franco gives up premiership - Admiral Carrero Blanco made premier
Dec 20	Prime Minister Admiral Luis Carrero Blanco assassinated
1975	"Political Associations" permitted
Nov 20	Franco dies
	Juan Carlos de Borbón becomes king

The Reasons for Franco's Survival

1. The victorious powers were unwilling to remove Franco after the war, because it suited them to have Franco prevent a possible Communist take-over in Spain.
2. Fear of the return of the divisions, death and destruction of the Civil War made many Spaniards who did not support Franco, reluctant to remove him.
3. Franco included in his governments many different important interests, and held them together in mutual rivalry, so that it was not in the interests of any one of them to stand out against Franco.
4. Despite the difficulties and the opposition, Franco remained steadfast in his belief in his religious mission to save the character and integrity of Spain.

The Nature of Francoism

1. Despite the trappings of fascism:
   - (i) his headship of the Falange, a fascist organisation;
   - (ii) the title *Caudillo* (CF *Duce* and *Führer*);
   - (iii) an apparently fascist style raised arm salute and shout of "Viva España");
   - (iv) Franco's close relations with Mussolini and Hitler;

   it seems clear that Franco was *not* a fascist:

   (a) The title "Caudillo" recalled the greatest leaders of Catholic Spain against the Muslims: Rodrigo Díaz de Vivar, popularly known as El Cid Campeador and "Catholic monarchs" Ferdinand and Isabella.

   (b) The raised arm salute and shout of "Viva España" was traditional in Spain.

   (c) The power of the Falange was always strictly limited.
   - (i) In 1937 Franco forced the Falangists to merge with the Carlist Requetes* in the new *Falange Española Traditionalista*.
   - (ii) During the Second World War some Falangists were sent to the Eaastern Front:
       - *a.* as an "offering" to appease Hitler;
       - *b.* to get rid of them.
   - (iii) After the civil war, some Fascist leaders were imprisoned.
   - (iv) Under Franco, Falangism was gradually divested of its radical populist character.

   (d) Although Franco was sympathetic to Mussolini and Hitler, he was using them for what he could get out of them. He took from them, and gave them nothing very much in return.

2. Franco saw himself as Saviour of traditional Spain – a crusader rather than a fascist. He always took important political decisions while resting his forehead on a golden reliquary containing the arm of Saint Theresa of Avila, a relic carried before him on his visits to different parts of Spain. Some of those who knew him well have testified that he believed that he was sent by God to save Spain.

3. Under Franco Spain was a totalitarian state, but it was a traditional Catholic totalitarianism.
   - (a) Catholicism was dominant in educational and social life.
   - (b) There was an armed police and a secret police force.
   - (c) Censorship was rigid.

4. On the other hand there were limits to his totalitarianism:
   - (a) Spain did not have a single party structure parallel to and dominating the administration of the state.
   - (b) The economy was largely in the hands of private enterprise.
   - (c) Franco's regime depended upon:
       - (i) public exhaustion after the Civil War and apathy;

(ii) the satisfaction of several pressure groups within the establishment;

(iii) the exclusion of certain groups and interests;

(iv) the division and mutual suspicions of his enemies.

5. It was an old-fashioned, Spanish-style, Catholic military dictatorship. Despite showing some elements of fascist style, it was not fascist because it was not a revolutionary state which replaced traditional authorities with a new elite under a charismatic demagogue. It preserved traditional authorities, and Franco was neither charismatic nor a demagogue. It was not a new populist conservatism, it was an old, authoritarian conservatism.

The Achievements of Francoism

1. Franco succeeded in keeping Spain out of the Second World War.
2. Considerable economic progress was made during the Franco years.
3. The problem of extreme social and political divisions in Spain was gradually defused. By the end of Franco's life most people had moved towards the political centre, and a younger generation was more concerned with economic betterment than ideology. Simply by being there and preventing change, he had allowed the bloody rivalries of the 1930s to wither and die.
4. By contrast, the problem of separatism was simply suppressed. Violent police suppression of local nationalism exacerbated the frustration of the separatists and led to the development of ETA the Basque terrorist movement.
5. The huge cost of these achievements, however, was great: massive state repression, hardship for the majority, economic migration, suppression of womens' rights, etc.

Glossary

africanistas army officers who had made their careers by serving in the Moroccan campaigns.

Alcazar citadel

Alfonsists monarchist supporters of the main Spanish royal line, constitutional monarchists

Carlists supporters of a dispossessed branch of the Spanish royal line, absolute monarchists, based largely in Navarre

Catholic Action an organisation of Catholic laymen with the aim of influencing society

caudillo "Saviour": a traditional title of the "Catholic Monarchs" Ferdinand and Isabella

CEDA *Confederación Española de Derechas Autónomas* - right-wing monarchist group led by Gil Robles

CNT *Confederación nacional de Trabjo* - anarchist syndicalist trades union

concordat an agreement with the Papacy

crusade a holy war

entourage those who accompany and surround a powerful figure

ETA *Euzkadi Ta Azkatsuna* - "Basque Homeland and Liberty", the Basque independence movement

Falange Fascist movement founded by Jose Antonio Prima de Rivera in 1933

Freemasonry a world-wide secret society which in the past resisted Catholic and clerical control of society, but which is now chiefly a mutual aid society for business and managerial elites and their children

Generalissimo supreme commander

IMF International Monetary Fund

JAP *Juventud de Acción Popular - CEDA* youth movement

Jefe nacional title of the leader of the falange

junta a group of military officers which has seized power

limpieza "cleansing" of political opposition by Franco

masonic associated with the Freemasons

Opus Dei a secretive Roman Catholic religious order, very influential in Franco's Spain

personality cult the deliberate cultivation of devotion to a public figure, usually a leader

popular front alliance or coalition of left-wing parties

POUM *Partido Obrero de Unificación Marxista* - Non-Stalinist Socialist Party

primus inter pares first among equals

paranoia a liability to hold irrational convictions, especially of being threatened

proselytise to attempt to gain new adherents to a religion

Requetes Carlist paramilitary organisation

sycophantic having a flattering and servile character

technocrats those with valuable practical technical knowledge and skills

Adolf Hitler

Hitler's Germany

"I shall go down in history as the greatest German!" (Adolf Hitler, 15th March 1939)

Hitler's Rise to Power

The First Crises of the Weimar Republic

The Weimar Republic was born in crisis and defeat.

1. By October 1918 the situation of Germany was desperate:

   (a) It was clear that Germany could not win a war of attrition after the USA entered the war. Desperate attempts in spring 1918 to break through on the Western Front before US forces arrived in large numbers had failed, so that it was impossible for Germany to win the war of attrition;

   (b) Germany's allies were in the process of collapsing or breaking up;

   (c) The government was deeply in debt.

   (d) The Allied blockade* and poor management of the economy had led to a desperate food shortage, which, together with an epidemic of influenza, was devastating the population;

   (e) Strikes and criticism of the government had been suppressed with ferocity, but this could not go on indefinitely.

2. In October 1918, Hindenburg and Ludendorff, the military leaders of Germany, tried to smooth the path to an armistice* by advising Kaiser Wilhelm to appoint a civilian government under Prince Max of Baden. Moderate members of the Social democratic Party (SPD) were brought into the government.

3. The naval chiefs, wishing to undermine the new government, ordered the fleet at Kiel to sea, to face the British battle fleet. Instead, the sailors mutinied and seized the ports.

4. This unleashed a wave of protest across the country and a collapse of the existing political order:

   (a) army mutinies seemed imminent in various places

   (b) Kurt Eisner declared Bavaria an independent republic

   (c) Nov. 9th Prince Max resigned and was replaced by Friedrich Ebert, leader of the Social Democrats

   (d) On the same day the Kaiser abdicated* in favour of a republic, in order to dissociate the Germany the Allies would deal with during the peace negotiations from the Germany of the war, and went into exile in Holland.

(e) A republic was proclaimed.

5. A provisional government was established under President Ebert containing Social Democrats (SPD) and Independent Socialists (USPD) Afraid of the extreme left, Ebert:

(a) retained the officer corps of the Imperial Army and the Imperial Civil Service

(b) postponed the nationalisation* of heavy industry.

6. This annoyed the left:

(a) The Independent Socialists (USPD) resigned from the coalition.

(b) the Spartacists demanded the sovietization of Germany.

7. Right-wing former soldiers formed paramilitary organisations to prevent a Bolshevik revolution in the various towns of Germany. These were collectively known as *Freikorps*.* There were five such independent groups in Berlin alone. They may be compared with the Blackshirts in Italy.

8. In January 1919 the Spartacist rising of left-wingers, headed by Karl Liebknecht and Rosa Luxemburg, led to the occupation of almost every major city in Germany. President Ebert was besieged in the Chancellory. The revolt was put down with great brutality with the help of the *Freikorps*.

9. After elections in January a Constituent Assembly met in Weimar to draw up a constitution for a republican government. This came to be known as the **Weimar Republic**. It was a very liberal constitution, using an electoral system based upon proportional representation,* but residual emergency powers were given to the president. Friedrich Ebert became first president.

10. In April troops were sent to Munich to put down a Communist Republic there.

11. In June 1919 the Weimar Government lost credibility by agreeing to the terms of the Treaty of Versailles. Resentment was generated by:

(a) The fact that the treaty was a *diktat*;*

(b) The "war guilt" clause;

(c) The loss of territory in Europe and the colonies overseas;

(d) The limitations on national sovereignty suffered:

(i) limitations on the size and nature of the armed forces;

(ii) the demilitarization and temporary occupation of the Rhineland;

(e) The war indemnity of 6,600 million pounds imposed, fixed in 1921.

12. The legend of the "**November Criminals**" (Jews, Communists and Liberals) who had stabbed Germany in the back" began to grow. Ironically, Field Marshall von Hindenburg expressed such sentiments. It had been forgotten that it was the Imperial Government which had negotiated the armistice terms at the behest of Hindenburg and Ludendorff.

13. In March 1920 there was a communist uprising in the Ruhr, put down by the army with great brutality.

14. At the same time, right-wingers tried to seize power in Berlin when the government tried to disband the *Freikorps*. Berlin was occupied by a *Freikorps* regiment and the government fled to Dresden. In what was known as the **Kapp *Putsch,*** Dr. Wolfgang Kapp was declared Chancellor by the rebels. Berlin workers staged a general strike and ended the *Putsch*.* Except for Kapp, who was imprisoned, the guilty escaped punishment.

15. Several hundred political assassinations were carried out, mostly by ex-*Freikorps* members; e.g. killing Walter Rathenau, the Jewish Foreign Minister and Gustav Erzberger, leader of the armistice delegation.

16. Whereas left-wing leaders were dealt with harshly, right wing leaders who had endangered the state were generally given derisory sentences and treated sympathetically by the police, judiciary and prison officials, who themselves despised the state they represented.

The Hyperinflation Crisis

1. Already in 1919 the government was close to bankruptcy because of the cost of the war.
2. Payment of the war reparations of 132 billion gold marks was laid upon Germany. It was to be paid off at the rate of 2 billion per year plus 26% of Germany's exports. This was an additional huge burden.
3. The French became exasperated when:
   (a) The USA stayed out of the League of Nations and signed its own peace treaty with Germany;
   (b) The US and Britain seemed more intent on recovering wartime debts from France that in getting reparations from Germany;
   (c) the marks in which the Germans paid much of the indemnity were losing their value.
4. In August 1921, after paying £50 million due, the government requested a breathing space to allow her economy to recover. France refused, and in 1922 Germany could not manage the full payment.
5. In 1923 **French and Belgian troops occupied the Ruhr** to seize goods from mines and factories in lieu of payment.
6. The German government ordered passive resistance, and a general strike in the Ruhr.
7. The government printed money
   (a) to pay the workers on strike;
   (b) to pay war pensions;
   (c) to pay war reparations.
8. The value of the mark collapsed, resulting in **hyperinflation**.* By Nov. 1923 the mark was 4,200,000,000,000 to the dollar. Over 2,000 printing presses worked 24 hours a day to produce bills. Notes were sometimes overprinted before leaving the printing house, because by the time they were ready, they were worth so little it was not worth sending them out. Shops employed people to relabel goods, putting the prices up. When they had finished, they had to start again from the beginning. Some people were being paid twice daily, so that they could spend their morning's pay before prices rose again. Wages were collected in baskets and wheelbarrows. When the price of coal went up, many people burned their pay instead of coal.
9. Gustav Stresemann became Chancellor in a coalition government.
   (a) Hjalmar Schacht closed the banks for a week and brought out a new currency, the *Rentenmark*, based upon the value of the German land. 10,000,000,000,000 old marks could be replaced by one new *Rentenmark*.
   (b) Stresemann ordered German workers in the Ruhr to cooperate with the French, and
   (c) Resumed reparations payments.
10. In 1924 new arrangements known as the **Dawes Plan**, were made for the indemnity:
    (a) The payments were rescheduled over a longer period;
    (b) Germany was offered loans from the US to help it pay the indemnity;
    (c) The French agreed to evacuate the Ruhr within a year.
11. The consequences of this hyperinflation crisis were:
    (a) Many middle class people lost their life savings, which became worthless overnight. This permanently alienated them from the Weimar Republic.
    (b) Some people made a profit out of the misery:
       (i) farmers, who had food to sell;
       (ii) large industrialists, who exported goods and were paid in foreign currency were able to buy up smaller bankrupt businesses, and so came to dominate the economy. It has been argued that big business engineered this crisis deliberately, with precisely this result in mind.
    (c) Germany became dependent upon US loans.

Hitler: Personal Background

1. Adolf Hitler was born April 20, 1889 at Braunau Am Inn, in the Austro-Hungarian Empire. His father, Alois, a customs officer, who was 42 when Hitler was born, had been an illegitimate child, who for a time called himself by his mother's name Schickelgruber.
2. Hitler spent most of his childhood in Linz, in upper Austria. His mother, who was much younger than his father, spoiled young Adolf. Hitler's father died in 1903, when Hitler was 14 years old, but he left an adequate pension to support his wife and children.
3. After a poor record at school, when Hitler was 16, in 1905, he went to Vienna, and tried to enter the Academy of Fine Arts to study architecture, but twice failed the entrance examinations.
4. Hitler lived in Vienna from 1908 until 1912. Some accounts portray him as a homeless down and out, moving from lodging house to lodging house, surviving on the few pitiful watercolours he was able to sell. Other accounts say that Hitler lived a reasonably secure life based upon funds left by his parents and other relatives.
5. This part of his life is very important, in that many aspects of his personality and ideas may have been formed between 1908 and 1914, in particular authoritarianism, nationalism and racism.
   In this period he showed traits that were later to dominate his behaviour. He developed an intolerance and hatred for the bourgeois world and non-German people, and a loathing of Jews in particular. Hitler tried to portray life, and particularly his own life, as a great struggle between those who were fit to survive and those who were not (Social Darwinism). It is considered to be of some importance whether Hitler did in fact struggle during his early years or whether his subsequent claims in *Mein Kampf* ("My Struggle") were lies.
6. In 1913 he moved to Munich. In February 1914, he was recalled to Austria for military service, but was rejected as unfit. When World War I broke out in August, he volunteered for the German army and was accepted into the 16th Bavarian Reserve Infantry Regiment.
7. Hitler, who remained a corporal throughout the war, served with distinction while being a courier during four years of combat. (The average life-expectancy of a courier on the Western Front was said to be about six weeks) He was wounded in October of 1916 and gassed in 1918. For bravery in combat he received the Iron Cross Second Class in 1914, and the Iron Cross First Class in August 1918.

The Munich Nazi Party

1. After the War, Hitler became a spy for the army and was sent to Munich to watch a small group known as the German Workers Party (DAP), which had been founded by a locksmith, Anton Drexler.
2. Hitler joined the party and quit the army to devoted his life to building up the party. He discovered that he could speak in a powerful manner, and through numerous beer hall harangues he built the membership of what in 1920 became the **National Socialist German Workers' Party (NSDAP)** or Nazi Party.
3. Germany, at this time, was in a terrible condition:
   (a) People resented the defeat, and particularly the Treaty of Versailles. They blamed the "November Criminals" and the Weimar Government.
   (b) There was considerable disorder, with both communist and right-wing attempted coups. The right wing formed paramilitary units, called Freicorps, to defend Germany against the danger of social revolution.
   (c) The economic dislocation after the War affected many Germans, but most particularly the middle classes. There was widespread unemployment, lack of economic growth, failure to pay

reparations and consequent French occupation of the Ruhr, and for a brief period in 1923 runaway inflation which broke the back of the financial security of the middle classes. Savings were wiped out as people had to carry money in wheelbarrows in order to buy even the most basic goods.

4. Bavaria, the province of which Munich was the capital, scene of a brief revolution and civil war, became a gathering place for discontented ex-soldiers and persons who hated the Republic that been established in Berlin. The Nazi party grew under these conditions. During this early period people like Alfred Rosenberg, Rudolf Hess, Hermann Göring, and Julius Streicher joined the party.

5. In 1920 the party acquired a newspaper, the *Völkischer Beobachter* or "Peoples' Observer" published in Munich.

6. Hitler took over the presidency of the party from Drexler in 1921.

7. In the same year Ernst Röhm founded the party's own paramilitary force, the **Sturmabteilung (SA)** or Brownshirts, a *Freikorps* group, created in imitation of Mussolini's Blackshirts. Röhm had influential friends in the army in Bavaria and the Bavarian police.

The Munich Beer Hall *Putzsch*

1. From February to September 1923 Röhm persuaded other right-wing parties in Munich to combine with the Nazis in a common front: the *Kampfbund* or German Fighting Union.

2. In response to the French occupation of the Ruhr, in September the Weimar Government declared a state of emergency and placed the Minister of Defence and Army Commanders in charge of the government of the country. In Bavaria the government declared its own state of emergency, appointing Gustav von Kahr as State Commissioner with dictatorial powers.

3. From Berlin, General von Seeckt ordered the Bavarian government to arrest right-wingers in Munich. Von Kahr refused.

4. By November 1923, Hitler had decided to attempt a *Putzsch*, seize power in Bavaria, and call for a nationwide "march on Berlin" (modelled on Mussolini's 'March on Rome').

5. Von Kahr and the heads of the army and police in Munich met to address a meeting of leaders of the community in the *Bürgerbraukeller* on Nov. 8th. They were to consider a plan to restore the Wittlesbachs as the ruling dynasty in an independent Bavaria.

6. The *SA* surrounded the building and Hitler took the three prisoner, offering them jobs in his administration if they would join him, and proclaim a national revolution, while sending a message to General Ludendorff (who lived nearby) to join them, which he did very reluctantly. (He resented being summoned by a mere former corporal.) Other *SA* were to take over public buildings.

7. When Hitler left the *Bürgerbraukeller* to see to a clash between the *SA* and regular soldiers, the Bavarian leaders slipped away and organised resistance.

8. The Nazis then decided to march on the centre of the city. They were stopped by police when 16 of them were shot by police, and Hitler was arrested.

9. Hitler stood **trial** and was sentenced to 5 years in prison. Although he had been less than heroic during this so-called revolution, he was able to turn the trial to his advantage. A sympathetic judge allowed him to make long speeches in his defence, which received nationwide publicity in the newspapers.

10. In prison Hitler lived comfortably and with his second-in-command, Rudolf Hess, and produced the first volume of *Mein Kampf*. This outlined Hitler's view of history and of the future.

11. Hitler appointed Alfred Rosenberg as his deputy while he was in Landsberg prison, but Rosenberg was soon being challenged by Julius Streicher, and the party fell into chaos.

12. In December 1924 Hitler was released, after serving just 9 months of his sentence.

Reasons for the Failure of the Munich Beer Hall *Putzsch*
1. Commissioner Kahr would not co-operate with Hitler.
2. The Munich police were not sympathetic.
3. The Nazi Party had virtually no support outside Bavaria, and not enough inside.
4. Despite appearances, the republic was not in danger of collapse at this time.

Advantages of the Attempted *Putzsch* for Hitler
1. The trial provided nationwide publicity, making Hitler's name familiar across the country.
2. Stephen J. Lee points out that it provided Hitler with "revolutionary credentials."
3. Hitler's period of imprisonment taught the Nazis that they needed his leadership to stay united.
4. The failure of the *Putzsch* pointed Hitler towards a more likely path to power – through conventional party politics.

The Years of Peace

Nazism
1. In Landsberg Prison, Hitler expounded the philosophy of Nazism in *Mein Kampf.*
2. *Volkisch** nationalism was an extreme form of nationalism, underpinned and justified by an extreme form of racism, which exhibited features additional to the almost universal racist beliefs current at the time:
   (a) In Germany, racism had assumed quasi-scientific status even before the First World War.
   (b) The white race was said to be superior to all others, but due to intermarriage with people from other races it had been "diluted" in many places. The purest form of the white race was the blond-haired, blue-eyed Aryan* who had inhabited the forests of Germany during the Dark Ages. They formed a master-race (*Herrenvolk*), destined to rule the world, (Ironically, virtually no leading Nazi was both blond-haired and blue-eyed; but they never seemed to notice).
   (c) Jews were an able people, but morally inferior. This made them dangerous. They were a universal scourge which only the Aryan race could resist.
   This racism was justified by reference to Social Darwinism. *[See Chapter One]*
3. The state was thought to be all-important, a familiar theme in German philosophy:
   (a) National unity must be maintained, and the class struggle avoided;
   (b) Strong government is necessary for this, including the "leader principle";
   (c) Democracy must be rejected as degenerate.
4. The strength of the state is based upon the health of the race, which must be protected:
   (a) by eugenics:* Only the healthy must beget children;
   (b) by the elimination of the physically deformed, the mentally ill, and the morally corrupt.
5. Existing élites were degenerate. A revolution was necessary to replace them with the biological élite. Distinctions of birth, education and wealth profited only social parasites. Existing élites must be swept away by people of genuine talent, who would rise to the top by a process of natural selection. (Social Darwinism again)
6. Belief in the superiority of the Aryan race was reconciled with the defeat of 1918 by arguing that Germany had been stabbed in the back in 1918-19 by the "November Criminals."
7. There was a romantic attachment to feeling, a glorification of force and will, and a revulsion from reason, again justified by Social Darwinism.
8. In a hostile, competitive world, the state must aim at autarchy* (economic self-sufficiency)
9. These central ideas were spread by a well-organised propaganda department, headed by Josef Göbbels, but Hitler himself was the ultimate propagandist
10. This is a form of fascism, with racism added.

The Creation of a National Party

1. When Hitler emerged from prison it seemed that his chance had passed. Germany had passed into a period of comparative peace and prosperity.

   (a) The hyperinflation crisis had passed, the **Dawes Plan** allowed the rescheduling of the war reparations and the French withdrew from the Ruhr.

   (b) The economy picked up. There was a **boom** in coal, iron, steel, electrical goods and the chemical industry.

   However:

   > (i) Unemployment remained relatively high.

   > (ii) The textile industry was in difficulties.

   > (iii) Small farmers experienced difficulties.

   > (iv) The apparent prosperity was dependent upon short-term loans from the USA.

2. Despite the positive signs of a return to peace, there is much evidence that Germans were not accepting their defeat and its consequences:

   (a) Leading politicians and members of the general staff are on record as referring to the need one day for the revision of the Treaty of Versailles, and of preparing for war with France and in the East.

   (b) The terms of the Treaty were sometimes evaded:

   > (i) the abolished general staff surreptitiously continued in being;

   > (ii) military research was conducted by private industry;

   > (iii) military factories were secretly built, and military training carried out, in the USSR;

   > (iv) "police" units carried out basic military training;

   > (v) nearly half the soldiers in the smaller German Army were NCOs,* in preparation for its expansion into a much larger army.

   (c) In 1925 the Germans elected war hero Marshall Hindenburg as President. Before accepting he wrote to the *Kaiser*, addressing him as "Your Imperial Majesty," to secure his permission to accept the post. In September 1927 President Hindenburg renounced Germany's responsibility for the war.

3. Hitler had decided, after his failure in Munich in 1923, that he must come to power by legal means. He recognised that the army would never let him take power by force. Therefore he set out to build a mass party which would bring him to power through elections. Hitler was allowed to refound his party in the *Bürgerbraukeller* on 27th February, 1925, as a constitutional party to fight elections.

4. Hitler avoided producing detailed policy proposals; (he did not like to be pinned down as a conventional politician of the right or left) so as:

   > (a) personally to remain above conflict;

   > (b) to avoid rifts in the Party;

   > (c) to avoid alienating potential supporters.

5. Controversy and infighting continued within the Party:

   (a) Leaders in the north disagreed with the new policy of being a constitutional party;

   (b) Gregor Strasser, together with leaders in the west wanted a more socialist party to compete with the left for the support of the workers. Some even favoured an alliance with the USSR against the "Jewish capitalist West," regarding the USSR under Stalin as a nationalist power.

   At the Bamberg Conference (1926) Hitler overcame Strasser and won over Joseph Göbbels.

6. The party was organised on a regional basis, Germany being divided into districts called *Gaue*. Each *Gau* was under a regional party leader, or *Gauleiter*. An administrative machinery was built up, largely by Gregor Strasser.

7. Propaganda was organised locally by Gauleiters personally appointed by Hitler, and leading party activists. New branches would be set up when there were about fifteen members in a town or village.
8. A host of subordinate organisations were founded for different types of people in the party by age, sex and profession.
9. The Party acted as a welfare society. It collected money and distributed food and clothing to those in need during hard times.
10. In 1928 Hitler allied his party with the National Party. This placed at Hitler's disposal the resources of Hugenberg's chain of newspapers and big business contacts.
11. Despite all the organisation and propaganda, in 1928 the Nazis received only 2.6% of the total vote, and 12 seats in the *Reichstag*. But the means for receiving and holding on to new members was ready for the day when a new crisis would create renewed interest in the party.

The Second Crisis of the Republic

1. In 1928 an agricultural crisis developed.
2. In 1929, the **Young Plan** reduced Germany's war reparations from £6600 million to £200 million and rescheduled the payments to end in 1986. But it was already too late to help.
3. Following the **Wall Street Crash** (October 1929) the US stopped further loans and began calling in loans previously made to Germany. This undermined the currency and caused a run on the banks. Many collapsed. Gustav Stresemann, perhaps the best politician to deal with the crisis, died of a heart attack during that month.
4. There was a slump in world trade and factories closed everywhere, but Germany was hard hit. **Unemployment** rose to 6 million by 1932. This polarised the voters, who once more turned to the parties on the extremes.
5. In the elections of September, 1930, the number of National Socialist Deputies in the *Reichstag* rose from 12 to 107 with 18.3% of the votes.
6. The government of Chancellor **Brüning** (Catholic Centre Party) took **emergency powers** and ruled by decree. It:
    (a) reduced social services, unemployment benefit and the salaries and pensions of government officials;
    (b) introduced high tariffs to protect German farmers;
    (c) bought shares in factories hit by the slump;
    (d) stopped making reparations payments.
    Effectively, parliamentary democracy in Germany was already at an end.
7. On 27th January 1932 Hitler made a successful appeal for support to industrialists at the **Düsseldorf Industry Club**. This substantially increased donations to the Party from wealthy industrialists fearful of a Communist revolution which would deprive them of their wealth and power, at a time when the Nazi Party desperately needed funds to fight elections.
8. These drastic measures produced some results by late summer 1932. But they were very unpopular, and in May 1932 Brüning was replaced as Chancellor by **Von Papen** (Conservative Monarchist), who had no body of supporters, either in the Reichstag or in the country. His cabinet was called the "cabinet of barons." Hitler would not agree to be second-in-command. In order to gain Hitler's support, von Papen lifted a ban on street armies.
9. In the first election of 1932, in July, the Nazis won their highest vote total in free elections. The total vote for the Nazis in this election was 37.4% of the vote. This gave them 230 seats as the largest party in the *Reichstag*.
10. Hitler decided to stand against Hindenberg in the presidential elections. He lost by 13 million

to 19 million votes, but the campaign established him in the minds of many Germans as an alternative national ruler.

11. In the election of November of 1932, the Nazi vote declined by 2 million and they lost 34 seats in the *Reichstag*. It began to look as though they were past their peak of popularity. This probably had something to do with a delayed improvement in the economy brought about by Brüning's measures.

12. The drop in the Nazi vote led von Papen and von Schleicher to believe even more strongly that Hitler could be controlled. Hindenberg would still not appoint Hitler. Instead he asked General **von Schleicher** to become Chancellor.

13. Schleicher tried to split the Nazis by inviting Gregor Strasser into his government. Strasser quarrelled with Hitler and resigned from the Party to join him. But when von Schleicher presented his government's programme, he could not get the support of the *Reichstag*.

14. A conspiracy of right-wing politicians, including Von Papen and Von Schleicher, decided to bring Hitler into government:
    (a) They were afraid of a Nazi *Putsch*, and wished to pre-empt it;
    (b) They believed they could control Hitler better inside the government than outside it;
    (c) They believed that the Nazi votes in the *Reichstag* would give them sufficient majority to replace the Weimar Republic with the monarchy, their ultimate aim.

They first tried to persuade Hitler to enter a government with Von Papen as Chancellor and Hitler as Vice Chancellor, but he would not agree. Von Schleicher, Von Papen and Hindenburg's son, Oscar, then persuaded Hindenburg to invite Hitler to form a government with two other Nazis in the cabinet. He reluctantly agreed.

The Nazis Come to Power

1. In January 1933, Hitler was appointed chancellor of Germany in a cabinet with only three Nazis.
2. Once in power Hitler began to take the steps to establish an absolute dictatorship, somewhat following the example of Mussolini in Italy.
3. He immediately announced parliamentary elections for March 5, 1933.
4. Hermann Göring was placed as Minister in charge of Prussia, and Wilhelm Frick was Minister of the Interior. These used their positions to ensure a high vote for the Nazi Party. Senior police officers were replaced by Nazis. 50,000 auxiliary police officers were appointed, mostly *SA* and *SS*. They intimidated rivals and attacked rival party meetings. The police took action against their opponents only. The media were extensively used for Nazi propaganda.
5. On 27th February the *Reichstag* building was burned down, allegedly by a Dutch Communist. Hitler claimed it was part of a planned Communist uprising. He used the incident to:
    (a) create a climate of fear to persuade people to accept the removal of their civil rights;
    (b) frighten voters into supporting a self-styled "strong leader";
    (c) justify outlawing the Communist Party.
6. The Nazi party received 288 seats in the elections, but only 44% of the vote, despite their campaign of propaganda and terror.
7. In order to gain a majority in the *Reichstag*, Hitler declared the communists' seats null and void.
8. When the *Reichstag* met in the Kroll Opera House (March 23, 1933) the members were intimidated by the *SA* and *SS*. The Communists, if not already arrested, were not allowed to enter. He then made a political deal with the Catholic Centre Party, which gave him the two-thirds majority necessary to pass the **Enabling Act.** This gave Hitler the power to govern by decree for four years without reference to the constitution or the Reichstag. It passed by 441 votes to 94. Only the Social democrats voted against it.

The Consolidation of Power

1. Despite his dictatorial powers, there were still forces in Germany that could restrain Hitler:
   (a) President Hindenburg, although senile was widely respected, and no one could dismiss him.
   (b) The *SA* or "brown shirts" under Ernst Röhm:
      (i) the radical wing of the party, expected some sort of social revolution;
      (ii) expected the rewards of their service to Nazism.
   (c) The army, contemptuous of Hitler and resentful of the *SA* was appraising him.
2. Hitler nevertheless initiated a policy of **Gleichschaltung** (forcible co-ordination) and took steps that allowed him to eliminate or control virtually all areas of German life:
   (a) All political parties except the Nazis were banned.
   (b) The separate parliaments of the *Länder* lost their powers to Nazi officials or *Gauleiters*. For the first time, Germany was no longer a federal state.
   (c) The *SA* and *SS* simply took over town halls, police stations and newspaper offices.
   (d) The civil service was purged of enemies of the Nazis, especially Jews.
   (e) Trade unions were abolished and replaced by the German Workers Front, to which all workers had to belong. Union leaders were arrested, and strikes forbidden.
   (f) Schools and colleges were forced to indoctrinate Nazi ideas. Teachers were closely watched for signs of disloyalty to the regime or anti-Nazi ideas. The Hitler Youth and League of German Maidens, etc. supplemented regular education.
   (g) The media were supervised, and dominated by Göbbels' propaganda.
   (h) The economy was placed under some control:
      (i) Industrialists were told what to produce;
      (ii) Food prices and rents were controlled;
      (iii) public works schemes were introduced (e.g. *Autobahns,* land drainage, (CF Mussolini));
      (iv) barter was sometimes substituted for money trade.
   (i) All opposition was crushed by the Gestapo (*Geheime Staatspolizei*) who routinely used torture. Concentration camps were set up for political prisoners. They did not actively spy on ordinary citizens; ordinary citizens spied on each other, and reported each other to the Gestapo.
3. *Gleichschaltung* did not lead to a monolithic society. Nazi organisations were created to oversee existing organisations, and were often created in competition with each other. Independent conflicting policies were pursued by their heads, Hitler acting as referee. This was a deliberate policy of "divide and rule." (CF again Mussolini)
4. These measures were generally popular with many Germans:
   (a) Hitler promised action and seemed to begin to implement his promises;
   (b) Purges of Jews and other opponents of the regime created jobs for Germans;
   (c) Wealthy Germans felt much safer from the threat of Communism.
5. The Churches were "tamed."
   (a) In 1933 Hitler concluded a Concordat* with Pope Pius XI, which compromised the Roman Catholic Church by affording recognition of his regime. Having given a promise that the Church would not be interfered with, Hitler then promptly dissolved the Catholic Youth League, a rival to the Hitler Youth.
   (b) A *Reich* Church was organised for all Protestants under a Nazi "First *Reich* Bishop". Some who protested were interned in concentration camps.
6. The *SA* became a problem to Hitler once he was in power. Under Ernst Röhm:
   (a) their numbers had risen to over four million, outnumbering the *Reichswehr* (German Army).
   (b) Many of th *SA* were radicals who took very seriously the word "Socialist" in the name of their party, and were expecting a social revolution. (There had been an embarrassing revolt of the *SA* in Munich in 1930, when they occupied Party headquarters, which had been put down by the *SS*

and the German police).

(c) They were expecting a reward for their service now that Hitler was chancellor. They and their ambitious leader threatened:

(i) the leadership of the Nazi Party: This was especially felt by Göring and Himmler.

(ii) the *Reichswehr:* Röhm wanted the *SA* to be merged with the *Reichswehr** and himself to be made a general.

(iii) the state: Both President Hindenburg and the non-Nazi vice-chancellor in the coalition government, Franz von Papen, had complained to Hitler about them. They had a reputation of being thugs, and were an embarrassment in government.

(iv) Even Mussolini, who had suffered from problems with his own paramilitary organisation, the Blackshirts, advised him to rein them in.

On the "**Night of the Long Knives**" (30th June 1934):

(i) having secured the support of the Army for his becoming president after Hindenburg's death in return for emasculating the *SA*;

(ii) being panicked by false reports of an imminent *SA* coup fed to him by Himmler;

Hitler had Röhm and other *SA* leaders murdered, using the *Schutzstaffel (SS)* – an elite military formation run by Himmler, which had grown out of Hitler's bodyguard.

At the same time, Hitler also took the opportunity to settle some old scores others he considered dangerous to him, including Gregor Strasser, Kurt von Schliecher and Gustav von Kahr. All were accused of plotting against Hitler and the state. The *SA* were little more than a parading force afterwards.

7. President Hindenburg died on August 2, 1934. Hitler immediately combined the office of president and chancellor. The armed forces duly swore an oath of loyalty to the *Führer*.

8. In September, 1934, Hitler proclaimed that the German form of life was settled for the next thousand years. Officers in the army had to take an oath of allegiance to Hitler personally.

9. With economic recovery apparently taking place, Hitler held a plebiscite in which it was reported that 90% of the German people said that they approved of Hitler's policies and actions.

10. Hitler could now turn his attention to the subject that interested him the most: foreign policy.

Why Hitler was able to Gain Power

1. The Weimar republic began with several disadvantages which it never entirely shook off:

(a) It was associated in the mind of the public with defeat. Most people failed to notice that it was General Ludendorff who had asked for an armistice while the Kaiser was still on the throne.

(b) It was associated with Germany's acceptance of the humiliating and unpopular *diktat* of Versailles, and therefore with defeat and dishonour.

(c) The republic was originally adopted only as a temporary measure to placate the Allies, until the monarchy could safely be restored.

(d) There was no tradition of democracy in Germany. This led to:

(i) Inexperience of governing among the leadership of the political parties, since before 1919 the Reichstag had not controlled policy;

(ii) A lack of respect for democratic governments;

(e) There was no tradition of civilian leadership in Germany. The governments of the Kaiser had been packed with army officers, who had great prestige in the eyes of the public. By contrast the civilian leadership of the Republic, mostly middle class and containing many Jews, commanded little respect. At that time Germans mostly respected uniforms.

(f) The Parliamentary system of voting by proportional representation led to a succession of minority governments. This led to coalition governments which were often unable to carry out

Timeline of Hitler's Rise to Power

1919	Hitler joined the German Workers' Party (DAP)
1920	DAP became the National Socialist German Workers' (Nazi) Party
	Röhm founded the *SA*
1921	Hitler became leader of the Nazi Party
1923	
January	Franco-Belgian occupation of the Ruhr
August	Hyperinflation crisis – Stresemann became chancellor
Nov 8	Failed *Bürgerbraukeller Putsch*
1924	Hitler tried and imprisoned – *Mein Kampf* written
1925	
Feb 27	Nazi party refounded in the *Bürgerbraukeller*
1929	The Wall Street Crash – Death of Stresemann – Young Plan
1933	
Jan 30	Hitler appointed Chancellor
Feb 27	Reichstag Fire
Mar 5	"Managed" election
March 23	Enabling Act passed
May 2	Trades unions banned
	Concordat with the Papacy
1934	
June 29	Night of the Long Knives
Aug 2	Death of President Hindenburg – Hitler combined offices of president and chancellor

their programmes. The average life-span of a government was eight months, creating a permanent sense of crisis.

(g) The Weimar Republic appeared weak:

(i) It began with a series of risings which were quelled only with difficulty. In putting them down, the leaders of the Republic allied themselves with the established centres of authority and against the revolution, alienating much of its support.

(ii) Whereas left-wing leaders were dealt with harshly, right wing leaders who had endangered the state were generally given derisory sentences and treated sympathetically by the police, judiciary and prison officials, who themselves despised the state they represented.

(iii) Many politicians were assassinated, mostly by ex-Freikorps members; e.g. Walter Rathenau, the Jewish Foreign Minister and Gustav Erzberger, leader of the armistice delegation.

(iv) Although disorder died down during the period 1924-9, it re-emerged during the early 1930s as unemployment grew. Private armies expanded and street fighting was rife. Political meetings were regularly broken up by rival groups. The police seemed powerless to prevent disorder.

2. The Republic was plagued by economic problems.

(a) In 1919 the government was close to bankruptcy because of the cost of the war.

(b) Payment of war reparations led to hyperinflation. Although Stresemann stabilised the currency during 1924, the middle classes had lost their savings.

(c) Although during 1924-9 the economy improved, and the reparations instalments were paid under the Dawes Plan (and from 1929 the Young Plan), there were still problem areas: especially the textile industry and small farms.

(d) The recovery was based upon loans from the USA. With the Wall Street Crash (October 1929) the US immediately recalled short-term loans. This caused a run on German currency and on German banks, and some closed. Foreign trade also almost disappeared. This produced the economic slump and mass unemployment.

(e) The measures taken by the government of Chancellor Brüning were unpopular.

(f) during economic instability people sought drastic solutions and their votes polarised to the political extremes. The connection between the failure of the economy and the rise of the Nazis can be seen by looking at the voting figures:

Economic Conditions in Germany and the Nazi Vote		
March 1924	32 seats	economy still unstable after the hyperinflation
December 1924	14 seats	economy recovering after Dawes Plan
1928	12 seats	comparative prosperity
1930	107 seats	unemployment rising (Nazis 2nd largest party)
July 1932	230 seats	massive unemployment (Nazis largest party)
November 1932	198 seats	some improvement in the economy
March 1933	288 seats	using the media, police, SA and SS.

3. The Nazis began to appeal to people at this time because:

   (a) When the traditional politicians had been seen to fail, the Nazis promised strong, competent government.

   (b) They promised to restore full employment and to get the economy straight.

   (c) They promised to rid Germany of the causes of the trouble: Communists, Jews, Gypsies, etc.

   (d) They promised to overthrow the terms of the hated Treaty of Versailles and to restore German honour and power.

   (e) Wealthy landowners and industrialists feared a Communist revolution and thought they could use Hitler and his SA to protect themselves.

   (f) The lower middle class feared loss of status.

4. Despite his firm convictions on many points, Hitler constantly reformulated party policy so as to appeal to new segments of the population alienated from the Republic.

5. The Nazi Party had built up a nation-wide organisation during the years 1925-9, so as to enable it to take advantage of the crisis at the end of the 1920s. Discontented Germans thus had somewhere to go in order to express their dissatisfaction with conventional politicians, i.e. their local Nazi Party and its many associated organisations.

6. The Party had an excellent propaganda machine led by Joseph Göbbels.

7. Hitler was a skilful politician and demagogue. He articulated all the resentments and prejudices of his audience.

8. Wealthy capitalists and landowners and many conservatives and catholics saw Hitler and the Nazis as a buttress against the "Red Menace" of Communism.

9. Most voters for the NSDWP were:

   (a) lower middle class white-collar workers: small-businessmen, shopkeepers and people on fixed incomes who were anti-capitalist, anti-Communist, anti-Semitic Pan-Germans;

   (b) conservative Protestant farmers in the East;

(c) young working class unemployed in non-industrial areas.

10. The provision of the Weimar Constitution which allowed the President to govern by decree ignoring the Reichstag was used by Brüning from 1930. This:

(a) established the idea that strong government was achieved by suspending normal constitutional government;

(b) provided Hitler with the machinery he was to use to become a dictator.

11. Many conservatives disliked the intellectual and artistic freedom of the Weimar Republic, which shocked them.

12. The manoeuvring of Von Papen and Von Schleicher brought Hitler to power as a temporary expedient:

(a) to pre-empt a Nazi *Putzsch;*

(b) the better to control Hitler;

(c) Their long-term aim was the restoration of the monarchy. They mistakenly thought that the Nazi votes might be employed for that purpose. They had fundamentally mistaken Hitler's radicalism and purposes. They may have seen him as another Mussolini, outwardly radical but a supporter of existing elites.

13. The opposition failed to unite against Hitler. Since they thought that he would not be able to govern for long, the Communists were content to "let him try and fail," for then they would be the only alternative.

14. Hitler often appeared to be deliberately following the path laid out by Mussolini, but as a pupil more able and ruthless than his teacher.

The Third Reich

Gleichschaltung

The policy of ***Gleichschaltung***, or forced co-ordination, which was immediately implemented by the Nazi government, was intended to constitute a revolution, changing the very character of the German state.

1. The new government armed itself with new powers of coercion and terror:

(a) The **Decree for the Protection of People and State** (February 1933) gave the authorities the right to detain people indefinitely without trial.

(b) Several **Agencies of coercion** were necessary to enforce *Gleichschaltung,* including:

The *Schutz Staffel* (*SS*) had been a branch of the *SA*. This developed several components:

(i) the *Liebstandarte*, Hitler's bodyguard;

(ii) the *Sicherheitspolizei* (*SiPo*), or security police;

The *SiPo included the* Gestapo (*Geheime Staatspolizei*)

(iii) the *Sicherheitsdienst* (*SD*) or Security Service;

In 1939 the *SiPo* and *SD* were merged into the *Reichsicherheitshauptamt* (RSHA) or Reich Main Security Office under Reinhard Heydrich, which had over a hundred sections

(iv) the *Totenkopfverbände*: the "Death's Head" units which ran the concentration camps.

These organisations were associated by being under the overall direction of Heinrich Himmler, who came to wield immense power.

(c) Denunciation by hostile neighbours was the ordinary person's greatest source of danger.

2.. The justice system was incorporated into the totalitarian state:

(a) Judicial autonomy was abolished, and the judges subject to the Ministry of Justice.

(b) Judges could be retired if they did not act in the interests of the National Socialist state.

(c) Prosecutors usurped many of the functions of judges.

(d) Draconian* punishments became the norm, particularly following the outbreak of war, e.g. people were executed for telling an anti-Nazi joke.

(e) retroactive legislation* became common, usually to the advantage of the regime.

(f) From 1936 the courts were routinely bypassed:

(i) people found not guilty in court would be rearrested on release.

(ii) "undesirables" would be rounded up and interned in camps without any trial.

(iii) Prisoners would not be released at the end of their sentences.

3. All **political parties** except the NSGWP were outlawed.

4. The **state parliaments** (*Länder*) were deprived of their powers when most of their functions were taken over by Special Commissioners (*Gauleiters*). Germany became a unitary state for the first time in its history.

5. The **civil service** was purged of all likely opponents of the Nazis.

6. The **trade unions** were abolished, their funds confiscated and their leaders arrested. They were replaced by the German Labour Front, membership of which was compulsory for all workers. Strikes were outlawed.

7. The **educational system** was co-opted as a propaganda agency of the Party. This was not difficult as teachers were a conservative section of the population who conformed readily to Nazism.

(a) Schools and universities became agencies of propaganda.

(i) All teachers were closely supervised. Membership of the Nazi Teachers' Association was compulsory. A teacher's duty was to propagandize rather than to educate.

(ii) The curriculum was adjusted, and the textbooks rewritten, to conform to Nazi ideas. e.g. The teaching of biology incorporated Nazi racial theories.

(iii) Religious education and the participation of priests in education was phased out.

(b) The Nazis were essentially anti-intellectual, and in consequence:

(i) Educational standards plummeted.

(ii) Research suffered. e.g. The "Jewish physics" of Albert Einstein was banned.

(c) Compulsory youth organisations (*Jungvolk, Hitlerjugend, Jungmädel, Deutscher Mädel*) sought to:

(i) indoctrinate Party ideology;

(ii) prepare young people for later roles as soldiers or mothers;

(iii) abolish class differences.

8. The **mass media** were controlled by Joseph Göbbels Ministry of Propaganda.

(a) Books, newspapers, films, etc. were censored.

(b) Writers, artists and scholars were attacked for failing to express opinions in conformity with Nazi teachings.

9. Culture was to be employed as an instrument of ideology.

(a) Unacceptable works, particularly works by socialists and Jews, were destroyed. There were ceremonial book-burnings in the universities.

(b) "Aryan art," which glorified the *Herrenvolk* was fostered.

(c) Modern art was banned as "degenerate."

10. The Churches were "tamed."

(a) In 1933 Hitler concluded a Concordat with Pope Pius XI, which compromised the Roman Catholic Church by affording recognition of his regime. Having given a promise that the Church would not be interfered with, Hitler then promptly dissolved the Catholic Youth League, a rival to the Hitler Youth.

(b) A *Reich* Church was organised for all Protestants under a Nazi "First *Reich* Bishop". Some who protested were interned in concentration camps.

11. New Nazi festivals and rituals were created to replace traditional Christian observations: the annual Party Rallies at Nuremberg, the celebration of Hitler's birthday, the commemoration of the Munich *Putsch*, etc. Some Nazis introduced artificially designed pagan festivals to revive the religion of the early Germanic tribes, such as sun rituals. Hitler did not take these seriously.

12. The Nazis regarded the proper place for women as in the home (*Kinder, Kirche, und Kuche* - "children, church, kitchen"). Accordingly, working women were encouraged to stay at home and have babies. However, as war approached women were moved into the factories, eventually forming three-fifths of Germany's labour force.

13. Populism was maintained by symbols which stressed the classless "folk community" and by spreading some of the advantages of the middle class to the working class:

    (a) Hitler would frequently speak to workers, stressing his own humble origins as a worker.

    (b) Grammar-school boys were encouraged to burn their distinctively coloured caps.

    (c) In 1935 two titled women were executed for espionage on behalf of Poland as a sign of the new egalitarianism* of the law.

    (d) More than a million gained advancement through appointment to the Party administration.

    (e) Holidays with pay were virtually doubled.

    (f) The *Kraft durch Freude* or "Strength through Joy" movement provided subsidised holidays away from home, often foreign cruises for workers on the basis of a lottery draw in which managers were not allowed to take part. In addition they took block bookings at sports events, concerts and theatres. In 1938, one worker in 200 took a trip abroad.

Economic Policies

1. The initial aims of Nazi economic policy were:

    (a) to secure the support of the population;

    (b) to revive the industrial and military power of Germany;

    (c) to prepare for war by:

      (i) achieving autarchy (economic self-sufficiency);

      (ii) and rearmament.

2. Hitler was uninterested in the details of economics and never developed a distinctive theory of the economy. He appointed able men, e.g. Hjalmar Schacht, Head of the *Reichsbank,* and let them get on with it.

3. The Party programme included radical measures, e.g.

    (a) communalization of department stores and their lease to small traders; In 1933 some enthusiasts tried simply to take over department stores, but were thrown out on Hitler's orders.

    (b) land reform;

    (c) the abolition of interest on mortgages;

    (d) Cessation of payment of foreign debts.

4. To stimulate the economy and reduce unemployment:

    (a) Taxes were reduced;

    (b) Farmers guaranteed prices for their produce;

    (c) Grants were made to industry to install new machinery;

    (d) Public works enterprises were initiated, e.g. autobahns built and slums cleared.

    These were initially paid for through bills discounted by the banks, but later by taxes on corporate profits and incomes and forced loans from businessmen.

5. Craft guilds which controlled entry to, and regulated, artisan professions by examination were fostered, together with associated rituals. The guilds became centres of corruption and nepotism.

6. From 1934 the economy came to be known as a *Wehrwirtschaft* (war economy), i.e. an economy preparing for war. In May 1935 Hitler appointed Schacht Plenipotentiary for the War Economy. There is disagreement about whether Hitler was planning for total war (e.g. Richard Overy) or for a series of short *Blitzkrieg* campaigns.

7. In order to pay for rearmament, Schacht:
   (a) manipulated the currency markets to Germany's advantage;
   (b) negotiated barter deals with other countries;
   (c) issued "Mefo" bills accepted by German banks to pay armaments manufacturers.

8. Hitler became discontented with progress, and a Four Year Plan was implemented from Sept. 1936 under the control of Hermann Göring, in imitation of the Soviet Five Year Plans, with the aim of achieving autarchy in four years:
   (a) Imports were reduced to a minimum, factories being set up to make synthetic replacement products inside Germany;
   (b) severe controls were placed on wages, prices and dividends.

9. From 1936-7 great changes in the economy were made by the growing power of the state in the economy and the increasing dominance of the arms industry. Competition for markets was replaced by competition for raw materials and labour.

10. In 1937 a state owned steel corporation, the *Reichswerke Hermann-Göring*, was set up in order to correct a blockage in iron production, despite opposition from the steel barons.

11. Some historians, e.g. Tim Mason see an economic crisis during the late 1930s. Rearmament put pressure on exports and foreign currency earnings and created a shortage of labour. This problem could only be solved in one of two ways:
    (a) by giving up rearmament;
    (b) by fighting short wars of conquest which would enable the Germans to obtain resources from the conquered countries.

12. The German wartime economy was a continuation of the peacetime economy, since:
    (a) a degree of mobilisation of the economy had already occurred.
    (b) for the first two years of the war Germany did not wage total war; it was not even properly prepared for *Blitzkrieg.*
    (c) Hitler was unwilling to impose too much sacrifice upon the population
    (d) The chaotic organisation of the Nazi state led to a proliferation of competing authorities which compromised mobilization measures
    (e) Many in the Nazi leadership were disinclined to mobilise women.
    (f) Instead the occupied countries were exploited for:
        (i) confiscation of foodstuffs and manufactured goods,
        (ii) slave labour,
        (iii) foreign exchange,
        (iv) favourable trade terms.

13. From 1942 Hitler was forced into a war of attrition. War production was put under the control of Albert Speer and a Central Planning Board.
    (a) Changing of jobs was discouraged
    (b) Many male workers were retrained for the armaments industry
    (c) Attempts were made by the *Gestapo* to enforce military discipline in the workplace
    There were significant increases in production, despite massive Allied bombing, but the German economy could not outproduce those of the USSR, Britain and the USA.

14. In general, Hitler ignored the interests of the small businessmen who had been his supporters before he came to power, and benefited the capitalists who held large concerns useful for the

Timeline of Hitler's Economic Policies	
1935 May	Hjalmar Schacht appointed Plenipotentiary for the War Economy.
1936 Sep	Four Year Plan, under the control of Göring
1942 Feb	Albert Speer appointed Minister of Armaments
1945 Mar	Hitler issues the Nero Decree

Wehrwirtschaft or war economy.

15. Economic considerations were always subject to ideology.
   (a) In 1935 Economics Minister, Hjalmar Schacht, criticised the Anti-Jewish boycott and terror action against the Jews as harmful to the German economy. He was ignored.
   (b) The first Polish Jews gassed in the extermination camps were trained metal workers from the Polish armaments factories. This was at a time when Germany desperately needed such workers.
16. The war economy was to some extent sabotaged by *Gauleiters* who resisted Speer's attempts at imposing central control in the interests of their own autonomy:
   (a) delaying the ending of the production of consumer goods;
   (b) hindering the transfer of skilled workers out of their districts;
   (c) circumventing instructions designed to intensify work or lower standards of living.
   This would be justified by the need to bolster morale in their districts.
17. On March 19th 1945, with defeat certain, Hitler issued the **Nero Decree**, ordering a scorched earth policy, that retreating German administrators and forces should destroy all facilities and infrastructure in advance of the enemy advance. This was not carried out by some Nazis, e.g. Albert Speer.

The Racist State

1. In July 1933 the Sterilization Law made sterilization compulsory for people with hereditary defects or illnesses, together with some anti-social conditions such as alcoholism.
2. In 1939 Hitler secretly authorised the killing of the congenitally ill and insane throughout Germany to free resources for the war effort. Most were denied medication or killed over a period of months, the deaths being recorded as "natural" e.g. from pneumonia, by the doctors who killed them. In 1941 Count Galen, the Roman Catholic Bishop of Munster, denounced the **euthanasia* programme** from the pulpit, and it was halted.
3. Certain groups were persecuted, and ultimately attempt was made to exterminate them. Among these groups were Jews, One and a half million Roma* were killed, as well as the entire Polish *intelligentsia*, Communists, homosexuals, Jehovah's Witnesses, etc. Their fate is accorded less publicity than that of the Jews.
4. David Mazower points out in *Dark Continent: Europe's Twentieth Century*, that what most horrified Europeans about Hitler's *Reich* was that non-Aryan Europeans were treated by the Nazis in ways that Europeans had traditionally treated non-Europeans outside Europe.

Anti-Semitism
The Origins of Anti-Semitism

1. Anti-Semitism has a long history in Europe, dating from the days of the Roman Empire. Yet while anti-Semitism has been almost constant, the reasons for it have not.
2. Medieval anti-Semitism was religious. It was based upon the rejection of Christ by the Jews, and

their part in securing his crucifixion. Since Christians believe Christ to be God, the Jews were considered deicides, that is, people who had committed the uniquely evil crime of "murdering God." Jews were also widely reputed to kill Christian boys and drink their blood on Good Friday (the so-called "blood-libel"), and consort with the devil.

3. With the coming of the Age of Reason and the decline of religious belief, this form of anti-Semitism declined. But intellectuals in the Age of Reason frequently became anti-Semitic because they were against religion as such, and noted that the claim to possess the final truth about everything important in a particular book, and the aspects of bigotry, intolerance and hypocrisy which they most detested in the Christian Church, were an inheritance from Judaism.

4. Yet religious anti-Semitism survived in religious circles, and was widespread throughout Europe during the 1920s and 1930s.

5. An urban people engaged in trade, with family members in different cities, the Jews of Western Europe and North America were exceptionally well placed to take advantage of the development of capitalism. Many New York, London and Manchester Jews became very wealthy. Thus Jews, traditionally associated with moneylending, came also to be associated with international capitalism, in which the value of money was supreme.

6. Anti-Semitism in Austria and Germany came to be incorporated into a general pseudo-scientific theory of racism. But the Jews were culturally very productive, particularly in Vienna: e.g. Mendelssohn, and Mahler in music; Heine in poetry; Freud and Adler in psychology; Einstein in physics, etc. Many Austrians and Germans felt that German culture was under threat from this alien influence. Romantic nationalists like influential opera composer Richard Wagner and mayor of Vienna Karl Leuger tied the pseudoscientific ideology of racism to anti-Semitism. Given their cultural contribution, the Jews could not be described as culturally inferior, so they were designated morally inferior — an able race, but a hostile and dangerous alien threat.

7. Hitler was dissatisfied with religious anti-Semitism "based on religious ideas and not racial knowledge." Personally influenced by Wagner and Leuger, he sought to turn the religious antipathy of the Germans towards the Jews into a racial hatred. In this he was supported by figures such as Alfred Rosenberg, the party's chief ideologue, although in propaganda, the imagery of the earlier religious antipathy could be employed with modern racial ideas.

8. In 1917 the world was shaken by the Bolshevik Revolution in Russia. Many of the leading Bolsheviks were Jews. Late in 1918 when Germany faced collapse, such revolts broke out across the country, especially in Berlin and Munich. Many of the leaders of these revolts, such as Kurt Eisner and Rosa Luxemburg, were Jews. Thus Jews figured large among "the November Criminals" who, responsible for the disorders of 1918-21, were seen as responsible for the defeat of Germany, and Bolshevism came to be seen as part of a World Jewish Conspiracy.

9. When, in 1919, the Weimar republic, a liberal democracy, was foisted upon a defeated Germany by the Western Allies, it seemed to some right-wing Germans like the triumph of international capitalism and Jewry over their nation and its culture.

10. Hitler himself had an extreme personal loathing for Jews. He saw Jewish "robber nomads" as parasitically corrupting other peoples while seeking world domination. As early as 1920 he proclaimed his purpose as "the inexorable resolve to strike the evil at its root and exterminate it root and branch." In 1922 he declared that if he gained power "the annihilation of the Jews will be my first and foremost task."

Anti-Semitism in the Third Reich

1. When he became Chancellor in 1933, anti-Semitism became the basis of government policy. Systematic discrimination by the general population was encouraged.

2. Legislation against the Jews began almost immediately with the **Career Civil Service Act,** which excluded from employment in the civil service anyone who had one Jewish grandparent. Similar acts soon excluded Jewish doctors from hospitals, Jewish professors from universities and Jewish officers from the armed forces. Jews were systematically excluded from the arts, media and sports. This discrimination was generally popular, since it removed competition and created new career opportunities for "pure Aryan Germans."

3. **The Nuremberg Laws**, promulgated on 15th Sept. 1935, deprived Jews of *Reich* citizenship, and so of public rights. **The Blood Protection Act** prevented marriage or sexual relations between Jews and Germans in the interest of the "survival of the German race."

4. There was a temporary lull in anti-Semitism during 1936, when the Olympic Games were held in Berlin; e.g. Discriminatory signs were temporarily removed.

5. After a seventeen-year-old Jew assassinated an embassy secretary in Paris, on 9th November 1938, Göbbels launched a *pogrom** against Jewish businesses on what came to be known as *Kristallnacht*. "Spontaneous" attacks were organised by the Party. More than thirty thousand Jews were imprisoned and hundreds murdered. Every synagogue in the *Reich* was burned down or demolished.

6. During the following years, a further wave of discriminatory laws was enacted:
    (a) Jews were excluded from schools and universities, places of entertainment, sports stadia, swimming baths.
    (b) forbidden to practice as doctors, dentists or vets.
    (c) had to surrender all gold, silver and jewellery in their possession.
    (d) lost their tenancy and property rights, and were increasingly driven into "communal Jewish houses" and forbidden to be out of doors after 8.00 pm in winter and 9.00 pm in summer.
    (e) had all their radios confiscated.
    (f) were strongly encouraged to emigrate, although forbidden to take out their wealth.

7. The chief aim of the Nazis at this time was to force the emigration of Jews. This coincided with the aims of Haganah, the Jewish paramilitary force formed in Palestine to fight the indigenous Arab population, who wished to increase the Jewish population there to take over the country. Thus Adolf Eichmann met Haganah representatives in Cairo for talks to facilitate Jewish emigration from Central Europe to Palestine. By 1939 the British stopped this as it alarmed the Arabs.

8. During 1940 Göring ordered Heydrich to begin the enslavement of all Jews in the German occupied territories. Jews were made to wear the distinguishing mark of the yellow star, and the first mass deportations began. Many were sent for slave labour.

9. Consideration was given to moving all Jews to the tropical island of Madagascar.

10. In 1941 corps of SS men known as *Einsatzgruppen** accompanied the *Wehrmacht** into the USSR to eliminate systematically "undesirables" from the occupied territories. This included Jews.

11. At the **Wannsee Conference** in January 1942 the "Final Solution" to the Jewish Question was considered and probably planned.

12. Rations for Jews were drastically reduced, and they were forbidden to use public transport.

13. Shortly afterwards the first **gassings** began. Initially this was done using vehicle exhaust gasses in specially fitted closed vans.

14. Later gas chambers and ovens were built at special "**extermination camps**" (Auschwitz-Birkenau, Belzec, Chelmo, Maidenek, Sobibor and Treblinka) for the systematic extermination of the Jews and other groups considered undesirable.

15. When, during 1944, the camps were threatened by the advance of the Red Army into Poland and

Germany, imitating the practice of the Turks by adopting the **Death Marches** by which they had sought to exterminate the Armenians, the SS drove the surviving inmates into the interior ahead of the liberators. Most perished, as had clearly been intended. At the very end, in April 1945, in his *Last Testament,* Hitler urged the Germans to "merciless opposition to the universal poisoner of all peoples, International Jewry."

16. Perhaps up to six million Jews were murdered during those years, in what the Jews call the "Holocaust."

17. Most historians accept that most Germans were unaware of the extermination programme, although Daniel Goldhagen, in *Hitler's Willing Executioners* argued that most Germans were fully aware of what was happening, and supported it.

Conditions which Made the Holocaust Possible

1. The background of religious anti-Semitism:

   (a) gave Hitler's racist anti-Semitism a missionary fervour it would otherwise have lacked.

   (b) It provided a conceptual framework for the demonization of the Jews: "the personification of the devil as the symbol of all evil assumes the living shape of the Jew."

   (c) Hitler did not persecute the Jews single-handedly. He was assisted, particularly in the earlier stages, by willing Germans, and in the later states by the other peoples of Eastern Europe.

      (i) The more traditional religious anti-Semitism of the conservatives made Hitler's racist anti-Semitism more acceptable.

      (ii) Many religious anti-Semites vigorously supported the actions of the Nazis with their own more traditional propaganda and cooperation. Thus the German Catholic Church supplied the Nazis with records of Jewish converts.

2. Anti-Communism: Kurt Eisner, Rosa Luxemburg and many of the revolutionary leaders of 1919 had been Jews. The Nazis were thus able to combine anti-Semitism with Anti-Bolshevism, managing to blur the distinction between the two. Martin Bormann said that Nazism was anti-Semitic because it was "both anti-Communist and anti-Christian."

3. Anti-capitalism: The Jews were scapegoats for the German leaders of big-business, who were not attacked in the Nazi revolution.

4. Hitler introduced the persecution gradually and almost unobtrusively.

   (a) Initially he awarded state pensions to dismissed Jewish civil servants.

   (b) He suspended action during the 1936 Olympic Games.

   (c) After *Kristallnacht,** aware of public disquiet, he proceeded more slowly.

   (d) The "Final Solution" was decided and carried out in semi-secrecy; Hitler himself never signing a paper which would later have provided unequivocal evidence of his responsibility.

Timeline of Hitler's Racist Rule	
1933 July	Sterilization Law passed
1935 Sep 15	Nuremberg Laws enacted
1938 Nov	*Kristallnacht.*
1939	Hitler secretly authorized euthanasia programme
1941	Catholic Bishop of Munster denounced euthanasia programme
1941 Jun 6	Hitler and Croat fascist leader Anton Pavelic plot ethnic cleansing of Serbs, Roma, etc. in Croatia
1942 Jan	Wansee Conference

The *Reich:* Popularity and Opposition

The Popularity of the Third Reich

1. Because of the long period of chaos and humiliation dating from 1918, people yearned for strong government by a strong man would knock the country into shape. Hitler seemed to be that man.
2. Hitler provided spectacles for the people: military parades, torchlight processions and fireworks displays, especially the Nuremberg Rallies. These:
   (a) reassuringly demonstrated the imposition of order upon society;
   (b) gave Germans a new sense of national pride.
3. Hitler was successful in eliminating unemployment. When he came to power in 1933 there were 6,000,000 unemployed; by 1935 under 2,000,000 and by 1939 none. This was due to:
   (a) Public works schemes, e.g. the autobahns.
   (b) A large Party bureaucracy provided thousands of new jobs.
   (c) The purges of Jews, Communists, Socialists and others created new job vacancies.
   (d) Rearmament began in 1934.
   (e) Conscription was reintroduced in 1935.
   (f) Women were returned from working like to the kitchen.
4. Hitler was careful to keep the loyalty of the workers:
   (a) The *Kraft durch Freude* (Strength through Joy) organisation provided:
      (i) subsidised holidays;
      (ii) cheap theatre and concert tickets;
      (iii) convalescent homes.
   (b) Rents and many prices were controlled.
5. Wealthy industrialists were pleased to:
   (a) feel safe from Communists;
   (b) get rid of the trades unions;
   (c) enjoy the profits of economic recovery.
6. Farmers were pleased because:
   (a) Prices paid for agricultural produce were fixed, ensuring a reliable return;
   (b) farms became inherited and could not be mortgaged to pay off debts.
7. The Army was pleased at:
   (a) Hitler's plans for rearmament, ignoring the provisions of the Treaty of Versailles.
   (b) The way he dealt with the *SA* in the "Night of the Long Knives."
8. Hitler's anti-Semitism was very popular with much of the population.
9. Although the people did not want another war like the First World War, Hitler's early foreign policy successes in removing the humiliation of Versailles and expanding German territory were very popular, and Hitler gained in popularity with every success.

Opposition to the Hitler and the Reich

1. Hitler was a controversial politician, and aroused great opposition. There were to be over 40 attempts on his life – all unsuccessful.
2. On taking power Hitler was able to rely upon several already existing Nazi organisations, in addition to state organisations, to impose control over society, e.g. the *SA* and *SS*; while the Gestapo was set up.
3. The groups who would have been expected to oppose the coming to power of the Nazis were the Communists and Socialists, the trades unions, the Jews and old-fashioned monarchists. All were targeted on coming to power, and subjected to ruthless repression.

(a) Leaders of opposition groups were immediately arrested.

(b) On May 1st 1933, the trades unions were replaced by tame Nazi organisations (following Mussolini).

(c) Extra-legal action was frequently taken against those considered as trouble-makers. e.g. Accused people found not guilty were arrested on leaving the court and taken away to concentration camps. The Gestapo was not numerous; it usually merely investigated information volunteered to it by citizens.

(d) Concentration camps were opened to hold and intimidate the opposition. By 1939, 150,000 Communists and Social Democrats had been interned. Many had fled the country. These were mostly workers.

4. The Churches, as alternative sources of ideology and authority, were dealt with next by bringing religion under state control.

(a) The Catholic Church compromised itself when the Pope signed a concordat with Hitler, recognising the legitimacy of his regime. Having given a promise that the Roman Catholic Church would not be interfered with, Hitler then promptly dissolved the Catholic Youth League, which was a rival to the Hitler Youth. In 1937 the pope expressed his disquiet about what he saw as the infringement of traditional Church rights in an encyclical letter *Mit Brennender Sorge.*

However, increased attendance at public rituals and the practice of applauding Church leaders in public expressed continuing support for the Church under adverse circumstances.

(b) A *Reich* Church was organised for all Protestants under a Nazi "First *Reich* Bishop". Some who protested were interned in concentration camps. Subsequently, a "Confessing Church" was founded by Pastor Niemoller for those Protestants who refused to conform to the state. In 1938 Niemoller was interned in a concentration camp.

5. Otto Strasser, brother of Gregor Strasser, formed the **Black Front**, based in Prague, of ex-Nazis and Jews who made several attempts n Hitler's life, but Strasser was forced to flee to Canada when Hitler put pressure on Czechoslovakia during the Sudeten Crisis.

6. When the Nuremberg Laws began to exclude Jews from German society, the large number of young Jews forced out of university provided potential plotters against Hitler. Thus one assassinated the leader of the Swiss Nazis.

7. The *SA* became a major problem to Hitler once he was in power, because of the size and radical nature of its membership, and the ambitions of its leader, and were emasculated during the Night of the Long Knives, using the *SS*. The *SA* were little more than a parading force afterwards. But although the mass of *SA* remained loyal to Hitler, during the next year there were more than 150 assassinations of SS men by betrayed SA men known as "**Rohm's Avengers.**"

8. The *Wehrmacht* remained the only organisation capable of unseating Hitler.

(a) His policy of immediate rearmament in defiance of the terms of the Treaty of Versailles was popular with the generals.

(b) Conscription brought many Nazis into the army in the lower ranks.

(c) Hitler appeased them over the *SA* with the Night of the Long Knives.

However, some leaders were alarmed at Hitler's war plans and reckless approach to international relations. They formed a small secret anti-Nazi movement under the protection of Admiral Canaris, head of the *Abwehr* (the German military intelligence agency). When it was clear that Hitler intended to invade Czechoslovakia in September 1938, Colonel Ludwig Beck, Chief of the Army General Staff, resigned in protest. He and his successor, General Halder, together with former economy minister Schacht, planned to depose and kill Hitler to prevent a general war. They made contacts with the British and French, and asked them to stand firm over the Munich Crisis. They would kill Hitler to defuse the crisis. Instead Chamberlain followed a path of appeasement. (exposed by Patricia Meehan in *The Unnecessary War: Whitehall and the German Resistance to Hitler* (London: Sinclair-Stevenson, 1992)) and the coup collapsed. this was to be the last chance to prevent the world war.

(d) When sixteen generals were retired and forty-four relocated, the army was transformed into a body dominated by Hitler. Thus War Minister Blomberg and Army Chief of Staff Fritsch were dismissed on false charges. Others were bribed into acquiescence with money or promotion.

9. As Hitler's many foreign policy successes, and then the initially overwhelming German military victories, conspired to make Hitler's position unassailable after 1938 except by assassination.

Opposition during the Second World War

1. Throughout the war Hitler carefully cultivated the support of the general population. He never asked them to undergo the hardships which e.g. the British population were asked to undergo by the British government.
2. The resistance working under the protection of the *Abwehr*:*
   (a) gave the allies important information about Hitler's secret war plans;
   (b) gave people advance warning if the Gestapo was seeking them;
   (c) covered resistance actions;
   (d) helped Jews escape from Germany;
   (e) communicated between the different circles of the resistance.
3. The **Kreisau Circle**, including Graf Helmut von Moltke, Adam von Trott, and others, planned for a Germany "after Hitler" during winter 1941-2.
4. Several attempts were made by anti-Nazis under the protection of the *Abwehr* to kill Hitler:
   (a) General von Treskow put a bomb in Hitler's plane, in a package that looked like bottles of spirit, but it failed to go off.
   (b) Colonel Freiherr Von Gersdorff agreed to sacrifice his life to ensure that Hitler would die with him. Army Group Centre organized an exhibition of war flags taken from the defeated Russian army in the Military Museum in Berlin. Gersdorff carried two bombs. They needed ten minutes to go off, and Hitler rushed through in eight, so they were defused.
   (c) Axel von dem Bussche was supposed to "model" new uniforms in front of Hitler and his Nazi leaders. It was planned that Bussche would wear a bomb. But the new uniforms were destroyed in an air raid, and Bussche was wounded on the front, so the modelling session was cancelled.
5. When the commanders of the *Abwehr* smuggled 15 Jews from Germany to Switzerland with a large amount of money, the Gestapo discovered what had happened. Soon after that, the *Abwehr* was dissolved and its functions taken over by the SS. Klaus Schenk count Von Stauffenberg met Beck and he started to work immediately. He collected the ruins of the military section of the resistance and got it on its feet again. He convinced many officers to join the movement, including his brother, Berthold Von Stauffenberg, who was a high military judge in the navy.
6. During 1942-3 a student resistance group in the university of Munich known as the **White Rose** wrote leaflets, left them in public places, and mailed them to students and professors all over Germany. They attacked the regime and its crimes: from the extermination of the Polish nobility and intellectual elite and the Jews, to the elimination of the personal freedom of the Germans. On 13th July, 1943, the Gauliter of Bavaria, Paul Gisler, called all the students in Munich to a rally. He announced that male students who could not serve in the army must work in factories, and the female students must bear a child for Hitler every year! All the female students walked

Timeline of opposition to Hitler's Rule	
1937	Encyclical letter *Mit Brennender Sorge*
1938	Abortive Generals' plot
1941	Catholic Bishop of Munster denounced euthanasia programme
	Kreisau Circle formed
1942-3	White Rose formed and suppressed
1944	
Jul 20	Failure of the Stauffenberg Plot

out in protest, and when Gisler ordered their arrest, the male students took the Nazi student leader hostage, and ejected Gisler. They then demonstrated. Leaflets calling upon German youth to overthrow the regime were handed out by the White Rose and other students.

The demonstrations were suppressed, and the members of the White Rose received death sentences.

7. When the Red Army was advancing on Berlin Stauffenberg and others decided that they must kill Hitler and overthrow his regime to prove the world that there were moral Germans. Stauffenberg was to attend a meeting with Hitler and General Keitel on 20th July 1944. He was to leave two bombs in a briefcase, excuse himself, and return to Berlin and launch a military coup. After Stauffenberg had left the room one of the officers kicked Stauffenberg's bag, and pushed it behind the table. The heavy wooden table protected Hitler from the blast.

The coup plotters delayed until Stauffenberg reached them, so did not have time to implement the coup before the Nazis could take control of the situation. The plotters were executed.

Reasons for the Ineffectiveness of the opposition to Hitler and the Nazis

This was due to the following:

1. Once Hitler took all the reins of power into his hands, there was no legitimate constitutional authority above the dictator, like the king in Italy, which could be used to dismiss him.
2. The popularity of Hitler and his ideas with a significant sector of the public, increasing with diplomatic and military successes. This led to a willingness by the population to spy on each other on behalf of the regime, so that people enforced conformity on each other.
3. The speed and ruthlessness with which Hitler and the Nazis acted to decapitate opposition movements in 1933 and afterwards deterred opposition.
4. The repeated refusals of the British Foreign Office to act on information, warnings and pleas from the German anti-Nazi opposition, destroyed an opportunity to engineer a coup, replace Hitler and prevent a world war.
5. By demanding unconditional surrender, instead of offering a gesture of support to any post-Nazi government, the allies made it difficult for the opposition to recruit support.
6. The opposition consisted of isolated and rival groups from the right and left wings which could not work together.
7. During the last years of the war the inexorable advance of the victorious Red Army upon Germany paralysed the German people with fear. :
   (a) Racist propaganda had convinced them that the Slavs were sub-human.
   (b) Most probably knew something of the excesses of the German soldiers in their "racial war" in the East, and must have felt guilt, or at least fear of revenge.
8. Hitler was incredibly lucky in surviving many attempts on his life.

Assessment of Hitler's Rule

Hitler's Domestic Policy (1933-41)

Two opposing views are:

1. Hitler's domestic policy was very successful. Had he avoided war he would have imposed a new order on Germany. His regime was only undermined by the war.

    (a) Full employment was restored by 1939.

    (b) Wages rose by 50% on average between 1933 and 1937. Together with fixed rents and a decline in the cost of living, this meant a rise in the standard of living for most Germans.

    (c) The support of the workers was purchased with benefits:

        (i) holidays with pay;

        (ii) controls on rents;

        (iii) The **Strength through Joy** Programme (*Kraft durch Freude*), which provided subsidised holidays and cruises, and reduced price theatre and concert tickets.

    (d) Farmers benefited from the struggle for autarchy:

        (i) Fixed prices assured farmers of a profit;

        (ii) Farms could no longer be seized for debt, but had to be passed on to the next of kin on the death of the farmer;

    (e) Businessmen:

        (i) felt safe from Communist revolution;

        (ii) were no longer troubled by strikes;

        (iii) could make profits from public works schemes and rearmament.

    (f) The Army were content with the purge of the *SA* in the Night of the Long Knives.

2. Hitler's successes were superficial, and his policies were doomed to failure anyway, even without the war. The reasons for this are:

    (a) Full employment was achieved only by:

        (i) rearmament;

        (ii) the creation of a party bureaucracy;

        (iii) the purges of various sections of the population;

        (iv) the removal of women from the workforce.

    (b) Autarchy was not possible for Germany without military expansion. It crucially depended upon the exploitation of other countries, and this would necessitate war.

Hitler as a War Leader

Initially, Hitler was very successful.

1. The *Blitzkrieg* method of fighting initially produced spectacular results.

2. By the Molotov-Ribbentrop Pact he had effectively modified the Schlieffen Plan to achieve the defeat of France.

3. As a result of his conquests, he dominated the continent more than any other figure in history. By 1941 Hitler had succeeded in warfare as no German leader ever had before.

    (a) The Treaty of Versailles was overthrown,

    (b) France defeated

    (c) the pre-1918 boundaries of Germany exceeded,

    (d) all ethnic German areas included within the Reich,

    (e) Germany dominated Europe from Scandinavia to the Balkans.

But after 1941, his leadership was a catalogue of errors.

4. Hitler probably never took his war against Britain seriously. He was always prepared to do a

deal. So he did not commit Germany militarily to the invasion of Britain. At a critical point he diverted the *Luftwaffe* to the bombing of cities, allowing the RAF to recover.

5. The *Blitzkrieg* invasion of Russia was his chief mistake. With Britain unsubdued, he chose to enter upon a war on two fronts. So sure of victory was he that his soldiers had not been equipped for the coming winter. This failed *Blitzkrieg* landed him with a war of attrition he could not win. He clearly underestimated the Soviets due to his racial contempt for the Slavs and his belief in the superiority of the Aryan master race.

6. At and following the siege of Stalingrad, when on the defensive, Hitler
   (a) refused to allow tactical retreat, and so lost forces, thus he refused to allow von Paulus to make an orderly withdrawal, losing the Sixth Army;
   (b) placed his hope in the ultimate dissolution of the Grand Alliance.

7. Hitler gratuitously declared war on the USA after Pearl Harbour, considering it:
   (a) a racially mixed state, and degenerate power for that reason;
   (b) "permanently on the brink of revolution";
   (c) preoccupied with the war in the Pacific, which the Japanese would win.
   Hitler's contempt was misplaced, since the USA would be an important factor in a war of attrition.

8. Despite everything, Hitler was unprepared for the war of attrition which he had brought about by 1942.
   (a) He faced two of the greatest industrial powers in history. The German economy could not hope to outproduce those of the USA and the USSR.
   (b) In any case, the German economy never adjusted to war as well as that of eg. Britain.
      (i) The Nazis refused to conscript women into industry, preferring slave labour;
      (ii) They depended upon plunder of newly-acquired territories to supply resources, and when these ceased, they fell short.

9. Hitler failed to co-opt the conquered people in his support. In large areas of Eastern Europe, the invading Germans were initially treated as liberators. They forfeited this support by their arrogance and cruelty, justified by their racist beliefs, exemplified by arbitrary punishment of civilians, slave labour, etc. In the later years of the war they did recruit non-Germans to the *SS,* and even established a Russian anti-Soviet regiment. But by that time it was too late.

10. During the invasion of the USSR, Hitler frequently changed his mind about the most important objectives, e.g. moving from Leningrad to the Ukraine.

11. Allied equipment was often better than that of the Germans: Soviet *KV* and *T-34* tanks, *Katyusha* rockets; British *Spitfire* and *Hurricane* fighter planes.

12. Hitler made his scientists focus upon rocket technology, which required some development, instead of improving technology already available.

14. He placed too much confidence in the Atlantic Wall, the defences along the Channel coast.

15. He fell back upon the hope that the Allied coalition would break up, and that this would save him.

16. In the end he totally lost contact with reality, ordering the movement of armies which had already ceased to exist.

Hitler as a Dictator

1. Hitler was portrayed as a "strong leader," and some historians, e.g. Alan Bullock agree.
2. Other historians, eg. Martin Brozsat, argue that Hitler was a weak dictator.
 The Government of the Third Reich became increasingly chaotic as time passed.
   (a) Hitler seems to have followed a policy of "divide and rule":

Hitler's Allies	
Hermann Göring	World War I ace fighter pilot - joined Nazis 1922 as leader of *SA* - 1933 Minister for Prussia, imposed *Gleichschaltung* - from 1935 Head of the *Luftwaffe* - from 1936 controlled the economy
Ernst Röhm	professional soldier - joined Party in 1919 - in 1930 took over *SA* and expanded it - reluctantly killed in the Night of the Long Knives 1934
Gregor Strasser	Joined Party in 1920 - reorganised the Party structure after 1925 - developed a socialist approach to Nazism- offered vice-Chancellorship in 1932 by von Schliecher - killed in the Night of the Long Knives 1934
Heinrich Himmler	*Reichsführer SS* - responsible for concentration camps, *Einsatzgruppen* and extermination camps - responsible for "racial cleansing"
Joseph Göbbels	Joined Party 1924 - Gauleiter of Berlin - from 1933 Propaganda Minister
J. von Ribbentrop	Joined Party 1932 - Foreign Minister 1933-45
Rudolf Hess	Joined Party 1922 - became Hitler's deputy - in 1941 flew to Scotland to negotiate peace - imprisoned
Albert Speer	Party architect - friend of Hitler - designed future Reich capital - from 1942 Minister of Armaments

(i) often creating two or more positions with overlapping duties;

(ii) blurring the lines of command.

Although he did permit the development of some large accumulations of power, e.g. by Göring and Himmler.

(b) He worked by using relations of personal loyalty rather than bureaucratic hierarchy. Thus he usually supported the right of his *Gauleiters* to govern their *Gaue* as they wished, even though they might be pursuing policies at cross-purposes with each other or with the central government. Thus his rule was feudal rather than bureaucratic. The most important decisions were made by his confidants, not the relevant government ministers.

(c) Hitler's personal style of rule was undisciplined, non-bureaucratic and idiosyncratic

(i) He was lazy.

(ii) He rarely bothered to put his orders in writing, many took the form of casual remarks.

(iii) He was inclined to ignore or brush aside matters he regarded as too trivial for his attention.

(d) Hitler was distrustful of traditional centres of power and influence, such as cabinet ministers, civil servants and judges. Traditional government was not demolished but bypassed and compromised. Thus he rarely held cabinet meetings or met with ministers.

(e) A charismatic* leader, he was extremely careful of his public image and popularity, for his legitimacy was based upon his direct personal relationship with the German people. He was always afraid that loss of his personal popularity would lead to a domestic crisis. Thus he frequently refrained from making decisions until it was clear which would be the most popular alternative, and avoided unpopular decisions. Thus at times his leadership was remarkably passive.

(f) A believer in Social Darwinism, Hitler was inclined to let supporters of rival positions fight it out, then side with the winner. He was also tolerant of infighting among his subordinates, regarding it as healthy.

The Uniqueness of Hitler and the Nazi Movement

This question is seen as important because of the destructiveness of Hitler and the Nazi regime.

1. Golo Mann argued that Hitler was an anomaly in German history. He and his Nazis imposed their will on the country like foreign conquerors.
2. Alan Bullock argues that Hitler and the Nazis stood squarely in the tradition of German political thought, and was its natural outcome. Hitler's ideas were all taken from German tradition:
    (a) nationalism,
    (b) racism,
    (c) Social Darwinism,
    (d) glorification of war,
    (e) expansionism and the wish to dominate Europe and find *Lebensraum* in the East,
    (f) admiration of the leader,
    (g) anti-Semitism.
   He was unique only in being ruthless and dynamic in applying them.
3. Hitler and Nazism could be regarded as:
    (a) A logical development of earlier German racist nationalism
    (b) A reaction to the instability and chaos of the times, and the need for order and national unity and the recovery of national self-respect (CF Italian Fascism)
    (c) A creation of the *bourgeoisie* as a defence against the threat of Bolshevism.
    (d) A result of the stresses of the move from a pre-capitalist to a capitalist form of society.

Glossary

abdicate give up the throne

Abwehr German Military Intelligence

anti-Semitism prejudice against Jews

armistice a cease-fire

Aryan blond-haired, blue-eyed race from which the Germans derived their ancestry according to Nazi doctrine

autarchy (autarky) economic self-sufficiency

blockade a siege by sea

charismatic able to command by force of personality

concordat a treaty concluded with the Pope

Confessing Church a Protestant movement which refused to accept the Nazification of the German Protestants

DAP German Workers' Party

draconian very severe

egalitarianism stressing equality of status among people

Einsatzgruppen SS execution squads

eugenics control of the breeding stock to ensure the health of the race

euthanasia normally: mercy-killing; but here: deliberate killing of biologically imperfect people to ensure the health of the race

Freikorps right-wing paramilitary groups composed of ex-servicemen

Gauleiters Nazi officials responsible for control of a region (*Gau*)

Gestapo (*Geheime Staatspolizei*) political police force

Holocaust the attempted genocide of the European Jews

hyperinflation extreme runaway inflation

Kristallnacht "the night of broken glass," *pogrom* against the Jews

Länder local parliaments

Lebensraum living space

nationalization a state takeover of private enterprises

Liebstandarte Hitler's bodyguard, a section of the *SS*

NCOs Non-commissiond officers

November criminals name given to all those who were held to have "betrayed Germany" in 1918: Communists, Jews, liberals, etc.

NSDAP National Socialist German Workers' Party

pogrom

proportional representation an electoral system which ensures that the relative proportion of Members of Parliament elected reflects the relative proportion of the total votes cast

Putsch attempted coup d'état

racism an ideology which justifies unequal treatment of different races

Reichstag the German Parliament

Reichswehr The German Army (term used until 1935)

retroactive legislation laws which turn actions performed in the past into crimes

Roma gypsies

Schutzstaffel (SS) originally Hitler's personal bodyguard it was reorganised for wider duties in 1925. In 1929 Himmler became its head and greatly expanded its responsibilities and numbers.

Slums old, poor-quality housing

social Darwinism an ideology based upon the survival of the fittest

Spartacists members of Rosa Luxemburg's extreme leftist Spartacus League

Sturmabteilung (SA) Nazi paramilitary organisation - the Brownshirts, Röhm became its head in 1930.

Totenkopfverbände the "Death's Head" units of the *SS*, which ran the concentration camps

Völkisch to do with the nation (conceived racially as a common blood stock)

Wehrmacht the German Army (term used after 1935)

Wehrwirtschaft the war economy

*Nikita Sergeevich
Khrushchev*

Khrushchev's USSR

"Without Khrushchev there would have been no Gorbachev." (Martin McCauley)

Khrushchev's Rise to Power
The Soviet leadership on Stalin's death

1. No successor had been nominated by Stalin, as this would have been too dangerous to his own position. The old, smaller Politburo of ten members was restored. The leading members decided upon a collective leadership:

    Malenkov - Chairman of the Council of Ministers, First Secretary of the CP;
    Voroshilov - Chairman of the Presidium of the Supreme Soviet;
    Beria - Chief of Security Police;
    Molotov - Foreign Minister;
    Bulganin - Minister of Defence;
    Mikoyan - Minister of Foreign Trade.

    Clearly, Malenkov had the leading position as head of both the government and the party.

2. Georgy Malenkov, born near Moscow, entered the Red Army (1919) during the civil war, joined the Communist Party of the Soviet Union (CPSU) in 1920, and rose swiftly through the ranks. He became closely associated with Stalin, and was deeply involved in the purges of the late 1930s. A candidate member of the Politburo in 1941, he served during World War II on the State Defence Committee. After the war Malenkov won full membership on the Politburo (1946) and was second secretary of the Central Committee and deputy prime minister. He became involved in a bitter rivalry with A. A. Zhdanov, as a result of whose charges he was relieved of one of his party posts (1946). But within two years he had regained his position as one of Stalin's chief lieutenants.

3. Unlike Lenin and many other Soviet leaders, who had generally middle-class backgrounds, Nikita S. Khrushchev was the son of a coal miner; his grandfather had been a serf. After a village education, Khrushchev went to Yuzovka (later Stalino, now Donetsk), a mining and industrial centre in the Donets Basin, where he began work as a pipe fitter at the age of 15. Because of his job, he was not conscripted in the tsarist army during World War I. He became active in workers' organisations, and in 1918 he became a member of the Party.

.   In January 1919 he joined the Red Army and served as a junior political commissar. His first wife, Galina, died during a famine. In 1922 Khrushchev entered the new workers' school in Yuzovka, where he received a secondary education. He became a student political leader and married Nina Petrovna, a schoolteacher. In 1925 Khrushchev became a full-time party worker, and came to the notice of Kaganovich, secretary general of the Ukrainian Party Central Committee.

In 1929 he received permission to go to Moscow to study metallurgy at the Stalin Industrial Academy. There he was appointed secretary of the academy's Party Committee. In 1931 he went back to full-time party work in Moscow. By 1933 he had become second secretary of the Moscow Regional Committee.

During the early 1930s Khrushchev supervised the completion of the prestigious **Moscow subway**, became a full member of the Central Committee of the Communist Party of the Soviet Union (CPSU), and in 1935 first secretary of the Moscow party, in effect, the mayor. Khrushchev was a supporter of Stalin and participated in the purges. He was one of only three provincial secretaries who survived the Yezhovshchina, and was sent to Kiev as first secretary of the Ukrainian party, and made a full member of the Politburo. In 1940, when Soviet forces occupied eastern Poland, Khrushchev presided over the "integration" of this area into the Soviet Union. This work was disrupted by the German invasion in June 1941. Khrushchev was charged with evacuating as much of the Ukraine's industry as possible to the east. Then he was made a General in the Red Army to stimulate the resistance of the civilian population and maintain liaison with Stalin and other members of the Politburo. He was political adviser to Marshal Andrey Yeryomenko during the defence of Stalingrad (now Volgograd) and to Lieut. Gen. Nikolay F. Vatutin during the huge tank battles at Kursk. After the liberation of the Ukraine in 1944, Khrushchev worked to restore the civil administration. During the famine of 1946, he fought to restore grain production and distribute food supplies to local people, against Stalin's insistence sending production from the Ukraine to feed other areas.

In 1949 he took over his old job as head of the Moscow City Party.

The Primacy of Malenkov (1953-55)

The First Power Struggle

1. The purge of those involved in the Doctors' Plot was immediately stopped on Stalin's death and the arrested doctors released, although two were already dead.
2. Without consulting is colleagues, Beria amalgamated the MVD and MGB under his command.
3. Malenkov was made to give up the post of First Secretary of the CPSU as it concentrated too much power into his hands.
4. 10th July 1953 Beria was "unmasked as a capitalist agent." He was reported shot with accomplices six months later. He was feared by the Politburo as a potential Stalin, and his Security Police were a threat to the CPSU.
5. In Sept. 1953 Khrushchev was appointed First Secretary of the CPSU.
6. Malenkov worked during 1953-55 to:
    (a) reduce arms appropriations,
    (b) increase the production of consumer goods at the expense of heavy industry,
    (c) provide more incentives for collective farm workers.
    His policies produced a thaw in the Cold War
7. Policy differences arose between Malenkov and the majority of the Politburo, headed by Khrushchev:

(a) The current five-year plan was going badly;

(b) Agricultural output was little higher than in Tsarist times;

(c) Malenkov proposed raising the standard of living by concentrating on light industry and housing;

(d) He urged a conciliatory approach towards the West, since a third world war would mean the end of civilisation.

He was opposed by Khrushchev, (who was later to take up precisely these policies himself).

8. During late 1954 it was clear that Malenkov was in trouble. In Feb. 1955 he was replaced as by Bulganin, a nominee of Khrushchev, but kept his Politburo seat. Khrushchev emerged as the most powerful leader, having the support of:

    (a) the army,

    (b) the Ukrainian CP,

    (c) a majority in the Central Committee.

Destalinization

1. On gaining power on Stalin's death, the main problem of the Soviet leadership was to

    (a) dismantle Stalin's dictatorship;

    (b) yet prevent his entire system from collapsing, and bringing chaos to the USSR.

2. Stalin's unconstitutional and powerful private secretariat was abolished.

3. News of the death of Stalin and the execution of Beria caused major risings in the labour camps e.g. Norilsk (N. Siberia) May 1953, and Kengir (Kazakhstan) May 1954.

4. The insurgents took over the camps, disarming the guards, and refused to work, demanding:

    (a) a re-examination of all sentences;

    (b) better rations;

    (c) shorter working days;

    (d) the right to frequent correspondence;

    (e) the right to frequent visitors;

    (f) the elimination of numbers from prison clothes,

    (g) the removal of bars from the windows,

    (h) the removal of bolts from the doors of the huts within the wire compounds;

    (i) no reprisals for the revolt;

    (j) (in Kengir) punishment for those responsible for shooting prisoners.

5. The principles behind these demands were:

    (a) better conditions for the prisoners;

    (b) some respect for basic human dignity.

6. The disturbances were dealt with by a mixture of compromise, duplicity and bloody repression, but the outcome was an improvement in living conditions in the gulag:

    (a) numbers were removed from uniforms;

    (b) bars from windows;

    (c) barracks were unlocked at night;

    (d) restrictions on correspondence eased;

    (e) visits allowed;

    (f) health care, clothing and food improved. A few *zeks** were reported sending food to relatives on the grimmer *kolkhozy.**

7. The execution of Beria set off a wave of letters and petitions from all over the country calling for charges against imprisoned relatives to be re-examined, since the official denunciation of Beria

cast doubt upon all the acts of security police under his command.

By the end of 1955, some 10,000 prisoners had been freed, and the Procuracy* began the process of rehabilitation of those convicted under Stalin as victims of "legal distortions" – many posthumously.* The Procuracy was asserting its independence of the MVD.

8. After Beria's death the Prosecuting Dept. of the MVD and the special tribunals which passed summary sentences, were abolished. In future, criminal investigation was to be carried on before the regular courts, under authorities answerable to the Party and the government.

9. The security police was downgraded:

    (a) detached from the MVD empire and renamed the KGB (Committee of State security);

    (b) placed under the control of the Council of Ministers;

    (c) run by men who had made their careers in the Party and not the NKVD;

    (d) the number of paid agents and informers was drastically reduced.

10. These measures ensured:

    (a) the accountability of the security police to the Party and the government;

    (b) at least outwardly that minimum standards of legality would be observed;

    (c) restoration of power to the Party from the security apparatus.

11. By 1954 the Central Committee had set up a special commission under P. N. Pospelov to collect evidence on Stalin's repression of party cadres. Khrushchev later claimed that the results of this inquiry surprised the leadership.

12. In May 1955, when Khrushchev made his first trip outside the Soviet Union, to Yugoslavia, he began to show his flexibility; he apologised to Tito for Stalin's denunciation of Yugoslav Communism.

The Denunciation of Stalin

1. In a special closed session, on the day after the official closing of the Twentieth National Congress of the CPSU, Khrushchev denounced Stalin for:

    (a) his personality cult;

    (b) usurping power from the party;

    (c) the purges and repression since 1934;

    (d) his conduct of the war;

    (e) Khrushchev claimed that socialism could be developed in ways other than Stalin's;

    (f) and suggested that peaceful coexistence with the west was essential to avoid nuclear war.

2. But, he:

    (a) limited his accusations to Stalin and his principal security chiefs;

    (b) ignored his own and colleagues' responsibility;

    (c) ignored Stalin's repression of the kulaks, etc. before 1934;

    (d) affirmed the correctness of Stalin's:

        (i) super-fast industrialisation;

        (ii) and collectivisation of agriculture.

3. This speech led to:

    (a) a breakdown of some of the fear and doublethink, in Eastern Europe; (The Party no longer had to be considered infallible.)

    (b) severe unrest in Poland and revolution in Hungary;

    (c) discontent in the USSR;

    (d) further destalinization.

    (e) Some conservatives, e.g. Molotov, were shocked;

    (f) It contributed to the Sino-Soviet split.

The Second Power Struggle (1957)

1. The stresses in eastern Europe, especially in Poland and Hungary, helped crystallise opposition to Khrushchev within the Party. By 1957 an anti-Khrushchev majority had formed in the politburo: Molotov, Shepilov, Kaganovich, Malenkov, Bulganin, Voroshilov, Pervukhin, and Saburov. In June, he was almost overthrown.
2. The anti-Khrushchev group were opposed to:
   (a) Khrushchev's style of leadership;
   (b) his economic policies;
   (c) the speed and nature of destalinization;
   (d) the pursuit of peaceful coexistence;
   (e) and held him responsible for the troubles in E. Europe and discontent in the USSR caused by his "secret speech " to the 20th Congress of the CPSU.
3. In June 1957 Khrushchev was confronted by a demand that he step down and become minister of agriculture. He refused to resign, except at the behest of the Central Committee, as was his right, and kept them talking while Marshal Georgy Zhukov, the Minister of Defence, mobilised Khrushchev's supporters in the Central Committee and got them to the Kremlin. As party leader Khrushchev had filled the Central Committee with his supporters.
4. Khrushchev's opponents were labelled the **Anti-Party Group** because they opposed the Party's running the state, regarding that as the government's function.
5. The Central Committee supported Khrushchev since:
   (a) 60% were republic and oblast secretaries, he was their patron;
   (b) they mistrusted the old guard and were enjoying their new freedom;
   (c) Khrushchev was making a genuine effort to grapple with the country's problems;
   (d) he had raised the status and power of the party.
6. Molotov, Malenkov, and Kaganovich were removed from the Presidium and the Central Committee, and their political careers came to an end. The leaders of the "anti-party group" were demoted to honourable but distant posts,
   e.g. Molotov to be Soviet ambassador to Mongolia,
   Malenkov to run a power station in Siberia.
   This marked a new tolerance within the ruling elite.
7. In October Khrushchev dismissed Marshal Georgy Zhukov from his post as Minister of Defence,
8. In March 1958 Khrushchev became chairman of the Council of Ministers, uniting headship of the Party and the government in his own person. Khrushchev was by this time in full command of Soviet policy.

The Significance of the Power Struggle

1. The unchallenged dominance of the USSR by the Party was established at this time, and it was to remain the key institution in the government of the USSR until 1991.
2. The elite which had been created by Stalin had by now become an established ruling class, who could expect to enjoy privileges even if dismissed.
3. The bloodless result of the power struggle, due entirely to Khrushchev, marked an important stage in the process of dismantling Stalin's structure of state terrorism and restoring a sense of normality to political life.
4. The means Khrushchev used to gain power:
   (a) filling the Central Committee with supporters;
   (b) isolating his opponents by opposing unpopular policies, and later adopting them;
   were the same as those used by Stalin.

The Khrushchev Era (1957-1963)

Ideology

1. Khrushchev was not a doctrinaire Marxist, but he tried to restore the ideological basis of society which had been eroded by Stalin's tyranny.

2. He believed that Soviet society had achieved socialism, and needed to move on to achieve communism. All class struggle had ended, so that the state now represented the entire people. The next steps were:

   (a) the transformation of the instruments of state power into instruments of self-government as state power "withered away."

   (b) The Party would take the lead in this, and increasingly become the expression of the will of the community.

   (c) The Party should become more responsive to the wishes of its ordinary members.

3. He forecast that by 1980 the material prerequisites of communism would be achieved, and society would be able to reward "each according to his need."

Industry

1. There was a move towards lighter industry and the production of consumer goods: radios, televisions, washing machines, sewing machines, etc.

2. Managers were urged to make profits instead of merely achieving quotas.

3. Absenteeism and quitting a job were removed from the list of crimes. Thus military discipline in the workplace was ended.

4. Khrushchev discovered that industrial and local political networks had developed, which made it very difficult for the central authority to impose its will. There was a gradual dissipation of power from Moscow to the provinces, which strengthened the Russian regions.

Agriculture

1. The "**Virgin Lands Scheme**" was an attempt to convert large areas of steppe in N. Kazakhstan, W. Siberia and SE Russia into grain producing regions. Kazakh leaders protested as:

   (a) they thought the land was unsuitable;

   (b) they did not want an influx of Russians.

   The project was initially a success. Hundreds of thousands of young people had been mobilised by Komsomol, and thousands of tractors sent. By 1956 they had tripled the 1953 harvest. Then it began to fail:

   (c) For quick results Khrushchev had discouraged the use of a crop cycle and fallow land, but had failed to provide fertilisers. The fertility of the land disappeared; soil erosion and desertification followed. Between 1960-65 half the area used was ruined.

   (d) Most volunteers lost their enthusiasm after some time, and drifted back to their homes.

   (e) There was a drought in the areas of new planting.

2. In 1957 a **livestock increasing campaign** was announced, with the aim of overtaking the USA in the production of meat, milk and butter within 4 years. To achieve the high targets set many collective farms too to stock rustling, and subsequently to overkilling the stock, so that insufficient breeding stock was left. The bubble burst in 1958.

3. The traditional grain producing region of the Ukraine was turned over to produce **maize** for cattle fodder after Khrushchev had seen the maize prairies of Iowa in 1959. At the height of this campaign 37 million hectares were under maize, of which only 7 million could be

harvested. The Ukraine is at the same latitude as Iowa, but has a damper climate —- too wet for maize production, so there was a poor maize harvest. To make matters worse, the land used for grain had been wheat land, so here was no wheat harvest there.

4. Investment in agriculture had been increased by 400%, but it was often clumsy and counter productive.
5. Machine-Tractor Stations were abolished.
6. Higher prices were charged for the produce of the *kolkhozy* in order to provide a better return for labour.
7. In 1962 the government had to raise food prices, leading to bread queues in the Ukraine and riots throughout the USSR.
8. 1963 Khrushchev decided to use the precious Soviet gold and hard currency reserve to import grain. This signalled the failure of the soviet (Stalinist) system in agriculture.

Social Services

1. Housing:
    (a) The housing stock almost doubled between 1955 and 1964.
    (b) Individual citizens were given the right to join housing co-operatives putting 15-30% down on an apartment, paying the rest at 0.5% interest. It was mostly professional people who purchased their accommodation. This indicated a stratification of society.
2. Education.
    (a) Fees were abolished for upper secondary schools and colleges;
    (b) Khrushchev wanted two years compulsory labour between school and college:
        (i) to encourage young people to take up careers in skilled manual trades
        (ii) to break the inbuilt educational advantage of the children of the professional classes
    There was strong opposition from:
        (iii) The professional classes, who passed on their advantages by education (rather than property or money);
        (iv) University teachers, who wanted well prepared students with regular habits of study;
        (v) Enterprise directors, who did not want crowds of unruly, unskilled young people hanging about their factories

The Economy

1. In 1957, in an attempt to reduce over-centralisation and encourage efficiency, 100 Regional Economic Councils (*sovnarkhozy*) were set up to take decisions about local industries, allowing 25 central ministries to be abolished.
This did not work well as co-ordination and judgement were only possible on the basis of information available in Moscow.
2. Under Khrushchev the economy performed well at first but then deteriorated due to:
    (a) failure to correct imbalances;
    (b) an acute shortage of capital, not corrected by attempts to get loans from the West;
    (c) higher military spending during 1960-3;
    (d) investment and effort spread too widely;
    (e) ill-directed political interference.
The USSR had a higher GNP per head than either Italy or Japan, but:
    (i)the quality of life of the citizens was lower;
    (ii) the quality of goods produced was lower.

Destalinization

1. The Government: Khrushchev's radical innovations included abolishing most of the central ministries (except for the defence sector) and devolving economic decision making to more than 100 economic councils. This policy was intended to do two things:

(a) It would reduce the power of Khrushchev's main rivals in the Party Presidium, which was dominated by those holding government posts;

(b) it would improve economic performance by allowing decisions to be made at the local level.

2. The Party:

(a) Khrushchev's practice of giving jobs to defeated opponents, who would retain some of their privileges, meant new security for the governing class;

(b) At the 22nd National Congress of the CPSU it as decided that:

(i) The state must be replaced by the party as society moved towards communism;

(ii) Ideology was not to be a cover for the exercise of power, its real meaning should be restored;

(iii) There must be limitations on how long a cadre could hold office:

at Politburo level – not more than 3 terms of 4 years;

at Central Committee level - not more than 4 of 4 yrs. (unless supported by 3/4 of the members in secret ballot);

at SSR level – 3 terms of 4 years;

at *Oblast** level – 3 terms of 2 years;

at *Raion** and *gorod** level – 2 terms of 2 yrs.

(c) The party was to be organised at oblast level and below according to the "production Principle," with everyone specialising in either industry or agriculture.

(d) It was intended in time to replace many full-time cadres with part-timers or volunteers. All this was viewed as an affront by full-time cadres*, who assumed that they had a job with special privileges for life.

3. The Law:

(a) 1958 New Criminal Code was published:

(i) Civilians only to be convicted in properly constituted courts i.e. no military tribunals;

(ii) Civilians only to be convicted for contravening a specific article of the criminal code, i.e. no convictions for being a relative of someone previously convicted, or for belonging to a particular group, or under vague charges such as being an "enemy of the people."

(iii) No convictions on the basis of the unsupported confession of the accused;

(iv) Sentences to be sharply reduced.

(b) Absenteeism and quitting a job were removed from the list of crimes. Workplace military discipline had ended.

(c) The Comrade's Courts of the 1920s were revived to deal with minor offences. Local soviets, trade unions or housing committees could set them up. Penalties limited to fines up to 50 roubles, corrective labour without custody or recommendation for demotion, dismissal from work or eviction. They were little used, as they aroused petty jealousies and quarrels.

(d) Legality was circumvented by the authorities by use of the "Parasite Law (1957)", vaguely worded as "living on non-labour income," and used to sack someone disliked and to prevent re-employment, e.g. It was used against priests and monks.

4. The Nationalities:

(a) He rehabilitated nearly all of the deported nationalities; the accusations of disloyalty made against them by Stalin were declared to be false. This allowed many nationalities to return to their homelands within Russia. Exceptions were:

(i) The Volga Germans: Their lands had been occupied by Russians who opposed their return.

(ii) The Crimean Tatars were similarly not allowed to return to their home territory. Russians and Ukrainians had replaced them, and in 1954 Khrushchev made Crimea part of the Ukraine.

(b) Khrushchev considered that all Soviet national groups would come closer together and eventually coalesce; the Russians, being the dominant group. Instead, there was a flowering of national cultures during Khrushchev's administration.

5. The Arts: This was a period of uncertainty and inconsistency. Boris Pasternak was condemned for *Dr. Zhivago* and not allowed to receive his Nobel Prize, but on the other hand, Alexander Solzhenitsyn was able to publish *A Day in the Life of Ivan Denisovich*. This was followed by a wave of memoirs of *zeks*.

In 1962 the politburo set up an Ideological Committee to regulate censorship.

6. Religion: Religious dissenters were dealt with more harshly than under Stalin. Paradoxically, oppression of the church was part of Khrushchev's destalinization policy:

(a) It marked a return to "Leninist orthodoxy";

(b) It would gain him the support of anti-clericals and appease the purists he had otherwise alienated.

7. Khrushchev was a patriot who genuinely wanted to improve the lot of all Soviet citizens. Under his leadership there was a cultural thaw, and Russian writers who had been suppressed began to publish again. Western ideas about democracy began to penetrate universities and academies. These were to leave their mark on a whole generation of Russians, most notably Mikhail Gorbachev, who was the last leader of the Soviet Union. Khrushchev had led the Soviet Union away from the harsh Stalin period. Under his rule Russia continued to dominate the union but with considerably more concern for minorities.

Foreign Policy

[For a more detailed study of Khrushchev's foreign policy see the companion volume "The Cold War"]

1. Khrushchev came to adopt the policy of peaceful coexistence with the West, which he had first opposed under Malenkov, and then expounded in a speech at the 20th Congress of the CPSU. At the 21st Congress of the CPSU in 1959 he said: "We offer the capitalist countries peaceful competition."

2. On Aug. 26, 1957, the USSR announced the successful firing of an intercontinental ballistic missile. On October 4th, the first orbiting space satellite, *Sputnik 1*, was launched, followed on November 3 by *Sputnik 2*. The USA felt their world hegemony threatened.

3. Khrushchev decided to rely for deterrence upon rocketry. This led him to cut the size of the military. He also tried to use the USSR's missile resources as diplomatic weapons, threatening retaliation if the West attacked the USSR. But US leaders used this to convince their people of the need for greater defence spending, creating an expensive arms race.

4. Khrushchev visited the United States, the first Soviet leader to do so, and toured the country. He conferred with Presidents Eisenhower and Kennedy.

5. The US illegally spied on the USSR and other countries by overflying their territory taking photographs using high-flying U-2 spy planes, believing that these could not be shot down. But on May 1st 1960, one was shot down near Sverdlovsk (now Yekaterinburg) in the Urals, and the pilot, Gary Powers, was captured. The US Government lied, claiming that

they had not lost a plane, then the Soviets produced photographs of the wreckage, showing its American markings. Then the Americans asserted that it was a weather research plane which had got lost due to a navigational error. So the Soviets produced the pilot, one Gary Powers, who admitted everything, including the fact that he had been given a cyanide capsule to swallow in case he came down in Soviet territory. This led to the collapse of the Paris summit in the same month, when Khrushchev demanded that Eisenhower make an apology for violating Soviet air space and lying about it. Eisenhower refused.

6. In 1961 a conference in Vienna with the new US president John F. Kennedy, led to no agreement on the German question. Shortly afterwards, the Berlin Wall was built.

7. Relations deteriorated during the Cuban missile crisis of October 1962. In 1962 Khrushchev had placed Soviet medium-range missiles in Cuba:

   (a) to counter the similar threat of US missiles on the Soviet border in Turkey;

   (b) to prevent an invasion of Cuba which was being planned in Washington.

President Kennedy provoked a tense confrontation in October, when both the superpowers stood on the brink of war. The US navy blockaded Cuba, while Soviet ground commanders in Cuba had the authority to launch a missile to defend themselves if attacked, without approval from Moscow. As Kennedy was unwilling to back down, and nuclear war was the only alternative, Khrushchev backed off. The Chinese and Cubans criticised him for giving in to United States aggression, but Khrushchev had saved the world from nuclear war.

8. Made aware of the dangers of such confrontations, the USSR, USA and United Kingdom signed the Nuclear Test-Ban Treaty in August 1963. Direct communications were established between Moscow and Washington with the "hot line."

9. A split developed between the USSR and China.

   (a) The Chinese resented Khrushchev's denunciation of Stalin.

   (b) The Chinese were disappointed by the reluctance of Khrushchev to help China regain Taiwan (Formosa), in the hands of Jiang Jieshi and the Guomindang (GMD).

   (c) They insisted upon all-out "war against the imperialists," while Khrushchev favoured peaceful coexistence.

   (d) The Soviets refused to assist the Chinese nuclear weapons programme

   (e) There were border disputes in Mongolia.

   (f) The Soviets resented the independence of the Chinese Communist movement.

   Soviet technicians were pulled out of China in 1960-1. The **Sino-Soviet split** then became an open one.

The Fall of Khrushchev

1. By 1963 Khrushchev He had become unpopular because:

   (a) The party cadres resented his treatment of them and his constant reorganisations, and particularly his limitation of their time in office, which threatened their jobs;

   (b) Conservatives feared further destalinization, which might threaten "the leading role of the Party";

   (c) The military resented his neglect of the conventional armed forces in favour of missile technology;

   (d) a downturn in the economy was blamed on him;

   (e) his agricultural policies were mostly spectacular failures;

   (f) he was accused of an imprudent foreign policy (Cuba, China);

   (g) his style of leadership: with his impetuosity and indiscretion, etc. embarrassed the elite.

2. Brezhnev and others plotted to remove him, either by arresting or murdering him; but the head

of the KGB would not cooperate.

3. The conspirators on the Central Committee then took advantage when Khrushchev went on holiday to the Crimea. They plotted in his absence and called him back on 14 Oct. 1964.
   In the Central Committee Suslov took the lead and denounced him for:
     (a) the cult of his own personality;
     (b) attempting to be a specialist in every sphere;
     (c) continual meaningless reorganisations;
     (d) an imprudent and indiscreet foreign policy.

4. Khrushchev was forced to resign. He went into retirement, wrote his memoirs and became a suspected dissident.

Assessment of Khruschev's Regime

1. Khrushchev was a political pragmatist* who adapted his beliefs to the needs of the time.
2. He presided over a regime in which the Party dominated the government rather than the security apparatus, as had been the case under Stalin. The worst aspects of Stalin's rule were eliminated. The killing of Beria was to be the last political execution in the history of the Soviet Union. Deposed politicians such as Molotov and Malenkov could expect to enjoy their retirement in security and comfort.
3. He developed the USSR as a great power, launching the first orbiting space satellite, and as the chief centre of resistance to US domination of the globe.
4. He had a populist style and humanised authority in the USSR. Khrushchev valued his contacts with the Soviet people and had an instinctive empathy with their needs, which resulted in moves towards the development of a consumer economy and a relaxation of security controls, even if they met with only limited success.
5. Despite his repression of the Hungarian uprising in 1956, his acceptance of "different roads to Socialism" led to growing independence among European Communist parties.
6. His Russian nationalism, and his suspicion of Mao Zedong's distinctive form of Communism, helped create an unexpectedly deep fissure between China and the Soviet Union.
7. His imagination was limited to tinkering with the system, rather than radical reform.
   Yet:
     (a) This may have been a result of his lack of formal education
     (b) He may not have enjoyed the degree of power within the collective leadership necessary to enforce radical reforms.
     (c) There is evidence that near the end of his period of office, e.g. from his son, that he was coming to the conclusion that the CPSU was not capable, by itself, of governing the USSR.
8. His schemes were often ill-thought out. This was a consequence of:
     (a) his lack of education, particularly of a liberal education;
     (b) the remnants of Stalinist habits, which made subordinates fear to criticise any policy put forward by the leadership, however flawed;
     (c) his blunt personal style, which was intolerant of criticism.
9. He could be undiplomatic, e.g. banging a shoe on his desk at the UN. His offhand remarks occasionally generated concern, as when he told the United States, "We will bury you," and boasted that his rockets were being churned out like sausages, and could hit a fly over the United States. Such statements were employed by US governments to heighten public fears and so justify increased defence budgets. His inconsistency led to problems of inter-state relations, e.g. his statements over Berlin.

10. His liberalization of the regime opened peoples' minds to new possibilities, and despite the reaction under Brezhnev, they prepared the way for Gorbachev's later reforms.

11. **By being prepared to back down at the critical point during the nuclear confrontation provoked by Kennedy which we call the Cuban Missile Crisis, Nikita Khrushchev may be the one person in history to have really "saved the world" from nuclear disaster. Wherever we are sitting at this moment, we owe our existence, and that of the world we live in, to the humanity, common sense and courage of this man.**

Timeline of Khrushchev's Regime	
1953	Death of Stalin – Malenkov dominant – Beria shot Khrushchev appointed First Secretary of the CPSU
1954	The anti-Party Group defeated
1956	Khrushchev delivers his "secret speech"
1957	*sovnarkhozy* set up
1962	Cuban Missile Crisis
1963	Khrushchev deposed

Glossary

cadres professional party workers

Central Committee usually composed of about 300 voting and 170 non-voting members, it was the main policy-making body in the Party and contained the most important people in the Party, and normally met twice a year

Chairman of the Council of Ministers the Soviet prime minister

CPSU The Communist Party of the Soviet Union

gorod an administrative area, an urban district or city

Gulag the system of labour camps

kolkhozy collective farms

MGB The Ministry of State Security, responsible for the security police, part of the former NKVD.

MVD The Ministry of Internal Affairs, responsible for ordinary police, public order and the Gulag; part of the former NKVD.

oblast province

Politburo usually composed of about a dozen voting and half a dozen non-voting members, and chaired by the First (or General) Secretary of the CPSU, it was the real governing body of the party and country.

posthumous after death

pragmatist was concerned primarily with things that had a practical bearing on human interests

Procuracy the State Prosecutor's Department

raion an administrative area, a rural district

zeks political prisoners in the Gulag

Leonid Ilich Brezhnev

Brezhnev's USSR

*"Most people think of him as long dead, so great is the veneration of his talent. ... He lives on, and does not even think of dying, to the consternation of all." (*Anonymous article in *Aurora*)

Brezhnev's Rise to Power

The Soviet leadership on Khrushchev's Deposition

1. After the dismissal of Khrushchev a new collective leadership was set up:

     President - N. V. Podgorny
     Prime Minister - A. N. Kosygin
     First Secretary - L. I. Brezhnev

    For some time Kosygin seemed to be the dominant personality.

2. Alexei Kosygin was conscripted into the labour army during the Russian Civil War, and then worked in Siberia as an industrial manager, returning to Leningrad in the early 1930s and ascending the hierarchy. During the Great Patriotic War, Kosygin was a member of the State Defence Committee, with the responsibility for moving Soviet industry out of territories in the path of the German army. He later served in several ministerial posts.

    Khrushchev promoted him to Chairman of the State Planning Committee (Gosplan), and then First Deputy of the Council of Ministers.

3. A land surveyor in the 1920s, Leonid Brezhnev, became a member of the Communist Party in 1931, and studied at the Dniprodzerzhinsk Metallurgical Institute. After graduating in 1935, he became director of a technical school and held a variety of local party posts. By 1939 he had become secretary of the party committee of Dnipropetrovsk.

    During World War II Brezhnev served as a political commissar in the Red Army, advancing in rank until he became head of the political commissars on the Ukrainian front. After the war he again held posts as chief of several regional party committees in Ukraine. In 1950 he was sent to Moldavia as first secretary of the Moldavian Communist Party with the task of sovietising the Romanian population. In 1952 he became a member of the Central Committee* of the CPSU and a candidate member* of the Politburo. When Stalin died (March 1953), Brezhnev lost his posts on the Central Committee and in the Politburo* and had to accept the position of deputy head of the political department of the Ministry of Defence.

In 1954 Nikita Khrushchev appointed Brezhnev second secretary of the Communist Party of Kazakhstan. In the next year Brezhnev became first secretary of the Kazakhstan Communist Party. He was responsible for the implementation of the Virgin Lands Campaign. A year later, after he had worked against the "antiparty group" that attempted to remove Khrushchev, he was made a full member of the Politburo, and in 1960 became chairman of the Presidium of the Supreme Soviet i.e., technically the head of state. In July 1964 he gave up that position to become second secretary of the Central Committee. He came to be seen as Khrushchev's potential successor as leader of the party.

Three months later Brezhnev was a major figure in the plot to remove Khrushchev, and helped to forced him from power. Brezhnev became first secretary of the CPSU.

The Primacy of Kosygin

1. Kosygin first reversed many of Khrushchev's reforms:
    (a) ended the division of the party structure into industrial and agricultural wings;
    (b) abolished the limitation on cadres' occupation of their posts;
    (c) dissolved the *sovnarkhozy* or regional economic councils Khrushchev had set up, and restored the centralised ministries he had broken up.
2. In 1965 Kosygin launched economic reforms, known as the **Kosygin Reforms**, following the advice of economists like Aganbeygan:
    (a) He tried to make the planning system more responsive by setting targets in terms of "gross realised output", i.e. goods actually sold, rather than merely produced;
    (b) A small interest charge was levied on capital equipment in order to discourage enterprises from hoarding resources;
    (c) There was to be greater freedom for managers to decide how to use their profits, e.g.
       (i) as incentive payments to workers;
       (ii) for reinvestment;
       (iii) as payments to amenity funds.
    (d) Targets would be set 5 years in advance and not changed, so as to end arbitrary interference and demonstrate stability.
    (e) New technology bought from the west to make up for lack of Soviet innovation. The largest scheme was a 1966 contract with Fiat to build a car factory on the Volga, now called Togliatti. This sort of thing involved opening up contacts with the west.
    (f) Kosygin followed Khrushchev's policy of placing relatively heavy emphasis on the production of consumer goods, and he altered Khrushchev's objectives only by setting more realistic targets.
    (g) In agriculture:
       (i) 20-25% more investment in the countryside led to a rise in the standard of living there, to only 10% below that in the towns;
       (ii) From 1966 the workers on the *kolkhozy* were paid a regular wage;
       (iii) More collective farms (*kolkhozy*) were converted to state farms (*sovkhozy*);
       (iv) Some experiments were tried with the "link" (*zveno*) system, by which land on the *kolkhozy* was cultivated for private profit, were so overwhelmingly successful that they were suppressed;
    But it continued to be necessary to import grain to feed the population. Thus agriculture became a burden on the rest of the economy.

3. In terms of economic performance, the years 1965-75 were the most successful in Soviet history. The economy of the USSR was growing at some 6% annually. The standard of living rose, but only to South European levels. For a time, the military-industrial complex* achieved near parity with the USA.

4. By the mid-70s the economy had run out of steam.

   The reforms failed, as in order to succeed enterprise managers would have needed powers which they were not given:

   (a) to set the prices at which their products were sold;

   (b) to determine levels of employment in their enterprises;

   (c) Innovations are difficult in a system where success is measured in terms of the fulfilment of targets;

   (d) Serious implementation of the reforms would have threatened the priority given to military production;

   (e) The power of party secretaries would have been reduced, so they resisted change;

   (f) Events in Czechoslovakia (the "Prague Spring") gave reform a bad name;

   (g) Setting targets 5 years in advance made the system less adaptable.

5. Additionally:

   (a) Power production slowed up;

   (b) Agriculture continued to lag behind despite investment;

   (c) Shortages of manpower showed up in certain industries and the army. There was a decline in the birth-rate in the industrialised areas of the USSR, so that recruitment in the military had rely more and more on Central Asia. Industry could not rely upon this because the Muslims there would not migrate to find work.

6. Kosygin exercised a moderating influence on the other Soviet leaders. The government retreated from fully implementing Kosygin's reforms, but his sensible management style helped preserve efficiency and discipline in the Soviet economy into the 1970s.

The Power Struggle

1. These reforms were opposed by Brezhnev. In particular, Kosygin's emphasis on economic decentralisation and on expanding light industry placed him increasingly at odds with Brezhnev, and as a result of their failure Kosygin lost his pre-eminence. Power was once more exercised collectively.

2. In 1966 Brezhnev's title was changed from first secretary to general secretary, the title under which Stalin had controlled the USSR.

3. In 1970 Brezhnev tried to get himself made Chairman of the Council of Ministers in place of Kosygin, but was prevented by Suslov.

4. Brezhnev gradually manoeuvred his own supporters into key positions, but it was 10-15 years before he was clearly in sole charge of events. It took him longer than Khrushchev to become national leader, but that was because he accumulated power very gradually, like Stalin, instead of adopting the high-risk strategy of his predecessor.

5. In 1977, he forced the retirement of Podgorny and replaced him as Chairman of the Presidium of the Supreme Soviet of the Soviet Union, head of state, effectively becoming an executive president.

6. Over the next few years he also appointed himself:

   (a) Marshal of the USSR;

   (b) Supreme Commander of the armed forces;

   (c) Chairman of the Defence Council.

Brezhnev's Dominance of the USSR

Brezhnev's Foreign Policy

[For a more detailed study of Brezhnev's foreign policy see the companion volume "The Cold War"]

1. Brezhnev left domestic affairs to his colleagues Kosygin and Podgorny, chairman of the Presidium, while he focused on foreign and military matters.

2. Brezhnev set out to improve relations with the rest of the world, and at the same time, to make it clear the Soviet Union was a superpower.

3. Sino-Soviet relations continued to deteriorate. During 1969 there was armed conflict along the Ussuri River and on the border with Xinjiang. Both sides agreed to negotiate, but the USSR gave military aid to India, Pakistan, and North Vietnam in an effort to contain Chinese influence in the region.

4. The USSR and most of the Warsaw Pact nations invaded Czechoslovakia in 1968 when a relaxation of controls and public debate known as "the Prague Spring" threatened to get out of control and challenge the leading role of the Communist Party, destabilizing the entire region. By analogy with the earlier US Truman Doctrine, Brezhnev indicated that the USSR was prepared to intervene militarily if the Party's control of a socialist state was threatened by internal subversion. This policy became known as the **Brezhnev Doctrine**, .

5. Following the attack on its Arab neighbours by Israel in 1967, the USSR supplied arms to the Arab states, increasing its influence in the Middle East.

6. In general Brezhnev sought to ease international tensions so as to divert resources to civilian use. In order to do this **détente*** with the West was necessary. Military conflict with the West was ruled out, although ideological competition was to continue.

7. In a policy known as **Ostpolitik,*** the chancellor of West Germany, Willy Brandt, set out to improve relations with the states of Eastern Europe in 1969. In 1970 he signed treaties with Poland and the USSR recognising the inviolability of the post Second World War borders. This was an early example of détente.

8. The USSR, USA and the United Kingdom signed the **Outer Space Treaty**, which prohibited nuclear weapons in space, in 1967.

9. The Arab-Israeli War of 1973 resulted in temporarily increased tension in the Mediterranean.

10. On May 26, 1972, Brezhnev and US President Richard M. Nixon signed the first **Strategic Arms Limitation Treaty (SALT)**, which ruled out nuclear war as a feasible option.

11. On Aug. 1, 1975, 33 European governments and the United States and Canada, signed the Final Act of the **Helskinki Conference on Security and Co-operation in Europe**. The Helsinki Accords:

    (a) recognised as inviolable the post-war frontiers in Europe.

    (b) human rights in each European state were recognised to be the legitimate concern of all states.

    This last point was seized upon by various dissident groups in the USSR, who set up **Helsinki Watch Groups**.

12. The mid-1970s were a period of considerable success in Soviet foreign policy.

    (a) In 1975 the Vietnamese finally forced the USA to withdraw from their country.

    (b) Pro-Soviet regimes had been set up in:

        (i) Cambodia and Laos in South-East Asia;

        (ii) The former Portuguese colonies, Angola and Mozambique, in Central Africa;

        (iii) Ethiopia in the Horn of Africa;

        (iv) Yemen in the Arabian peninsula;

(v) Afghanistan in southern Asia.

13. US leaders became alarmed at the expansion of Soviet influence all over the world.

14. The SALT II treaty was signed in Vienna in June 1979 with US President Jimmy Carter.

15. The Soviet Union invaded Afghanistan in December 1979 on the invitation of their threatened allies. They:

  (a) underestimated the degree of Muslim resistance;

  (b) misjudged American reaction. President Carter:

  (i) failed to submit SALT II for ratification to the US Senate;

  (ii) imposed an embargo on grain exports to the USSR;

  (iii) through the CIA and the Pakistan Intelligence Service, began to organise and arm fighters from all over the Muslim world (Mujahedin), to fight the Soviets in Afghanistan, e.g. Osama bin Laden.

16. Ronald Reagan became US president in November 1980, determined on a more aggressive posture towards the USSR. In 1979, NATO decided to deploy cruise and Pershing II ballistic missiles starting in December 1983. Negotiations with the Soviets, **Strategic Arms Reduction Talks (START)**, to reduce or eliminate deployment of these missiles began in Geneva in June 1982.

17. Brezhnev's government supervised General Jaruzelski's suppression of Poland's independent-minded Solidarity trades union in December 1981.

18. Soviet foreign and security policy from the mid-1970s onward was disastrous.

  (a) The expansion of communist regimes in Southeast Asia, the Middle East, and Africa gave the hawks in the West the opportunity to panic the public into supporting a new bellicosity in relations with the USSR, and further arms spending.

  (b) The allies the USSR obtained were not very useful. Vietnam was a reluctant ally, and Yemen and the all the African regimes were engaged in civil wars.

  (c) The invasion of Afghan involved the USSR in a difficult and costly war and made it enemies in the Muslim world.

19. We know from Gorbachev that dangerously, during the late 1970s and early 1980s, the Soviet leadership came to believe that the West was planning a first-strike nuclear attack on the USSR due to the bellicosity* of the Reagan and Thatcher regimes. This began to induce paranoia among the Soviet leadership.

Human Rights and Dissent

1. After Khrushchev was deposed there were signs of a clamp down on dissent and an end to the process of destalinization, led by Suslov and Shelepin;

2. Arrest of the authors, Sinyavsky and Daniel, for sending their stories to the west, led to demonstrations in Pushkin Square. Accused of anti-Soviet propaganda and sentenced to 5 years in a labour camp.

3. Alexander Ginsburg transcribed their trial for *samizdat** circulation.

4. 1966-68 1,000 citizens signed petition objecting to the trials were subjected to harassment.

5. There was no Stalinist-style pogrom. Shelepin, who had plans to arrest 1,000 leading intellectuals, was eased into a trade union job.

6. The response of the regime was more moderate:

  (a) discrimination and harassment;

  (b) arrest for hooliganism, possession of drugs, speculating in foreign currency, parasitism, anti-Soviet propaganda, treason, etc.;

  (c) committal to a psychiatric hospital;

(d) internal exile;

(e) imprisonment in a labour camp;

(f) expulsion from the country.

7. The response of the people harassed was:

(a) to demand that the state observe its own constitution and laws;

(b) to publicise breaches of both internally by *samizdat* and externally in the west.

8. In April 1965 Brezhnev gave the signal for the rehabilitation of Stalin and Zhdanov.

9. Harassment of dissenters was more efficient after 1967, when Yuri Andropov became head of the KGB.

10. May 1976 Yuri Orlov founded the Moscow **Helsinki Watch Group** to check that the USSR was observing the terms of the agreement signed at the Helsinki Conference. He and fellow founders Ginsburg and Shcharansky were imprisoned.

11. In 1982 the last of the Helsinki Watch Groups was disbanded. The regime had been successful in suppressing internal dissent.

12. Under Brezhnev the state gradually lost its monopoly on information control. Capitalist propaganda began to seep into the USSR. A counter-culture, influenced by Western pop music spread rapidly. Russian youth had become enamoured of Western pop stars, and the advent of the audiocassette made it easier to experience their music. The widespread teaching of foreign languages further facilitated access to outside ideas. By the end of the Brezhnev era the Russian intelligentsia had rejected Communist Party values.

Stagnation

1. Under Brezhnev, Russia dominated the USSR as never before. Three-fourths of the defence industries, the priority sector, were in Russia, and the republic accounted for about three-fourths of the Soviet gross national product. The rapid expansion of the chemical, oil, and gas industries boosted exports so that Russia earned most of the union's hard-currency income.

2. Brezhnev had no policy for change. Leaders who had tried to change things had failed, and had been pushed out on account of it. Brezhnev was determined that this would not happen to him.

3. Khrushchev had been pushed out largely because of his attack on the Party cadres. Brezhnev's watchword was "Trust the cadres." Hardly anyone lost his job for incompetence. As a result, by the 1970s the USSR was ruled by a **gerontocracy**.*

4. Cliques and clientele groups flourished as a consequence of **nepotism*** and croneyism* (esp. the "Dnipropetrovsk Mafia," people Brezhnev had promoted behind him as he rose in the system. This was the outcome of years of operation of the *nomenklatura* system.

5. The increasingly sclerotic nature of the centrally-planned economy led to economic stagnation. Periodic scarcities became worse.

6. A huge black economy grew up to supply unavailable goods and services. Despite an army of state supervisory organs like the **Dept. for Combating Theft of Socialist Property (OBKhSS),** the state tolerated it as:

(a) It built some flexibility into a rigid system, and so made it more tolerable;

(b) Its operators were left doubly dependant upon state and party officials for their oversight since they were acting illegally and could be blackmailed.

7. Machinery and plant was poorly built and inadequately maintained.

8. The consequences of this were:

(a) a lowering in the standard of living of the people, e.g. overcrowding, poor diet, alcoholism:

(b) Lack of health care, e.g. the Soviet death rate:
>> 1966 - 6.9 per 1,000;
>> 1980 - 10.3 per 1,000;

(c) chronic inefficiency in industry, e.g. in 1986 70% of the 28,000 fires recorded in Moscow were caused by faulty TV sets.

9. Initiative and effort was discouraged: "We pretend to work and they pretend to pay us."

10. Many people looked back to the "efficiency" of Stalin's rule, and called for a return of discipline in society.

11. Corruption among party and government officials grew. It was found in the inner family circle of Brezhnev himself, in the friends of his daughter, Galina.

12. The ruling elite became alienated not only from the people, but also from the rising generation of leaders in institutions, enterprises and provincial governments. These were not dissidents, but they wanted greater efficiency and some improvement in the lives of the people.

13. There was a loss of belief in Communism as an ideology, and a prevailing attitude of **cynicism**.

Brezhnev's Decline

1. Because of Brezhnev's obvious senility, a power struggle began to develop before his death over who would succeed him, between:

>> (a) Konstantin Chernenko, his designated heir, supported by the centralised bureaucracy,
>> (b) Yuri Andropov, supported by the diplomatic service, the armed forces and the KGB.

2. Andropov used his position as Ideology Minister to combat corruption. This was used as a weapon against rivals from the end of 1981. Investigations were made of "Boris the Gypsy," the boyfriend of Brezhnev's daughter, Galina. Andropov involved Suslov in the investigation of Brezhnev's brother-in-law, Tsvigun, who committed suicide.

   After Suslov's death, in Jan. 1982, Boris the Gypsy was arrested. Other friends of Galina and party allies of Brezhnev were investigated.

3. When Brezhnev died Nov. 10th, 1982, he was succeeded by Yuri Andropov.

Timeline of Brezhnev's Regime	
1963	Deposition of Khrushchev
	Kosygin becomes Chairman of the Council of Ministers
	Brezhnev becomes First Secretary of the CPSU
1965	Kosygin Reforms – Rehabilitation of Stalin and Zhdanov
1966	Trial of Sinavsky and Daniel
	Brezhnev becomes "General" Secretary of the Party
1967	Yuri Andropov becomes head of the KGB
	Harrassment of dissenters increases
1968	Invasion of Czechoslovakia – Brezhnev Doctrine
1969-70	Ostpolitik – Beginning of Détente
1975	Helsinki Accords signed
1976	Helsinki Watch Group founded
1977	Brezhnev becomes governing head of state
1979	Soiet invasion of Afghanistan
1981	Andropov begins to attack corruption in the circle of Brezhnev
1982	Death of Brezhnev – Yuri Andropov succeeds him

Assessment of Brezhnev's Regime

1. Gorbachev dismissed the Brezhnev era as one of "stagnation." This was true, but incomplete.
2. Under Brezhnev's incumbency the USSR reached the height of its international power and prestige. However, since the underlying conditions for achieving parity with the USA were not there, e.g. the USA had a much greater "empire" from which it could draw resources, the challenge merely provoked the USA into responding.
3. Throughout this period, the policy of the USSR towards the West had been one of peaceful competition, that of the West towards the USSR became threatening at the end of the 1970s, creating a new "Cold War" atmosphere and bringing the danger of nuclear war much nearer.
4. The culture of empty cynicism, which spread to the entire population, removed the *raison d'être** for the Soviet regime, and led to decline.
5. At the same time, capitalist propaganda, which painted the West as a materialist paradise and ignored its insecurities and inequalities of wealth, and the exploitation of Third World countries upon which this wealth was based, began to replace the previous ideology.

Glossary

bellicosity an aggressive, threatening, warlike posture

candidate member non-voting member

Central Committee usually composed of about 300 voting and 170 non-voting members, it was the main policy-making body in the Party and contained the most important people in the Party, and normally met twice a year

Chairman of the Council of Ministers the Soviet prime minister

CPSU Communist Party of the Soviet Union

croneyism giving favours (such as appointments to jobs) not on merit but on the basis of friendship

cynicism no longer believing in ideological ends or unselfish motives

détente the easing of strained relations between the superpowers

gerontocracy rule by old men

military-industrial complex the enterprises which produced goods for the military, especially weapons

nepotism giving favours (such as appointments to jobs) not on merit but on family relationships

Ostpolitik the West German policy of a new openness towards the East

Politburo usually composed of about a dozen voting and half a dozen non-voting members, and chaired by the First (or General) Secretary of the CPSU, it was the real governing body of the party and country.

raison d'être reason for existing

samizdat spreading literature by typing many carbon copies of a document or book, passing each of them on to readers, who would in turn each retype and pass on to others many other carbon copies.

Mao Zedong

Mao's China

"The chaos caused was on a grand scale and I take responsibility." Mao Zedong

Mao's Rise to Power

The War Lord Era

1. China is a vast country, covering an area larger than the USA and containing a quarter of the world's population. Mountainous and covering many varied types of terrain, communications in the interior were often very difficult.

2. The country had long been subjected to pressure from the US and European powers who wished to take advantage of potential markets there by establishing foreign enclaves* where Chinese law did not run, and where Chinese (except for the very wealthy) were treated as inferiors. This provoked resentment and xenophobia.*

3. For centuries China had been ruled by emperors. Traditionally, a good emperor was a strong ruler, who:

    (a) strictly enforced the laws, so that the dykes were maintained and irrigation was not interfered with, agriculture flourished and flood and famine were avoided.

    (b) Kept the powerful in order, so that civil war and internal disorders were avoided and foreigners did not take advantage to invade and devastate the land.

    A strong, successful emperor was known as the "Son of Heaven," and was said to enjoy "the mandate of Heaven".

4. In 1908 the throne of China was inherited by Pu-Yi, a boy of two years of age - the most extreme form of "weak emperor". This weakened the control of the Manchu dynasty over the empire.

5. Near the end of 1911 Sun Yixian, head of the nationalist party the **Guomindang** or **GMD** (**Kuomintang - KMT**), set up a republic, while in Beijing Yuan Shih-kai took control as Prime Minister, determined upon personal rule.

6. In 1912 Pu Yi was forced to abdicate and a republic was proclaimed with Yuan Shih-kai as president. Yuan outlawed the Guomindang and dismissed parliament. The Guomindang then set up a rival government under Sun in Canton.

7. At the meeting of the first parliament of China in 1913 the Guomindang argued for a democratic

republic on the Western model, while Yuan favoured strong personal rule by himself.

8. In 1915 Yuan died. A number of generals seized control in different provinces, leading to a period of chaos and civil war known as the **War Lord Era**.

9. The Guomindang had been founded by Dr. Sun Yixian with three aims, called **The Three Principles**:

(a) Nationalism: To rid China of foreign interference and rebuild it as a strong united power;

(b) Democracy: To introduce democracy, following the education of the people;

(c) Land Reform: rent restraint, and after a period of time, a more equitable redistribution of land. The organisation of the GMD was modelled on that of the Soviet Communist Party.

10. The Guomindang had its own army, which fought the War-Lords. Little was achieved, since:

(a) the army was so weak that it had to rely upon the support of some of the War Lords.

(b) Sun Yixian was not an effective military leader.

11. In May 1919 there was a student demonstration in Beijing which led to some Chinese turning to Marxism-Leninism as a pattern for reform. In 1921 the **Chinese Communist Party (CCP)** was officially founded. Most meetings of the national party were held on a boat in a lake in Shanghai to avoid the attention of the police. Mao Zedong was present.

12. In 1923, under pressure from the USSR, the members of the CCP also became members of the GMT, forming a united front. The ideological reason for this was that the GMD would bring about the bourgeois revolution, which would be a necessary precondition for the subsequent proletarian revolution. The GMD:

(a) accepted Russian assistance

(b) received Russian advisers

(c) sent some members to Moscow for training

(d) and adopted, in part, the Leninist organisation of the Soviet Communist Party, although not its ideology.

13. In 1924, after witnessing demonstrations by peasants in his native village of Shao-shan, who had been angered by the news of the shooting of dozens of Chinese by foreign police in Shanghai, Mao Zedong became aware of the revolutionary potential of the peasantry. He had previously adopted the traditional intellectual's view of the peasants as ignorant. His Marxism had already forced him to change his view of the urban proletariat, and now he turned to the peasants for support. This was a policy for bringing about revolution which differed from those of Marx and Lenin, but was better adapted to Chinese conditions.

14. In 1925 Sun Yixian died, and General Jiang Jieshi (Chiang Kai-shek) succeeded him as leader of the GMD.

15. In 1926 Jiang set out on the **Northern March** to destroy the power of the War Lords in the centre and north of China. In 1927 he captured Shanghai and Nanjing (Nanking); and in 1928 Beijing.

The Chinese Civil War

1. In 1927 in Shanghai, Chiang Kai-shek organised a massacre of left-wing members of the GMD, especially those who were also members of the CCP. The Communists organised resistance. This was the beginning of the Chinese Civil War.

[For a fuller treatment of the Chinese Civil War, see the companion volume: "Wars and Warfare"]

2. The reasons for this were:

(a) Although the GMD was receiving help from Soviet Russia, Chiang supported the landowners and businessmen rather than the left-wing and the communists, and removed left-wingers from positions of influence in the party.

(b) Jiang was being threatened by a rival (Wang Jingwei) for the leadership of the GMD, and he probably felt that this strong action would confirm his position.

3. The CCP split into two parts:

(a) The Moscow-trained central leadership went underground in Shanghai. They called upon the members of the CCP to launch urban revolutions. Although Moscow sent an agent, Heinz Neumann to assist them, the urban revolts failed.

(b) Mao tried to lead a revolt against the GMD by the peasants of Hunan, but this failed, and he led a group to Jiangxi (Kiangsi), where they established an independent base known as the Jiangxi Soviet. There Mao and Zhu De (Chu Teh) founded the Red Army.

4. Between 1930 and 1934 Jiang launched a series of five military **Campaigns of Encirclement and Extermination** against the Communists in the Kiangsi Soviet. From 1931 Mao Zedong (Mao Tse-tung) used the failure of the Moscow-directed leadership to consolidate his power as the real leader of the CCP. During the extermination campaigns Mao and Zhu De (Chu Teh), the commander in chief of the army, successfully developed the tactics of guerrilla warfare from base areas in the countryside.

5. The Communists successfully fought off four campaigns using tactics of mobile infiltration and guerrilla warfare developed by Mao, but in the fifth, Jiang gathered about 700,000 troops and established a series of blockhouses around the Communist positions.

6. The Central Committee of the CCP abandoned Mao's guerrilla strategy and, following the advice of Li De, used regular warfare tactics against the better-armed and more numerous Nationalist forces. As a result, the Communist forces suffered heavy losses and were nearly crushed.

7. In order to avoid extermination, on Oct. 15, 1934, the remaining 85,000 troops and 15,000 administrative personnel broke through the Nationalist lines and fled westward on what became the **Long March.** During the first three months of the march the Communists were subjected to constant bombardment from Jiang's air force and attacks from his army, and lost more than half of their men. At the Zunyi Conference in January 1936, held during the march, Mao established his dominance of the party with the help of Zhou Enlai (Chou En-lai).

8. The remnants of the marchers arrived at Yan'an (Yen-an) in Shaanxi (Shensi) in October 1935 with only about 8,000 survivors. Only one tenth of the original marchers survived.

9. Objectively, the Long March was a near-disaster. Most of the Red Army had been destroyed. Yet it became a legend. Edgar Snow said that it was ":an Odyssey unequalled in modern times." It:

(a) decisively established Mao's leadership of the Chinese Communist Party;

(b) enabled the embattled Communists to reach a base area beyond the direct control of the Nationalists;

(c) established Mao in the minds of the peasants as a potential leader of all China with the mandate of Heaven, and was the origin of the cult of Mao;

(d) reinforced Mao's faith in the ability of the revolutionary spirit to overcome all obstacles and mould history.

10. The Communists settled in Yan'an in Shanxi, where they remained throughout the war with the Japanese. From this base they grew in strength.

11. Seeing the threat from Japan, the CCP began promoting the idea of a **United Second Front** against the external threat. This was popular throughout China, but Jiang remained more concerned to defeat the Communists that to protect the country against Japan. A truce was concluded only after Jiang had been briefly imprisoned by his ally Zhang Xueliang, the War Lord of Manchuria. Both groups then fought the Japanese in uneasy alliance.

12. The communists were the more successful. They fought a guerilla campaign as partisans and came to control vast areas of the countryside. As a result, they:

(a) expanded their military forces to somewhere between 500,000 and 1,000,000 at the time of the Japanese surrender

(b) established political control over a population that may have totalled as many as 90,000,000, where socialist agrarian policies secured broad support among the peasantry.

13. In Yan'an, Mao:

(a) developed the "**Sinification" of Marxism,** its adaptation to Chinese conditions with the help of his secretary Chen Boda;.

(b) established his control over the Party.

14. **Maoism,** Mao's interpretation of Marxism-Leninism, was created during this period in Yan'an, although not known by that name until the Great Proletarian Cultural Revolution.

(a) Mao thought "book-learning" useless if not accompanied by real-life experience: "There can be no knowledge apart from practice." The young cadres* were taught to listen to the old men from the countryside.

(b) He considered the peasants a the vanguard of the revolution.

(c) In place of **democratic centralism*** he preferred "the mass line", based upon the practical experience of the peasants.

(d) History was not moved merely by impersonal forces. The revolutionary will of the peasantry could, if harnessed, move mountains.

(e) Mao saw and accepted the need to retain and intensify state power to build socialism. Western writers debate whether Mao's ideology was:

(i) a new form of Marxism adapted to Chinese conditions and ways of thinking, or

(ii) a form of Stalinism.

15. The differences between Mao and the Soviet-oriented faction in the party came to a head at the time of the **Rectification Campaign** of 1942-43. This program aimed at:

(a) giving a basic grounding in Marxist theory and Leninist principles of party organisation to the many thousands of new members who had been drawn into the party in the course of the expansion since 1937.

(b) the elimination of "foreign dogmatism": blind obedience to the Soviet model.

16. In March 1943 Mao achieved official leadership of the party, becoming chairman of the Secretariat and of the Politburo. Shortly after that, the Rectification Campaign took the form of a purge of those disloyal to Mao.

17. The Yan'an legacy left a tradition of:

(a) Mao's leadership

(b) popular education

(c) the practice of organising campaigns in the villages to ensure that policies were properly carried out

(d) economic self-sufficiency

(e) it gave the CCP experience of government

18. US policy was ostensibly to create a strong central government under US influence. The US hoped to bring the GMD and the CCP together under the moderates of the Democratic League. In 1944 the **Dixie Mission** arrived in Yan'an and were favourably impressed by what they saw, which contrasted with US impressions of the government of Jiang and the GMT. The attempt at reconciliation failed as both sides were too suspicious of each other. Talks broke down over the failure to merge the two armies. The USA reverted to supporting the nationalists.

19. In 1939 Jiang gave up his truce and stated to attack the Communists. In 1941 he tried to destroy their armies in the south. This policy was very unpopular throughout the country. He probably did this because:

(a) He thought that the Americans, who were providing him with aid, would intervene to defeat their common enemy the Japanese if he waited long enough;

(b) He saw the Communists as rivals for his leadership of the Chinese people.

20. The Sino-Japanese War came to an end unexpectedly with the Soviet declaration of war on Japan and with the dropping of the atomic bombs, and without US intervention on the mainland, leaving Jiang to face the Communists alone.

21. Serious fighting broke out again between the armies of the GMD and CCP in Manchuria in April 1946.

22. The Nationalists seemed to be winning, but by mid-1947 the Nationalist army was overstretched in occupying all the areas gained, and a successful Communist counter-offensive began in Manchuria, sweeping the country.

23. Chiang resigned from the presidency Jan. 1949 and the GMD asked the US to mediate with the CCP, hoping to retain the south. The CCP, sensing victory, was no longer interested in an armistice. Their advance continued.

24. In April 1949 Stalin urged Mao not to cross the River Yanzi and take southern China.

(a) He wished to avoid the creation of a strong, united Communist China under the independent -minded Mao;

(b) He feared that the USA would use it as a pretext to intervene in China and establish its own bases there.

Mao ignored him.

25. On October 1st 1949, the Peoples' Republic of China was proclaimed by Mao in Beijing (Peking).

26. Mao thus came to power by means of a revolutionary war.

Reasons for the Success of Mao and the Communists

The nationalists had many advantages:

1. They were recognised and supported by the USA *and* the USSR.
2. They had a large, US equipped army.
3. The experience of the Communist forces was in fighting guerilla campaigns only.
4. The nationalists had a monopoly of air power.

However:

5. The CCP were shown to be more patriotic nationalists and effective fighters than the Nationalists, in seeking national unity to fight the Japanese.
7. Mao's policy of cultivating the peasants and using them as a power base was successful.
8. The land reform policy of the CCP was compromised during the war, being limited to restricting rent rises, and giving the land of only the largest landowners to the poorest peasants. This won the support of the smaller landowners.
9. The glamour of the Long March assumed the proportions of a national epic and its spell captivated the peasants, and suggested that Mao would be "an emperor with the mandate of Heaven".
10. Mao had able generals, e.g. Zhu De and Lin Biaou (Lin Piao) and did not interfere with their conduct of fighting.
11. While the Nationalists had little information about what the Communists were planning, the Communists had a spies in the Nationalist camp, and knew the Nationalist's plans in advance.
12. The Nationalist was a government of industrialists, bankers and landlords. It made no attempt to gain the support of the masses, and signally failed to introduce any democratic reforms, or show any intention of doing so.

13. The GMD was inefficient in everything it did, from fighting the Japanese to coping with the economy, to introducing much needed reforms:
    (a) Little attempt had been made to improve the lot of the masses.
    (b) High taxes and forced labour were resented.
    (c) The administration of the GMD was notoriously corrupt:
        (i) The laws were not applied impartially to rich and poor alike. What had been done in the way of reforming legislation, e.g. laws against child labour, was not seriously applied.
        (ii) During a series of droughts and consequent bad harvests and famines, the Nationalists had not prevented the hoarding of rice by profiteers. Many of the profiteers had links with the GMD.
        (iii) US aid did not benefit the people, but went straight into the pockets of officials. Even President Truman referred to the Nationalist leaders as "grafters and crooks."
14. The Nationalists had paid for their wars against the Japanese and the Communists by printing money. This led to inflation, which meant more hardship for the poor, and ruin for the middle classes. After the end of the Sino-Japanese War inflation got out of control.
15. The Nationalist army was provisioned by being allowed to loot the countryside, making it very unpopular. By contrast, the PLA did not. Instead they spread Communist ideals and introduced land reform in the areas they controlled.
16. The Nationalist government relied heavily upon a hated secret police system.
17. The Nationalist army was very badly led, with no good generals.
18. In the final stages of the Civil War, Jiang would not countenance retreats. This led to disastrous defeats and to mass desertions.

Timeline of Mao's Rise to Power	
1912	End of the monarchy
1915	Beginning of the War Lord Era
1921	Chinese Communist Party founded
1924	First United Front founded
1925	Jiang Jieshi becomes head of the Guomindang (GMD)
1926	Northern Expdition
1927	Shanghai massacre of Communists - Mao sets up Jiangxi Soviet
1931	Japanese invasion of Manchuria
1934	The Long March begins
1935	Mao establishes his dominance of the CCP
	Mao creates the Yan'an Soviet in Shaanxi
1936	Jiang Jieshi kidnapped at Xian
1937	Second United Front formed – Sino-Japanese War begins
1939	Jiang breaks the truce
1942-3	Rectification Campaign
1943	Mao officially leader of the CCP
1945	Surrender of the Japanese
1946	Civil War resumes
1949	Peoples' Republic of China founded - Jiang flees to Formosa

The Period of Reconstruction (1949-53)

Initial Problems

1. In 1949 Mao and the CCP took over after forty years of warfare and disorder, including:
   (a) The War Lord Era (1915-31)
   (b) Civil War 1(931-37);
   (c) The Sino-Japanese War (1937-45);
   (d) The Civil War (1946-49);
   which left many problems.
2. Parts of South-West China were still in the hands of the GMT.
3. Some areas of the empire which became independent during long periods when the central authority was weak, e.g. Tibet, had not been unified with the rest of the country by the Guomindang.
4. Large areas of the countryside were in the hands of, or preyed upon by, brigands.
5. The cities were plagued with crime and destitution. The Communists had no experience in city life A US scholar living in Beijing explained that many of the Communists had never seen a large city before, and did not even know how to turn off the electric lights.
6. Capital had fled the country;
   (a) Inflation had become staggering during the final Guomindang years, and had affected the whole country, so that the Communists inherited a valueless currency;
   (b) Unemployment was widespread in the cities, exacerbated by refugees from the fighting;
7. Warfare had left a legacy of neglect and destruction.
   (i) There was only a primitive system of communications and transportation. The railways were only used by the army, there was no general plan for their use, equipment had not been properly maintained or repaired for a long time;
   (ii) In factories the equipment had not been properly maintained or repaired for a long time, many had shut down completely;
   (iii) Dykes and canals had not been properly maintained, leading to floods and droughts affecting 40 million people;
   (iv) The merchant fleet had taken refuge in Taiwan, Hong Kong or Singapore.
8. Many problems were caused by the heritage of foreign interference:
   (a) Modern industrial production was concentrated in a few out-of-the-way centres which had come under foreign influence, Shanghai and the lower Yangzi, Tientsin and the NE
   (b) The communications network was imbalanced, concentrated around ports and the NE.
9. Traditional Confucian Chinese attitudes created problems:
   (a) The need for resignation to one's fate worked against change and reform;
   (b) The position of women in society led to the depression of half of the workforce;
   (c) Local and regional loyalties were very strong
10. Rural labour was depressed, with few technical skills and no tradition of initiative.
11. The Chinese Communist Party (CCP) came to power very rapidly with the collapse of the Guomindang or GMD (Kuomintang - KMT) army. Out of 540 million Chinese, there were about 4 million members of the CCP. In many areas opponents outnumbered supporters. It was necessary to ask unsympathetic civil servants to remain in office, defeated soldiers to re-enlist, and personnel of capitalistic-bureaucratic enterprises to stay on. Most intellectuals lived near the coast, and were totally unaffected by communist ideology.
12. The hostile forces of the Guomindang remained on the island of Taiwan (Formosa), where they could not be pursued without amphibious forces.
13. Hostility from abroad, particularly from the USA, made the regime defensive. This was to

increase with the outbreak of the Korean war, and then with Chinese participation in the war.
14. However, the CCP had some advantages:
    (a) Experience of government in the liberated zones, in Yan'an going back 12 years;
    (b) The support of the well-organised and prestigious Peoples' Liberation Army (PLA);
    (c) The massive support of the peasants;
    (d) A powerful secret police apparatus which they inherited from the Guomindang;
    (e) The almost universal antipathy to the Guomindang.
15. In view of:
    (a) the immense difficulties which Mao and the CCP faced (The outbreak of the Korean War must have been very unwelcome to the Communist rulers of China at this time);
    (b) the need to use all the help they could get simply to keep things running;
    Mao acted very cautiously at first.
16. In 1949 Mao announced that while in the past the Chinese revolution had followed the unorthodox path of "encircling the cities from the countryside," it would in the future take the orthodox road of the cities leading and guiding the countryside. In harmony with this view, he agreed in 1950 with Liu Shaoqi (Liu Shao-ch'i) that collectivisation of agriculture would be possible only when China's heavy industry had provided the necessary equipment for mechanization. This was a return to the Soviet approach and Marxist orthodoxy.
17. The CCP announced "three years of recovery – ten years of development" The aims of the new government as set out in the **Common Programme** of Sept. 1949 were to build a "society of transition" meeting the common aspirations of the four revolutionary classes: the peasants, the industrial proletariat, the middle classes and national capitalists. This would involve:
    (a) Reconstructing the economy;
    (b) Initiating socially progressive measures;
    (c) Political Reorganisation.
18. This was done in accordance with the Common Programme and the decisions of the Advisory Political Conference (a constituent assembly) containing many non-Communists.
19. The central peoples" government was headed by Mao Zedong; while day-to-day management of affairs was under the Council of State Affairs, headed by Zhou Enlai (Chou En-lai).
20. The country was divided into six political and military regions in which both powers were combined. Thus the country was effectively under military rule until 1954.
21. Pressure of foreign threats made the regime more increasingly more repressive.
    (a) GMD agents infiltrated China from Taiwan, Hong Kong and Burma;
    (b) US General MacArthur at one point threatened China with nuclear bombardment.

Political Reconstruction

1. In 1954 A new constitution was enacted:
   (a) A **National People's Congress** elected every four years. Its work was done in practice by a Standing Committee;
   (b) The **Council of Affairs of State** was elected by the National Congress. This was the executive.* Its leader was effectively the Prime Minister (Zhou Enlai);
   (c) The **Chairman of the Republic** was also elected by the National Peoples' Congress. (Mao Zedong);
   (d) The CCP was to be the "driving belt" of society.
2. The Party:
   (a) in 1949 had about 4.5 million members;

(b) A hierarchical structure of organisations was formed to extend its influence: e.g. women's groups, youth groups, professional and intellectual organisations.

(c) The CCP was to organise mass movements (***yundong***)* which would disrupt normal life, in order to:

    (i) Link the masses to important political decisions;

    (ii) Mobilise the masses, giving them an active role in developments;

    (iii) Consolidate ideological values through marches, discussions and poster campaigns.

These were a purely Chinese phenomenon, developed for a largely illiterate society.

3. Bureaucracy: The bureaucratization of the Party and country began. An immense army of cadres grew up, organised in eight hierarchic echelons, as in the old Confucian bureaucracy, with plurality of functions, some honorary.

4. Propaganda: The New China News Agency and the *Peoples' Daily* were set up to disseminate official propaganda.

5. In 1950 a campaign was launched against counter-revolutionaries. The revolutionary classes consisted of the **Five Red Categories:**

    (i) poor and middle peasants;

    (ii) workers;

    (iii) revolutionary soldiers;

    (iv) revolutionary cadres (party workers);

    (v) dependants of the revolutionary martyrs (those who had died in the wars).

Their opponents consisted of the **Seven Black Categories:**

    (vi) landlords;

    (vii) rich peasants;

    (viii) reactionaries;

    (ix) bad elements;

    (x) rightists;

    (xi) traitors;

    (xii) spies.

There were almost 1,000,000 victims in this purge.

6. In October 1950 troops were sent into Tibet, an area which became independent whenever there was not a strong central government in China. They proceeded to reintegrate that area into China.

Law and Order

1. The Ministry of Security organised a secret police force, mainly to counter GMD agents.

2. There was a crackdown on traditional organised crime (the triads) which were usually involved in trading illegal narcotics, which was very powerful in the eastern coastal cities.

3. Public gambling (a great social problem) was outlawed;

4. The brothels were closed down.

5. Prostitutes and drug addicts were not criminalized but treated as victims of a capitalist society. Thus e.g. the re-education and rehabilitation of opium addicts was organised by the government;

6. The dominance of foreigners was gradually brought under control:

    (a) Foreign businesses were made to register with the government;

    (b) then closely regulated;

    (c) finally the businesses were confiscated and nationalized;

    (d) and the foreigners expelled from the country.

Social Reforms
The Family
1. The Marriage Law (1950):
    - (a) women were given equality with men, and e.g. allowed to own and inherit property;
    - (b) Many widespread traditional practices were forbidden:
        - (i) child marriage;
        - (ii) arranged marriages
        - (iii) polygamy;
        - (iv) the killing or selling of children;
        - (v) binding the feet of girls.
2. This was followed by measures to improve the status of women:
    - (a) women were taken into the workforce;
    - (b) positions of importance in the state and party were opened to them.

Health
1. Clinics and child-care centres were set up;
2. There were campaigns to improve hygiene and health, e.g. against parasites, rats and epidemics.
3. The opium addiction problem was solved by 1952 by:
    - (a) drastic penalties (including death) for major suppliers and dealers;
    - (b) amnesty for petty dealers;
    - (c) rehabilitation for addicts;
    - (d) public education campaigns.

Education
1. Literacy campaigns were organised;
2. An Academy of Science was founded on the Soviet model;
3. Marxist thought became a compulsory part of education at all levels;
4. Some traditional Chinese culture was honoured, e.g. in script and medicine.

The Economy
1. The aim at this stage was to control capitalism, not to eliminate it. Five legitimate sectors were recognised:
    - (a) State enterprises - many confiscated from:
        - (i) the great landlords;
        - (ii) the GMD;
        - (iii) the Japanese;
    - (b) Private enterprises owned by "national capitalists";
    - (c) State capitalist enterprises, owned in part by the state and in part by national capitalists;
    - (d) Co-operatives;
    - (e) Small individual businesses.

    Through the 5-year plans, only the state could co-ordinate all activities, so there was some loss of independence.
2. The banks were nationalised;
3. Inflation was brought under control in 1950 by the Peoples' Bank. A new currency was introduced and the budget was balanced.

Agriculture

1. The pattern was set by the **Agrarian Reform Law** (1950) Reform was to proceed step by step, so as not to damage production.

    (a) Feudal services and forced labour were abolished.

    (b) Cadres were trained and dispersed throughout the countryside.

    (c) They supervised the setting up of local peasant associations and militias.

    (d) Landlords had to refund rent deposits.

    (e) The class status of the villagers identified.

    (f) "Speak bitterness meetings" were held: an opportunity for the oppressed to denounce their oppressors.

    (g) The property of the rich landlords was divided up by the poor and middle peasants without indemnity. The rich peasants were left alone (it was not a strictly egalitarian reform). The middle and poor peasants could exercise full rights over their new lands, they could sell or rent them. Dispossessed landlords were given share of land "to redeem themselves through work."

    (h) The process was completed by the end of 1952.

    Generally the position of the peasants improved:

        (i) The peasants gained self-confidence;

        (ii) Agricultural productivity increased;

Industry

1. The CCP at first had little contact with or knowledge of industry. The management had evicted foreign control and was in a powerful position. The state limited itself to price controls, allocation of natural resources and state orders.
2. Trade Unions were organised on the Soviet model to convert workers to the state points of view on relevant matters.
3. Transportation:

    (a) The army repaired and extended the railway system.

    (b) Roads and canals were repaired and extended.
4. These efforts were successful and production increased two and a half times by 1952.

Finance and Commerce

1. The state budget was balanced and inflation held in check during the Korean War.
2. Wholesale trade passed under state control during the early 1950s.
3. Commercial co-operatives were set up, which undercut private retail trade.
4. State stores began to be set up in the early 1950s.
5. Tight restrictions were placed on the private sector. Prices wages and working conditions were determined by the state.
6. Allocation of raw materials was controlled.

Law and Order

1. The First Thought Reform Campaign (1951) was directed at intellectuals. It enjoined:

    (a) intensive study of the writings of Mao;

    (b) mass meetings;

    (c) sessions of criticism and self-criticism, "confessions" and public humiliation.
2. The campaign called **The Three Antis** (*Sanfan)* in 1952 was directed against corruption waste and the bureaucratic spirit, was directed at bureaucrats, party members and owners of businesses.

3. The campaign against the Five Antis (*Wufan*) in 1952-3 targeted tax evasion, bribery, corruption on state contracts and the theft of government property, and was directed at the bourgeoisie.

Results of the Reforms

1. There was some resistance:
    (a) Two CCP veterans, Gao Gang (NE) and Rao Shushi (Shanghai) tried to develop their areas independently. Gao Gang killed himself and Rao Shushi was imprisoned.
    (b) There was resistance among intellectuals. Zhou Yang used authoritarian repressive measures. The writer Hu Feng challenged the cultural bureaucracy, and even China's choice of socialism. He was arrested as a counter-revolutionary.
2. Opposition: Movements were instituted against those resisting the reforms:
    (a) *sanfan*: against cadres who were corrupt and authoritarian;
    (b) *wufan*: against capitalists who defrauded the state by defaulting on contracts, fraud or theft.
3. There were dramatic developments in heavy industry.
4. Agriculture lagged behind. In order to cope with the failure, the movement towards agricultural co-operatives was accelerated by government action from 1955.
5. By-products of the Five-Year Plan were:
    (a) It favoured the development of a centralised bureaucracy; The CCP was transformed into a bureaucratic organisation. Cadres became bureaucrats, losing the old revolutionary spirit.
    (b) It stifled local initiative.

The Period of Transformation to Socialism (1953-1957)

Industry

1. Mao was determined to follow the Soviet model and institute a **Five Year Plan**. Delays were caused by:
    (a) Lack of experience in large-scale planning;
    (b) the Korean War.
2. The State Planning Commission was established in 1952, leading to increased bureaucratization and centralization. It resembled the Soviet structure.
3. The **Five-Year Plan** was drawn up in 1953 and finalised in 1955. An elite class of technocrats did the planning. 10,000 Soviet and East European experts assisted. The masses were encouraged to compete with each other in fulfilling the targets, like Soviet **Stakhanovites**. The main effort was to be directed:
    (a) at the comparatively undeveloped interior of the country;
    (b) at heavy industry;
    (c) at large-scale projects.
    At the time of the inauguration of the First Five Year Plan, the era of "transition to socialism" was announced. Due to disruption of war, when the First Five Year Plan was announced industrial production was at mid-1930s levels.
4. The First Five Year Plan provided China with a sound industrial base, although small compared with most industrial countries. Industrialization led to increasing wage differentiation
5. During 1956 in the towns and cities all small craft and industrial businesses were gathered into co-operatives organised on a neighbourhood basis.
6. The national capitalists were indemnified in the form of a fixed interest to be paid on the goods transferred for a period of 7 years.

Agriculture

1. By the mid-1950s there were problems in agriculture:
   (a) Some plots were too small, given the character of the land, to support them adequately and many poor peasants lacked equipment for proper cultivation and irrigation.. This led to:
      (i) the reappearance of usury, and some had to sell their land to pay debts.
      (ii) the eviction of poor peasants by richer ones,
      (iii) the reappearance of a kulak-type class and social polarisation.
   (b) Fragmentation inhibited the introduction of modern machinery.
   (c) There were poor harvests in 1953 and 1954.
   (d) Peasant migrants were driven to the cities.
2. The Agrarian Law Reform had been only a temporary measure before collectivization. This was to be a gradual process
   (a) the voluntary formation of seasonal, and then all-years round mutual aid teams of 6-7 households;
   (b) land would be pooled in cooperatives and profits divided;
   (c) Private ownership would be abolished, and team members paid in accordance with their contribution.
3. As one of the **Three Socialist Transformations**, in July 1955, Mao reversed the position on collectivisation, arguing that in China the social transformation could run ahead of the technical development. Deeply impressed by the achievements of certain co-operatives that claimed to have radically improved their performance without any outside assistance, he came to believe in the limitless capacity of the peasants to transform their environment at will when inspired by revolutionary goals. Those who did not share his vision he denounced as "old women with bound feet."
4. This created such enthusiasm for rapid collectivisation it became an unstoppable movement. From mid-1955 agricultural co-operatives began to be established throughout the countryside. By 1956 about 95% of peasants were in cooperatives of 100-300 families, sharing ownership of the farm and its equipment It took place very rapidly without disruption:
   (a) The rich peasants had not had time to consolidate themselves as a class;
   (b) Most Chinese peasants accepted the direction of the CCP.
5. Not only was the disruption to production caused by Stalin's collectivisation of the farms avoided, production increased by 5%.
6. The improvement was not as much as it might have been because investment in agriculture was low as the available resources were employed for the Five Year Plan.

Finance and Commerce

1. After 1953 private capitalist enterprises were increasingly nationalized.
2. By 1956 the private sector had ceased to exist in the cities.

Law and Order

The *Sufan* Campaign (1955) to wipe out hidden counter-revolutionaries was a purge of the CCP.

The Hundred Flowers Campaign

1. After Khrushchev had denounced Stalin in his Secret Speech to the 20th National Congress of the CPSU in January 1956, while defending Stalin, Mao returned to his former position that Chinese policies should fit Chinese conditions. He questioned:
   (a) the focus upon heavy industry;

     (b) the subordination of political to economic experts exercising centralised control over the economy.

2. Mao then called for open debate throughout the country in the **Hundred Flowers Campaign**: "Let a hundred flowers bloom, and a hundred schools of thought contend."

3. Criticisms offered included the following:

     (a) The cadres were overenthusiastic and incompetent.

     (b) There were too many full-time cadres, who had become a privileged class

     (c) The government was inclined to over centralisation.

     (d) The CP stifled discussion and debate, particularly in the *Sanfan* and *Sufan* campaigns.

4. There was agitation on the campuses and at Beijing University a "Democracy Wall" was opened where teachers and students freely expressed their views.

5. Some parts of the press opened up their columns to liberal intellectuals who questioned the socialist option.

6. The campaign was unpopular with the Party leaders and cadres:

     (a) who were exposed to criticism;

     (b) who feared the sort of disorders called forth by destalinization in Poland and Hungary.

7. When the debate threatened to get out of hand by calling into question the exclusive right of the party to rule by calling for a multi- party democracy, the critics were denounced as "poisonous weeds" Mao felt that the intelligentsia had betrayed his confidence.

8. Moves were made to end the new liberalism. An anti-rightist campaign was organised to attempt to stop the criticism. A purge of intellectuals, known as **The Second Rectification** (1957) resulted in hundreds of thousands being sent into the countryside for re-education.

9. The 8th National Congress of the CCP took the line that the authority of the party apparatus had to be strengthened and discipline maintained.

10. The Hundred Flowers Campaign has been interpreted as an attempt:

     (a) to win the intellectuals over to the regime by allowing them to express themselves more freely, particularly as the validity of Soviet models of development were being questioned;

     (b) to "divide and rule" by allowing the technocratic-managerial class to criticise the entrenched party bureaucracy;

     (c) to reinforce Mao's own authority, which was being circumscribed by the bureaucracy;

     (d) to avoid the disturbances in Poland and Hungary by providing a safety valve for protest;

     (e) to encourage critics of the regime to reveal themselves.

     (f) Philip Short argued that it was an experiment to attempt to combine a totalitarian system with the checks and balances of a democracy.

The Three Red Banners (1957-61)

1. During 1957 Mao succeeded in getting approval for his radical Twelve Year Plan, which involved a fundamental change of direction.

     (a) a rejection of the Soviet model

     (b) a return to the Yan'an experience,

     (c) an attempt to find a Chinese road;

     (d) a move from socialism towards communism.

2. It was prompted by:

     (a) The rejection of the Stalinist model in the USSR and Eastern Europe (following the 20th National Congress of the CPSU and Khrushchev's "secret speech");

     (b) Chinese disillusionment with the Stalinist model, due to the limited benefits of the First 5-Year Plan, and confirmed after Mao's visit to Moscow in Nov. 1957.

3. The Stalinist model:
    (a) was bureaucratic, too centralised, allowed too little initiative to local people;
    (b) vast industrial projects required capital, which China did not have;
    (c) it under-utilised China's chief resource: its huge peasant population;
    (d) it was not suited to the development of agriculture, upon which China depended for food.
4. Instead, the Chinese would:
    (a) build a more socialist, even communist, society;
    (b) do this in a Chinese way;
    (c) decentralise;
    (d) free the creative energies of the peasants;
    (e) dramatically increase output in agriculture as well as industry.
5. The basis of Mao's policy were the **Three Red Banners**:
    (a) The mass line;
    (b) The people's communes;
    (c) The Great Leap Forward.

The Peoples' Communes

1. The People's Communes were a development of the movement towards co-operativization. The movement was fostered by Mao, but impelled forward by popular enthusiasm.
2. The existing co-operatives were to be combined, usually on the basis of approx. 2,000 households, although vast communes of 10,000 - 20,000 households would also be created. Land, equipment and livestock would be the property of the commune.
3. Small livestock, poultry yards and a few trees were retained as private property, but not plots of land to cultivate.
4. Work on the communes was organised on the basis of teams, and teams in production brigades.
5. Payment was to be a share of the profits made by team and calculated on the basis of work done. Often it was apportioned according to need.
6. Many communes provided basic services, e.g. child care, mending of clothes, communal meals, the cleaning and upkeep of dwellings, etc., allowing women to be genuinely emancipated.
7. Popular militias, representing the idea of "armed communes" were set up.
8. Except in outlying regions, during 1958 most Chinese farms were communalized in this way.

The Great Leap Forward

1. The Great Leap Forward was an attempt to move from the Soviet to a Chinese model:
    (a) Industry was decentralised. The powers of the central bureaucracy were limited. Local authorities could fix part of the targets. Party committees were formed to oversee the work of large enterprises.
    (b) Smaller factories were to be built in the countryside they served, to provide machinery for agriculture. Mao talked of 600,000 backyard steel furnaces.
    (c) Low-level Labour-intensive technology was to be preferred to capital-intensive "high technology. During winter 1957 the peasants were mobilised under military discipline to labour on mass public works projects.
2. "Book learning" was downgraded, and an attempt made to break down the division between intellectual and practical labour. Cadres, students and one million intellectuals and teachers were made to work on construction sites or in the fields. Schools and universities were made to combine intellectual and productive labour.
3. Agriculture was to adopt practices based upon the "progressive biology" of Trofin Lysenko, a

discarded pre-Darwinian theory which asserting that characteristics of living things derived from the environment might be transmitted by inheritance, to produce crops with high yields.

4. High intensity farming practices, such as deep ploughing and close planting were adopted.
5. There was a new attack on traditional beliefs and superstitions:

    (a) Graves scattered through the countryside were levelled;

    (b) Women were called upon to abandon domestic duties with the creation of communal dining rooms. This annoyed many men.

The Results of the Campaign

1. Although initially it seemed to be successful, in time the campaign failed. Industrial and agricultural production at first increased but then fell, (and there were bad harvests during 1959-61, while much industrial production was poor qualitatively, e.g. much of the products of rural metallurgy ventures was waste.

    (a) The disappearance of the private plots removed an important source of production.

    (b) There was passive resistance was practised by many middle peasants, who hid grain, killed and ate their pigs;

    (c) the "progressive biology" of Trofin Lysenko was based upon unscientific error, and faked to produce crops with high-production yields.

    (d) High intensity farming practices, such as deep ploughing and close planting produced immediate improvements, but subsequently exhausted the land.

    (e) There was considerable lack of practical experience among the cadres, e.g. wells were sunk in places where there was no water;

    (f) Workers withdrawn from the land were not able to contribute to food production;

    (g) Over-enthusiastic propaganda and over-ambitious targets led to fictitiously inflated production figures. This lead to increased demand from the government from the peasants to feed the cities and to export for foreign exchange.

    (h) A breakdown of central planning led to inefficiencies and bottlenecks in the production and distribution of materials and goods.

    (i) When reports of what was happening reached Mao, e.g from Minister of Defence Peng Dehai, both the reports and those who made the reports were dismissed.

2. The bubble quickly burst. Famine followed in 1959-61. More than 20 million people may have died of starvation.
3. In April 1960 the Sino-Soviet split came into the open, and Soviet experts were summarily recalled from China, contributing to the dislocation and chaos.
4. Despite the disaster, the campaign produced some lasting positive results:

    (a) Many small rural industries were established relying upon local resources, e.g. small coal mines, oil refineries, chemical plants, etc.;

    (b) The peasants benefited from originally commune-operated workshops manufacturing and repairing agricultural implements.

The Bureaucratic Revival (1961-65)

1. Following the Wuhan Conference (1959) when the scale of the disaster was realized, Mao resigned as leader of the state and withdrew himself from everyday affairs. He remained chairman of the Party, and was accorded honour, but his speeches were applauded and ignored.
2. The Three Red Banners were never formally abandoned to avoid loss of face, but from 1960-62, after a series of high-level party meetings many aspects of the programme were dropped.

3. Mao's withdrawal after the failure of the Great Leap led to a reassertion of Party and government bureaucracies. They looked to Liu Shaoqi (Liu Shao-ch'i) and Deng Xiaoping (Teng Hsiao-p'ing) to restore Leninist democratic centralism.

4. Under Liu and Deng, there was a major retreat from radicalism. It began as emergency measures to deal with the famine.

   (b) The communes were successively reduced in size. They:

   (i) were to be small enough to link peasants' efforts with their remuneration;

   (ii) were administered by salaried employees of the state;

   (iii) exercised control of their commercial affairs, while militia, health and educational facilities was turned over to local government.

   (iv) Communalized property was returned to individual families.

   (v) The peasants' private plots of land were restored, together with private markets. Extensions could be made to the private plots.

   (vi) Untilled land could be appropriated by peasants for themselves

   (vii) Peasants were encouraged to take up additional trades.

   (viii) Scientific institutes were set up to develop improved seeds.

   (ix) 25 million unemployed ciry dwellers were sent to the countryside to help with the crops.

   (x) Grain was imported from Canada and Australia.

   (c) Industry:

   (i) In Feb. 1959 the rural blast-furnaces were closed down.

   (ii) Small uneconomical enterprises were closed down.

   (iii) Emphasis was laid on "profitability" in the operation of enterprises.

   (iv) Central economic planning was reintroduced.

   (v) The authority of managers and technocrats was strengthened.

   (vi) Material incentives were offered to improve production.

5. The economic policies pursued through this period have been compared to Lenin's New Economic Policy,* although it was much less of a retreat from socialism than Lenin's.

6. By the end of 1961, conditions had stabilized. Over the years 1961-65 the economy succeeded in regaining the level of output of 1957 in almost all sectors.

7. Results of these policies included:

   (a) increasing differentiation between the working class and a technological-bureaucratic class;

   (b) increasing differentiation between towns and countryside, worker and peasant incomes;

   (c) technical matters took precedence over ideology;

   (d) The revival of traditions such as religious festivals and cults, gambling and extravagant spending on holidays.

8. Mao disliked these developments:

   (a) He saw in the rise of the technological-bureaucratic class a new bourgeoisie which would be as deadly as the old, created by the power structures of the government and party. There would be a need for a new class struggle, lest China fall into the same plight as the Soviet Union.

   (b) The leadership was preoccupied with:

   (i) order;

   (ii) administrative efficiency;

   (iii) technological progress;

   (iv) economic development.

   Mao felt that they had become ideologically unsound.

9. Others gathered around Mao in opposition to these developments included:

(a) Mao's political assistant, Chen Boda (Ch'en Po-ta), who was an expert in ideology;

(b) Mao's wife, Jiang Qing (Chiang Ch'ing), who had strong policy views in the cultural sphere;

(c) Kang Sheng (K'ang Sheng), who was a Soviet expert;

(d) Lin Biao, who headed the PLA.

These united against Liu Shaoqi, Deng Xiaoping, and the remainder of the party leadership.

10. Mao built an alternative power base in the People's Liberation Army, which the new defence minister, Lin Biao (Lin Piao), had turned into a "great school of Mao Zedong Thought."

11. In the PLA, the cult of Mao was developed, and the "Little Red Book" of Chairman Mao's quotations, produced by Lin Biao and Chen Boda, which spread across the country.

12. Since 1962, Mao's thought had also been propagated through the Movement for **Socialist Education,** which was a campaign was launched against "bourgeois revisionists" inside and outside the party, and which sought to:

(a) educate the masses ideologically;

(b) counteract the spontaneous capitalist tendencies which had begun to appear.

Cadres went out in selected areas to practice the "**Four Withs**" in the community:

(i) eating with;

(ii) living with;

(iii) working with;

(iv) discussing with.

13. It was over the guidelines for this campaign that the major political battles were fought within the Chinese leadership. At the end of 1964, when Liu Shaoqi refused to accept Mao's demand to direct the main thrust of class struggle against "capitalist roaders" in the party, Mao decided that he would have to take over again."

14. People were divided between the **Two Lines:**

(a) The Rightist Line

(b) The mass line (the Mao Zedong line)

15. The immediate cause of conflict was the production, in 1965, of a play critical of Mao and the Great Leap Forward, written by Wu Han, deputy mayor of Beijing.

The Great Proletarian Cultural Revolution (1965-69)

1. The Great Proletarian Cultural Revolution was provoked by Mao and his supporters and the PLA, but quickly developed into a spontaneous mass movement.

2. It was launched:

(a) to destroy the rise of differentiation between the working class and a technological-bureaucratic class;

(b) to destroy the bureaucratic and elitist tendencies within the Party;

(c) to revitalize ideology;

(d) to destroy the relics of pre-revolutionary thinking and raise the consciousness of the people;

(e) as a vehicle to restore Mao's power and control of developments.

3. Inspired by Mao, a poster campaign began in Peking University. Students:

(a) denounced counter-revolutionary elements which had infiltrated the Party, government, army and cultural circles;

(b) demanded greater entry of workers and peasants to universities;

(c) An end to back-door entry to the Party and bureaucracy for children of cadres;

(d) a call for "red training" to replace that of "experts", i.e. political indoctrination should replace normal studies.

4. Liu Shaoqi tried to dampen this down by sending work teams into the universities. They attempted to deflect the violence towards traditional "class enemies": children of former capitalists, landlords, rich peasants and intellectuals.

5. The students took sides. Paradoxically:

(a) children of the former peasants were conservative, because they had done well out of the revolution, and tended to defend the Party.

(b) children of former landlords, rich peasants and intellectuals were radical and supported Mao. They had been discriminated against, especially in education, and responded to Mao's call to rise up against bureaucratic privilege.

6. In order to demonstrate his continued vitality, on 16th July 1965, in a spectacular publicity coup, 72-year-old Mao swam across the Yangtse River accompanied by 5000 young people.

7. In August 1966, the chief supporters of Mao set up the Central Cultural Revolution Group

8. Maoist students formed themselves into battalions of "Red Guards."

9. In a poster campaign Mao invited the students to "bombard the headquarters" of the Party which had become a "bourgeois dictatorship."

10. Lin Biaou invited students and Red Guards to campaign against the "**Four Olds**":

(a) old habits;

(b) old ideas;

(c) old customs;

(d) old culture.

Many priceless cultural monuments were destroyed as a result of this campaign.

11. During the late summer and autumn Red Guards toured the country:

(a) arguing Mao's case;

(b) purging schools, colleges and factories. Intellectuals were particularly singled out for attack as the "stinking ninth" class. Many were persecuted and driven to suicide. Liu Shaoqi and Deng Xiaoping confessed their errors and were purged;

(c) destroying the "four olds" including ransacking museums, and destroying cultural works.

12. Many mass rallies were held in Beijing in which Mao appeared to hundreds of thousands of Red Guards and students in Beijing.

13. Fighting frequently broke out between Red Guards and workers, Red Guards and peasants, and among rival groups of Red Guards.

14. Total chaos threatened: There was an anarchic atmosphere throughout the country. In addition to schools and colleges, the chaos spread to the factories. Many closed and production ceased.

15. In Shanghai young workers and students challenged the authority of the Party and state. Soon, two rival groups held the city in a state of almost civil war. In February 1967 they formed the **Shanghai People's Commune**. Revolutionary communes began to be set up in many cities.

16. The army began to intervene to restore order in some areas. .

17. In mid-May this led to popular risings against army action. Armed struggles broke out. There was a PLA mutiny in Wuhan.

18. Popular action led to foreign policy problems:

(a) crowds of Red Guards invaded the British mission and took the staff captive;

(b) When the Burmese government forbade children to wear Mao badges, there were riots in Rangoon and the Chinese called for revolution there;

(c) For a short period Red Guards took over the Foreign Ministry in Beijing and issued orders to Chinese embassy staff abroad.

19. Mao began to withdraw his support from the Revolution because:

(a) It had got out of control;

(b) the establishment of the Shanghai Peoples' Commune threatened the supremacy of the CCP;

(c) Army officers began to fear an extension of the disorders and purges into the PLA;

(d) There was a threat of war with the USSR.

20. The army was finally called in to restore order.

(a) military instruction was given in universities and schools.

(b) The PLA entered factories to ensure production.

(c) It suppressed many revolutionary committees.

(d) Many leaders of popular movements were arrested

21. The PLA took most of 1967 to restore order, and there were renewed outbreaks of violence in outlying provinces and in Beijing University early in 1968.

(a) These were suppressed by the Army;

(b) Mao ordered the Red Guards suppressed:

(c) In June 1968, perhaps 12 million students were sent to work in the countryside.

22. By late 1968 the situation had stabilised. The Cultural Revolution became institutionalised:

(a) The "Little Red Book" was ubiquitous;

(b) The uniform of the masses, blue jackets, trousers and caps was worn by all;

(c) The traditional Beijing Opera was replaced under the direction of Jiang Quing (Madame Mao) by new revolutionary operas;

(d) The cult of Mao was carried to new heights;

(e) Schools and universities reopened slowly, taught revolutionary consciousness, and held open book examinations.

23. The PLA continued a policy of repression until 1971.

The Nature of the Great Proletarian Cultural Revolution

It was:

1. A genuine mass movement characterised by popular hysteria, comparable to religious revivals in the USA;

2. An attempt to further the process of moving towards socialism - a revolution from above;

3. An attempt to root out pre-revolutionary ways of thinking and acting which survived into the era of developing socialism because of the speed with which the CCP came to power in the east;

4. An application of the idea of "continuing revolution", to block the growth of new power structures which could strangle the revolution, as were happening in the USSR;

5. A struggle for power between the two factions represented by the Two Lines; and an attempt by Mao to reassert his control over the country.

6. A diversion from the failure of the Great Leap Forward;

7. It was chiefly an urban movement. Most peasants were not involved.

The Effects of the Great Proletarian Cultural Revolution

1. Most obviously, the cultural revolution had disruptive and negative effects on society:

(a) Perhaps 500,000 people died prematurely.

(b) Many suffered torture and abuse.

(c) An entire "lost generation" missed much of its schooling. The universities resumed functioning only during 1970-72, under the direction of the army.

(d) The modernisation of China was delayed by:

(i) the disruption of normal life;

(ii) disruption of industrial production;

(iii) attacks upon the intelligentsia: Intellectuals suffered most, and this held back intellectual life in China. China faced a shortage of trained experts for a decade. The research and teaching of the universities came to an end.

(e) Divisions within the CCP were exacerbated*;

(f) Lin Biaou and the PLA increased their power;

(g) The loss of China's cultural heritage was immense.

(h) The Cultural Revolution brought about no significant reform of the Party or other political changes, and produced no new democratic institutions.

(i) It left a population sated with politics and disillusioned with ideology.

(j) China became even more isolated from the rest of the world.

2. However, there were some positive aspects:

(a) It helped to debureaucratize the administration.

(b) Move towards capitalism in the countryside were held up or reversed.

(c) The idea of the Great Leap to build small rural industries was revived, this time more successfully

(d) The health system was decentralised and health care taken into the countryside with:

    (i) mobile clinics

    (ii) barefoot doctors.

(e) Educational resources were moved into the countryside.

    (i) The system was decentralised. Schools were run by local authorities.

    (ii) Fees, entrance examinations and age limits were abolished.

    (iii) Students were admitted to university only after several years of productive labour, with priority being given to the children of poorer peasants, workers and soldiers .

The Years of Recovery (1969-76)

1. A power struggle began when Chen Boda and Lin Biao criticised Mao Zedong. Mao purged Chen and many of Lin's top supporters in the military forces. Differences centred around:

(a) Mao's desire to rebuild the Party organisation throughout the country to sideline the new revolutionary committees.

(b) Zhou Enlai engaged in secret diplomatic exchanges with the United States, and Mao agreed to a secret visit to Beijing by US national security adviser Henry Kissinger in July 1971. Lin strongly opposed the Sino-American rapprochement.*

2. In September 1971 Lin was killed in what was later said to have been an attempt to flee to the Soviet Union after an abortive assassination plot against Mao. Lin's son was said to have launched an attack on a train Mao was on, hit the wrong train, and Lin tried to flee by aeroplane to Mongolia, but he plane "had insufficient fuel and crashed." Virtually the entire Chinese high command was purged.

3. The facts were only revealed in July 1972. This disillusioned many who had supported Mao during the Cultural Revolution. Lin had been the high priest of the Mao cult. The details of Lin's assassination plot and flight seemed to reveal nothing more than a power struggle.

4. From late 1971 through mid-1973 Zhou Enlai tried to restore stability.

(a) He brought numerous people back into office who had been purged.

(b) He encouraged a revival of educational standards.

(c) China began again to increase its trade and other links with the outside world

(d) The economy developed from 1969.

5. Mao blessed these general moves but kept his distance, lest they call into question the validity of the Cultural Revolution itself.

6. During 1972 Mao suffered a stroke, while Zhou learned that he had a fatal cancer. In early 1973

they brought Deng Xiaoping back to power to groom him as a successor, but his re-emergence made Jiang Qing and the "**Gang of Four**" strive to return to a more radical path.

7. From mid-1973 there was a power struggle between:
   (a) Jiang and her followers, "the Gang of Four," who favoured:
       (i) continuing class struggle,
       (ii) anti-intellectualism,
       (iii) egalitarianism,*
       (iv) xenophobia,*
   (b) the supporters of Zhou and Deng, who tried to promote:
       (i) economic growth,
       (ii) stability,
       (iii) educational progress,
       (iv) a pragmatic* foreign policy.
8. Mao tried unsuccessfully to maintain a balance among these forces:
   (a) the radicals* gained the upper hand from mid-1973 until mid-1974,
   (b) By July 1974, economic decline and increasing chaos made Mao support Zhou and Deng.
9. With Zhou in hospital, Deng assumed increasing power from the summer of 1974 through to late 1975. During this time he sought to
   (a) promote the **Four Modernisation's:**
       (i) of agriculture,
       (ii) industry,
       (iii) science and technology,
       (iv) defence.
   (b) to rehabilitate victims of the Cultural Revolution,
10. The radicals convinced Mao that Deng's policies would lead to a repudiation of the Cultural Revolution and even of Mao himself, so Mao agreed to criticism of these policies in wall posters.
11. Zhou died in January 1976, and Deng delivered his eulogy, but Mao supported Hua Guofeng as a compromise candidate as his successor.
12. Deng was purged when massive demonstrations took place in Peking and other cities on the traditional Ch'ing-ming festival to pay homage to Zhou's memory, in an open challenge to the radicals. A campaign was launched to "criticise Deng Xiaoping and his right deviationism," and Hua Guofeng supported this criticism.
13. In July a large earthquake obliterated the city of Tangshan. In China natural disasters are traditionally seen as making the end of an imperial dynasty.
14. Mao died in September 1976.
15. In October 1976 Hua Guofeng ordered the "Gang of Four" were purged with the support of a coalition of political, police, and military leaders. Their hold upon power by Deng and the reformers was unchallenged.
16. Although it was officially ended by the 11th Party Congress in August 1977, the Cultural Revolution had in fact concluded with Mao's death and the purge of the Gang of Four.
17. In 1977 Deng was placed in charge f China's economy, and became the dominant figure in the government.

Assessment of Mao's Regime

1. The traditional culture of China was dominated by Confucianism, which valued order and obedience in a hierarchical system which was dominated by the emperor, the "Son of Heaven." Although this tradition was supposedly overthrown by the revolution this way of thinking was

Timeline of Mao's Regime

1949	Foundation of the Peoples' Republic of China
1950	Korean War begins
	Marriage Reform Law - Agrarian Reform Law
1951	Three Antis Campaign
1952	Five Antis Campaign
1953	First Five-Year Plan begins
1954	New constitution
1957	The Hundred Flowers Campaign
1958	Great Leap Forward launched
1959	Famine - Mao resigns as head of state
1960	Sino-Soviet split
1962	Mao launches Socialist Education Movement
1964	China explodes its first atomic bomb
1966	Mao launches Great Proletarian Cultural Revolution
1968	PLA suppresses the Cutural Revolution
1971	Death of Lin Biaou
	Peoples' Republic of China becomes member of the UN
1972	US President Nixon visits Beijing
1973	Deng Xiaoping rehbilitated
1976	Death of Zhou Enlai
	Death of Mao Zedong
	The arrest of the Gang of Four

hard to shake off. Mao simply became the new "Son of Heaven" in the minds of most Chinese.

2. Whereas Stalin favoured stability and continuity, suppressing all opposition, Mao allowed room for movements from below: "Let us not be afraid of troubles; the more troubles there are, the better for us."

3. The entire period of Mao's dominance can be considered a struggle between the **Two Lines:**

   (a) **The Revisionist Line**: based upon orthodox Marxism. Because the party had gained power the transformation of society into socialism was possible, but for this to come about the basic methods of production and distribution in China would need to be modernised in order to create the economic base necessary for a socialist society. Since industrialisation would be necessary for this, the support of the already industrialised nations would be desirable, since they would be able to provide the technology to make it possible.

   (b) **The Revolutionary Line**, or **the Mass Line**: Social relations would need to be transformed at the same time as the economic base for socialism was being built up. The old centres of interest and power and any tendency to elitism and bureaucracy would have to be destroyed.

4. Despite many blunders, Mao had lifted his country from being the foreign dominated "sick man of Asia" to achieve:

   (a) the territorial unification of the country (except for Taiwan);

   (b) the establishment of a strong centralised state;

   (c) the expulsion of the dominant foreigners and the elimination of foreign controls;

   (d) the elimination of landlord exploitation of the peasants;

   (e) great advances in the industrialisation of the country;

   (f) massive improvements in the living conditions of most of the people;

(g) a universal health service, which doubled life-expectancy;

(h) a universal educational service, which has all but eliminated mass illiteracy;

(i) the liberation of women;

(j) the virtual elimination of chronic traditional problems such as organised crime, child prostitution and addiction to drugs and gambling;

(k) China had achieved Great Power status, with nuclear weapons.

5. This had been achieved:

(a) without significant external assistance, since Soviet help had been limited, reluctant, and had to be paid for with interest;

(b) against the consistent and massive opposition and obstruction of the USA during the crucial years between 1949 and 1970;

(c) albeit at great cost to the people of China.

6. Mao had failed:

(a) to control China's population, which rose from 500 million in 1949 to 925 million in 1976;

(b) to build up the stability necessary for consistent growth;

(c) to build a Party and state responsive to the wishes of the masses.

Mao's policies were often counter-productive, and and hindered the progress he desired.

Glossary

abrogation the repeal of a law

bureaucracy administration by officials

cadres Party workers:

CCP Chinese Communist Party

collusion a secret understanding

commune a social unit in which work and goods are held in common

cooperative a society for the common production, distribution or sale of produce or goods

de-Stalinization the dismantling of Stalin's apparatus of terror

democratic centralism Lenin's idea that party policy, once agreed upon, must not be disputed

egalitarianism the ideal of equality

enclaves territory surrounded by enemy occupied territory

exacerbated made worse

executive the arm of government which carries out policy

Guomindang (GMD), (Kuomintang - KMT) Chinese Nationalist Party

PLA - Peoples' Liberation Army

pragmatic acting in such a way as to make a practical difference, rather than being doctrinaire

radicals those seeking fundamental change

rapprochement: a reconciliation between countries

Sino- Chinese

urban to do with the cities or towns, as opposed to the countryside

xenophobia fear and hatred of foreigners

yundang a campaign with advertisements, meetings, speeches and marches, etc. to mobilise the public

Leon Trotsky

Authoritarianism, Fascism and Totalitarianism

Right-Wing Single-Party States

Origins

1. The right wing single-party states of the 1920s and 1930s arose out of common circumstances:
   (a) the greatest man-made disaster in history: the First World War;
   (b) the greatest economic disaster in history: the Wall Street Crash and the Depression.
2. The fighting in the trenches demonstrated that the fate of the state now lay in the hands of the infantryman, and not, as before, with the aristocratic cavalrymen. Power tends to follow the ability to defend the country, so power moved from traditional leaderships to the masses.
3. But the masses in central, southern and eastern Europe had little experience of participation in government. Therefore they were vulnerable to the appeal of:
   (a) authoritarian military leaders attempting to buttress the fading power of existing élites; or;
   (b) demagogues,* who sought to gain power for themselves by placing themselves at the head of the masses using developments in the media of mass communication (radio, cinema newsreels) which allowed them unprecedented access to the masses for propaganda purposes.

Authoritarian Regimes

1. The right-wing regimes came to power as the result of coups or against the background of the threat of violence or civil war.
2. They were authoritarian, in that they:
   (a) suspended parliamentary constitutions;
   (b) ruled by threat of fear;
   (c) adopted a "black or white" posture: "He who is not with us is against us," so that anyone who dared to be faintly critical of the government was automatically branded as a traitor, and opposition was outlawed;
   (d) enforced their control by means of torture, arbitrary imprisonment and execution.
3. They claimed to be:
   (a) motivated by patriotism;
   (b) restoring law and order;

   (c) defending traditional values;

   (d) defending the country against the threat of Bolshevism;

   (e) leading a regeneration of the nation.

4. They were either led by army officers, or otherwise tended towards the militarization of society and increased police powers.

5. They employed, and censored, the media.

6. The majority were indifferent towards, or actively encouraged, the scapegoating of minorities.

7. Their most important purpose was to defend a **conservative establishment** and system of entrenched privilege which blocked movements towards radical changes to the social and economic order.

8. Some historians have argued that examples of traditional, authoritarian regimes in post World War I Europe would include Primo de Rivera's Spain, Franco's Spain, Salazar's Portugal, Metaxas' Greece, Horthy's Hungary, Antonescu's Rumania, Pilsudski's Poland and Papadopoulos' Greece.

Fascist Regimes

Many interpretations of fascism have been put forward, and no universally accepted definition of fascism exists.:

1. Seymour Martin Lipset regarded fascism as lower middle-class radicalism. A perceived threat from organised labour and big business during a period of economic distress drove the lower middle classes into authoritarian (racist and nationalist) radicalism.

  However, this fails to take account of:

   (a) the role of élites in bringing fascists to power;

   (b) the fact that fascism received support from all classes.

2. Marxists note that traditional élites tolerated or employed the dictators to capture the working classes and inoculate them against Bolshevism. Like nationalism, it was a deliberate diversion of the workers from their supra-national class interests. Fascist rulers were defenders of, and agents of, capitalism.

3. Nicos Poulantzas argues that established political authorities had been thoroughly discredited by the catastrophes of the First World War and the Great Depression. Fascism was a radical populist solution to the problem of restoring the hegemony of the dominant class. The typical fascist leader was a "man of the people," an ordinary foot soldier like the masses who had served in the trenches, who appeared to be a new kind of political authority. Yet in fact he was usually acting as "front man" for the old, discredited authorities.

4. It is often argued that fascist single-party states were essentially radical. They aimed to mobilise the masses to achieve some goal. K. D. Bracher contrasts this with authoritarian single-party states, which sought to immobilise or neutralise them. Eric Hobsbawm calls them "the revolutionaries of counter-revolution"

5. Some historians regard the differences between movements and governments regarded as "fascist" to be so important that no single account of fascism will fit them all.

6. If we define fascist regimes as essentially revolutionary in social and economic terms, then fascist regimes are very rare. In modern Europe, only Hitler's Germany would qualify. Even Mussolini's Italy, *the* fascist regime par excellence, after which all other fascist regimes are named, despite its original radicalism and Mussolini's rhetoric, soon became essentially a conservative authoritarian regime, supportive of, to some extent dependent upon, and in the end deposed by, the traditional centres of authority.

Comparison of Italian Fascism and Nazism

1. Both:
   (a) arose in countries which were:
      (i) recently united (comparatively speaking);
      (ii) recently industrialized;
      (iii) considered themselves to have been affronted by the peace treaties;
      (iv) suffered from deep social divisions;
      (v) suffered from deep economic problems.
   (b) The leaders of both were:
      (i) talented political agitators;
      (ii) social outsiders.
   (c) Both of the parties:
      (i) initially tried to establish themselves on the nationalist and populist left;
      (ii) stressed chauvinistic nationalism;
      (iii) were imperialist and expansionist;
      (iv) were intensely anti-Marxist and stressed national unity, as against class struggle;
      (v) attempted to destroy the power of organised labour.
   (d) In order to gain power, both:
      (i) used a mass party with support across the classes, but especially in the lower middle classes, to gain power;
      (ii) exploited the resentments of the population against other powers;
      (iii) used paramilitary movements which they later sidelined as too radical and crude;
      (iv) partly depended upon existing élites: political, economic, military, and bureaucratic;
      (v) ignored parts of their own programmes in order to achieve power;
      (vi) proceeded by stages to achieve their goals;
      (vii) made strong appeals to history;
      (viii) used revolutionary and populist rhetoric.
   (e) In power, both:
      (i) rejected parliamentary democracy;
      (ii) attempted to organise a totalitarian state, in which the Party controlled as many aspects of the life of the people as possible;
      (iii) used spectacles and the mass media to marshal, control and inspire the people;
      (iv) showed extreme intolerance to all other groups, suppressing them through violence;
      (v) appointed weak subordinates to prevent the emergence of an obvious successor;
      (vi) multiplied new special government agencies under subordinates, preserving the regular ministries but allowing them to drift, creating governmental chaos which only their own authority could cut through;
      (vii) adopted the methods of political gangsterism;
      (viii) attempted to achieve autarchy or economic self-sufficiency for their country;
      (ix) placed the needs of the state above those of the individual;
      (x) accepted Social Darwinism ;
      (xi) glorified war;
      (xii) stressed the cult of the leader;
      (xiii) foreign and domestic policy were related in the same way: internal consolidation was necessary for foreign conquest, and conquest was necessary for revolution at home.
2. There were, however, significant differences:
   (a) Mussolini's ideology was little more than an opportunistic device to take him into power;

Hitler had a worked-out ideology with deep roots in German history:

(b) Mussolini's expansionist goals were less ambitious than Hitler's.

(c) When in power, Hitler either controlled, subordinated or destroyed the existing élites, whereas Mussolini compromised with them, leaving them in place.

(d) Fascism was never accepted as wholeheartedly in Italy as Nazism was in Germany.

(e) Italian efforts at imposing totalitarianism were never as efficient as those in Germany.

(f) The Italian system was never as ruthless and brutal as the German system. There were no mass atrocities.

(g) Italian fascists were not anti-Semitic until 1938, when Mussolini was pressured into it by Hitler. Even then its application was half-hearted.

(h) Mussolini was always a national leader under a constitutional monarch; Hitler had no rival after the death of President Hindenberg.

(i) Mussolini compromised with the Roman Catholic Church in the Concordat of 1922, conceding that the Fascist party could not control certain aspects of Italian life. He never went back on this as Hitler did on his Concordat of 1933.

3. Most historians regard both Mussolini's Italy and Hitler's Germany as forms of fascism. However, some regard Hitler's Germany as so different from Mussolini's Italy that it should be regarded as a unique phenomenon.

Totalitarian Regimes

1. Totalitarianism is a form of government that seeks to subordinate all aspects of the individual's life to the authority of the government.

2. Mussolini coined the term in the early 1920s to describe the new fascist state of Italy, which he described as: "All within the state, none outside the state, none against the state." By the beginning of World War II, "totalitarian" had become synonymous with absolute and oppressive single-party government.

3. Carl Friedrich analysed the term as referring to regimes with:

   (a) an official ideology;

   (b) a single mass party;

   (c) terroristic police control of the population;

   (d) monopoly control of the media;

   (e) monopoly control of arms;

   (f) central control of the economy.

(To regard the state's monopoly of arms as a sign of totalitarianism is a peculiarly US view. Elsewhere, state control of the possession and use of weapons would be regarded as a precondition for civilised life.)

4. Karl Dietrich Bracher offered an alternative analysis:

   (a) the total claim to rule;

   (b) the leadership principle;

   (c) an exclusive ideology;

   (d) the fiction of the identity of rulers and ruled.

5. The totalitarian state pursues some special goal embodied in its ideology, such as industrialisation or foreign conquest, to the exclusion of all others. All resources are directed toward its attainment regardless of the cost. Like the building of the pyramids, it could have been chosen to enable the leaders to bind society together; for this reason, the goal could never be allowed to be achieved or it would remove the justification for the authority of the ruler and the sacrifices he demanded.

6. Some historians regard the concept of "totalitarianism" as not merely worthless but mischievous, regarding its use as a function of Cold War propaganda, employed to tie the Soviet system firmly together with that of the Nazis and the Italian Fascists in the minds of the Western public.

Comparison of Stalin and Hitler

1. Stalin arose from within a system, Hitler from outside it. Stalin was a committee man, Hitler was as unlike a committee man as it is possible to be.
2. Hitler placed considerable trust in his lieutenants; while Stalin trusted no one.
3. Stalin was an interventionist. He sought to centralise all decisions under his control and micro-manage the system. Hitler tried to stand aloof, above the level of administration, did not interfere in the work of his subordinates, and frequently left problems to solve themselves.
4. By contrast, in military matters Hitler micromanaged his wars, whereas Stalin learned to step back from making tactical military decisions.
5. Stalin's policies were at odds with the ideology of the movement he led; while Hitler's were consistent with Nazism, his own creation.
6. Stalin terrorised his supporters as well as his potential opponents. Hitler only terrorised opponents. The apparent exception of the Night of the Long Knives was not an exception, since he was removing supposed "allies" who he knew were potentially dangerous to him, to many of his ideas, and to his movement.
7. Hitler was a charismatic leader, whereas Stalin's personality cult was entirely artifice
8. Hitler's regime became increasingly radical; Stalin's became increasingly conservative.
9. Hitler was irreplaceable to Nazism as a movement in a way that Stalin was not to Soviet Communism.

For up to date information about Anagnosis books
·visit our website: www.anagnosis.eu
email: info@anagnosis.eu

Anagnosis, Deliyianni 3, Maroussi 15122 Greece
telephone: ++30-210-612-9572
fax: ++30-210-62-54-089